THE
NATCHEZ
INDIANS

THE NATCHEZ INDIANS

A History to 1735

James F. Barnett Jr.

UNIVERSITY PRESS OF MISSISSIPPI
JACKSON

www.upress.state.ms.us

The University Press of Mississippi is a member of the Association of American University Presses.

Illustrations courtesy of the author

∞

Library of Congress Cataloging-in-Publication Data

Barnett, James F., 1950–
The Natchez Indians : a history to 1735 / James F. Barnett Jr.
p. cm.
Includes bibliographical references and index.
ISBN-13: 978-1-57806-988-0 (cloth : alk. paper)
ISBN-10: 1-57806-988-2 (cloth : alk. paper) 1. Natchez Indians—First
contact with Europeans. 2. Natchez Indians—Government relations.
3. Natchez Indians—Wars, 1716. I. Title.
E99.N2B37 2007
976.2'4004979–dc22

2007008841

British Library Cataloging-in-Publication Data available

For my wife, Sharon, and my parents, Lois and Jim Barnett Sr.

CONTENTS

ILLUSTRATIONS

ACKNOWLEDGMENTS

I AM INDEBTED TO a number of people who helped in various ways with this project.

First of all, I want to thank Joseph V. "Smokye" Frank III for reviewing an earlier version of this manuscript and for generously sharing with me his extensive library of archaeological reports and his considerable knowledge of local sites, artifacts, and French maps. Frank was a member of Robert Neitzel's excavation crew during the 1962 investigations at the Fatherland site, also known as the Grand Village of the Natchez Indians. He is a longtime associate of the Lower Mississippi Survey and an indefatigable discoverer of archaeological sites representing the Natchez and the French colonial period. Ian W. Brown reviewed an earlier version of this manuscript and provided many useful comments and suggestions. Brown and his Lower Mississippi Survey colleagues Jeffrey P. Brain and Vincas P. Steponaitis have freely shared their files and insight with me ever since my arrival in the Natchez Bluffs some twenty-five years ago. Likewise, I am grateful to many people with expertise in the Lower Mississippi Valley who responded to my requests for information, including John Connaway, Jessica Crawford, Shannon Dawdy, Patricia Galloway, Marvin Jeter, Brad Lieb, Joe Saunders, and Tom Scarborough. I am grateful to Christine Wilson, editor of the *Journal of Mississippi History*, for providing me with a copy of the Smithsonian's *Handbook of North American Indians, Southeast, Volume 14*. Clark Burkett and Grover Stanton Jr. helped me with information about eighteenth-century firearms, Tamara Beane shared her knowledge of pottery making, Jean Claude Coullerez assisted with translations of eighteenth-century French texts, and Johnny Mott Guice helped me locate an archaeological site in Louisiana. Gordon Sayre graciously shared his translations of French colonial letters and narratives. Linda Walker Green and Nancy McLemore of

Copiah-Lincoln Community College's Willie Mae Dunn Library made numerous publications available to me through the interlibrary loan program. I want to thank Craig Gill, editor-in-chief of University Press of Mississippi, and an anonymous reviewer for their constructive criticisms and many helpful comments. Angelique Caine copyedited the manuscript for University Press of Mississippi and made helpful suggestions about organization. I am grateful for assistance from the Louisiana State University Library and the Bibliothéque nationale de France. This book would not have been possible without the encouragement and support of Elbert R. Hilliard and H. T. Holmes, past and current directors respectively of the Mississippi Department of Archives and History. Holmes also loaned me his personal copy of *Mississippi Provincial Archives, 1704–1743, French Dominion, Vol. III.* Recognition should likewise go to the staff of the Grand Village of the Natchez Indians who labor to tell the story of the Natchez Indians to the public: (at the time of this writing) Rebecca Anderson, Fred Green, Allen Hunt, J. W. Jackson, Avis King, Sharon Ogden, and Janice Sago. Sharon Ogden also typed portions of an earlier version of the manuscript. Finally, thanks to Walter Biggins, Shane Gong, Valerie Jones, and all of their colleagues at University Press of Mississippi.

INTRODUCTION

EARLY ON THE MORNING OF MARCH 11, 1700, a file of canoes manned by French Canadian soldiers and voyageurs snaked upstream against the Mississippi River's current. The sunlight flickered through the trees on the bluffs above the east bank. Along the river's west bank, the trees crowding the river were inundated in places by spring floodwaters. The expedition's commander, Pierre LeMoyne d'Iberville, surveyed the stretch of river ahead and occasionally laid aside his paddle to consult a map. The thirty-nine-year-old French officer was ascending the great river to smoke the calumet—a ceremony he detested—with the native tribes he hoped would become France's allies. Now Iberville and his men were entering the territory of the people whom the natives of the region called "Theloel." Securing the allegiance of their chief was crucial to Iberville's objective of countering English attempts to befriend the tribes controlling the Mississippi River. Shortly after midday, Iberville's party encountered Theloel fishermen near the tribe's river landing and the commander purchased some of their morning's catch. A short while later, the Frenchmen were given a friendly greeting by the chief, whom Iberville described as "a man of five feet three inches tall, rather thin, of intelligent countenance."[1]

Iberville's diplomatic mission in the spring of 1700 helped establish the Theloel, later known to the world as the Natchez Indians, as one of the most important tribes on the Mississippi River. Over the next three decades, the Natchez played host to a parade of voyageurs, missionaries, traders, colonial administrators, and soldiers, eventually condoning the establishment of a French fort and several tobacco plantations in their midst. As we will see, the Natchez played a key role in the early eighteenth-century struggle for empire between England and France. Tragically, the Natchez became one of the casualties of that contest between European superpowers and by the mid-1730s, Natchez refugees were driven from their homeland

and forced to join other tribes for survival. During the eighteenth and nineteenth centuries, the tribe's image acquired a romantic mystique throughout Europe and America, thanks, in part, to histories written by Le Page du Pratz, Dumont de Montigny, Pierre F. X. Charlevoix, and others, and to the popular novels of François-René de Chateaubriand.[2]

In the twentieth century, the Natchez Indians became the focus of intensive archaeological investigations, primarily at a small mound group near Natchez, Mississippi, known as the "Fatherland Site," named after the plantation on which it was located. The first archaeological work at the site was Warren K. Moorehead's limited testing in 1924.[3] In the 1930s, archaeologists Moreau B. C. Chambers and James A. Ford identified the Fatherland site as the place mentioned frequently in the French colonial records as the "Grand Village of the Natchez."[4] Chambers led the first extensive archaeological excavations at Fatherland in 1930 for the Mississippi Department of Archives and History. In 1962 and 1972, further archaeological investigations were carried out for the Department by Robert S. Neitzel, resulting in two landmark publications in Southeastern archaeology: *Archeology of the Fatherland Site: The Grand Village of the Natchez* and *The Grand Village of the Natchez Revisited: Excavations at the Fatherland Site, Adams County, Mississippi, 1972*.[5] Radiocarbon samples gathered during Neitzel's 1962 excavations indicate that the occupation at the Grand Village began around A.D. 1200, and the presence on the site of hundreds of European trade artifacts testified to occupation into the colonial period. Neitzel's work was undertaken with a keen awareness of the numerous French colonial descriptions of the site. In his analysis of his findings, he was able to draw correlations between what he was seeing in the ground and what the eighteenth-century Europeans had witnessed.[6]

In the broader geographic picture, twentieth-century archaeological studies in the Lower Mississippi River Valley linked the historic Natchez Indians with the prehistoric Plaquemine culture, which lasted from around A.D. 1200 until the late seventeenth century.[7] This work was spearheaded by a group of archaeologists known as the Lower Mississippi Survey (LMS), founded in 1939 by Philip Phillips, James A. Ford, and James B. Griffin. The LMS used pottery classification to establish a cultural sequence for the late prehistoric period in the Lower Mississippi Valley.[8] LMS archaeological investigations continued in the region during the last half of the twentieth century, led by Stephen Williams, Jeffrey P. Brain, Ian W. Brown, Vincas P. Steponaitis, and others.[9] Assisting the LMS team in the Natchez area were experts on the local archaeology, notably Joseph V. Frank III and Robert Prospere.

As mentioned above, the archaeological findings at the Fatherland/Grand Village site have been successfully correlated with the written documents generated during the French colonial period. In the early twentieth century, ethnohistorian John R. Swanton used the colonial sources to explore many aspects of Natchezan culture, including the tribe's language, religion, and social organization.[10] This information has provided archaeologists and historians with ethnographic data for interpreting the nature of late prehistoric mound-building societies that existed prior to European contact. Although the Natchez have been held up as an ethnographic example of a Southeastern chiefdom surviving into the early eighteenth century, Ian Brown has cautioned that the Natchez Indians of the late seventeenth and early eighteenth centuries were probably different in significant ways from their prehistoric ancestors because of the far-reaching impact of European contact. Therefore, one should not take the colonial descriptions to be accounts of a pristine native society.[11]

In addition to providing valuable cultural information, the colonial records illuminate the brief but tumultuous history of the Natchez through their relationship with French and English explorers, missionaries, empire builders, and colonists, which brings me to my purpose for writing this book. In twentieth-century syntheses of this history by Marcel Giraud, Verner Crane, Jack Elliott, and others, the Indians have been peripheral to the story of the Europeans themselves.[12] I want to use the colonial narratives to move the Natchez Indians to center stage. Swanton's sixty-six-page "History Since First White Contact" provides a beginning in this regard, while more recent and rather brief summaries of Natchez history are relegated to a sidebar role in essays that are primarily concerned with analyses of the tribe's intriguing social and ceremonial behavior.[13] The Natchez Indians' pivotal role in the contest between France and England and their interaction with neighboring tribes, both friendly and adversarial, warrant a more thorough examination.

Recent reevaluation of Swanton's model of Natchez internal political structure by scholars such as Marvin T. Smith and Karl G. Lorenz indicates that the tribe was not a single entity controlled by the hereditary chief the French called "The Great Sun," as viewed by Swanton and others, but rather a loose confederation of ethnically diverse villages or settlement districts. Chiefs who, in most cases, were apparently not members of the elite Sun family led these settlements and acted independently in their relationships with the French and English.[14]

Between 1682 and 1735, the French knew three Great Suns: the old man whom Iberville met, the Great Sun who lived out his life in the shadow of the

French and was their staunch ally, and the bewildered young heir to the Great Sun title who finished out his days as a slave on the sugarcane plantations of Santo Domingo. Clearly, these chiefs were venerated to some extent because of their position at the top of an elite lineage, but history reveals that they held no real power over the settlement districts.

The interpretation that the Natchez villages were autonomous throws a much different light on the recorded behavior of the Natchez. Indeed, I believe that this way of viewing them can help to explain the Natchez group's ability to sustain itself during the chaotic times between the tribe's initial encounter with the La Salle expedition and its tragic dispersal by the French in the 1730s. I will argue that it was this lack of central authority that gave the Natchez the flexibility to form alliances and do business simultaneously with both the French and English.

This book, then, is about the way that the Natchez coped with a rapidly changing world that became inescapably fused with the political ambitions of two European superpowers. Through a more or less chronological retelling of the history of the Natchez, I will examine the shifting relationships between the tribe's settlement districts and the settlement districts' relationships with neighboring tribes and with the Europeans. My work has been simplified by the translation into English of a wealth of documents generated by the principal European players on the colonial scene. These primary references include letters and journals by the early travelers in the Lower Mississippi Valley, including Nicholas La Salle, Tonti, Iberville, Nairne, and Pénicaut. Missionaries who left first-hand accounts of the Natchez include De Montigney, Saint-Cosme, Gravier, and Charlevoix. As the Louisiana colony expanded to eventually found a French settlement at the Natchez, a wealth of information about the tribe's activities appears in the letters and reports of soldiers, planters, and administrators, including Bienville, La Harpe, Perier, Dumont, and Du Pratz.

To discuss this history, I've divided this book into four chapters. In Chapter One, before taking up the colonial French and English interaction with the Natchez, I will look at the brief but spectacular encounter between the warrior boatmen of Quigualtam and the De Soto expedition in the mid-sixteenth century. The Quigualtam episode is the earliest documented glimpse of the people whom many believe represent the Natchez at or near the height of their power as a well-organized chiefdom in control of a territory roughly the size of New Hampshire. I will also explore the reasons for the drastic decline in population size in the Southeast during the century and a half separating the De Soto and

La Salle expeditions, when the number of native inhabitants dropped an estimated 33 percent.[15]

Chapter Two, "European Reconnaissance," covers the period from the spring of 1682, when the Natchez were met by La Salle and his party, through the years 1713–1715, when the French established a trading post at the Natchez. During this time, both the French and the English courted the Natchez as a strategic ally, and the tribe became ensnared, through the slave- and deerskin trade, in the seductive economy of Western Europe, with its irresistible flow of trade guns and other merchandise. During Iberville's first encounters with the Natchez in 1699 and 1700, the settlement district configuration of the tribe first becomes evident and we have the earliest description of the main ceremonial center, the Grand Village. The memoirist Pénicaut visited the Natchez during this stage in the tribe's history and the Seminarian missionary Saint-Cosme lived among them for six years.

Chapter Three, "European Occupation," tells how the First Natchez War led to a French settlement at the tribe's doorstep and how the Natchez reacted to the ensuing colonial encroachment. The doomed French colony at the Natchez was unique in Louisiana in the way the European settlers were obliged to interact with the native inhabitants because of the remoteness of the colony. The settlement's isolation forced the French to depend upon the Indians for sustenance, creating a complex interrelationship that erupted into violence with the second and third Natchez wars. As will be seen, another volatile ingredient in the ethnic mix of the French settlement at the Natchez was the burgeoning African population, comprised of both enslaved and free blacks. It is apparent from the colonial narratives that some of the Natchez group felt an affinity with the Africans and treated them differently than they did the Europeans; so much so, in fact, that the tribe's rebellion of 1729 was, in part, a slave rebellion. This ethnic mix was tested in the extreme by the continued tug-of-war between the French and English and their competing constituencies within the Natchez group. Ultimately, it was the failure of the French to recognize a major shift in political alignment among the circle of Natchez chiefs that spelled disaster for the colony.

The story of the massacre and rebellion that erupted at the Natchez in 1729 is told in Chapter Four. I will trace the French retaliation against the Natchez and examine the charges by colonial administrators that the Natchez uprising was not an isolated event but a part of a multi-tribal conspiracy instigated by the English. Under sustained attack by combined French and Indian forces, the Natchez eventually broke up into scattered bands of fighters, and their families pursued guerilla warfare.

The Natchez Rebellion of 1729 brought an end to the Company of the Indies' Louisiana enterprise and destroyed France's dreams of colonizing the interior of the Lower Mississippi Valley. Aside from illuminating a small but significant theater of North American history, the story of the Natchez Indians is a cautionary tale about what can happen when very different cultural groups are thrown together and expected to coexist for the attainment of larger political and economic goals.

THE
NATCHEZ
INDIANS

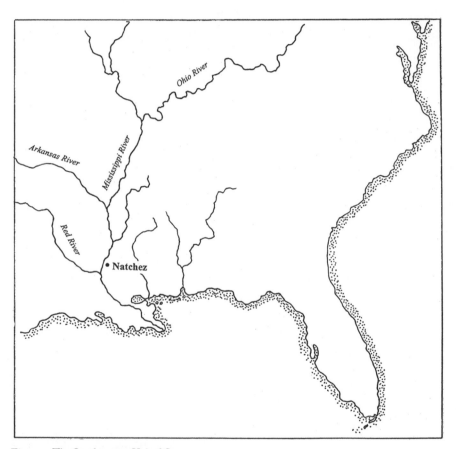

Figure 1. The Southeastern United States.

Chapter One

WARRIOR BOATMEN

⇀→ ─────────────────────────────────────── ←↼

IN APRIL 1542, Spanish soldiers encamped along the Mississippi River with Hernando de Soto first heard the name "Quigualtam." According to Indians living near the mouth of the Arkansas River, Quigualtam was a powerful nation led by a chief of the same name who controlled the great river a short distance to the south. For reasons outlined in the story that follows, the Spaniards would never meet Chief Quigualtam, nor would they set eyes on his citadel, but they would soon come to fear and respect his power.[1]

The De Soto expedition had landed on the west coast of Florida in May 1539 and followed a haphazard route across the Southeast in search of gold-laden native states such as those recently conquered by the Spanish in Peru and Mexico. By the time De Soto reached the Mississippi River, he and his army had covered close to two thousand miles. The Spaniards sustained themselves on this long campaign by taking advantage of the communal maize granaries they found at the ceremonial centers of the chiefdoms they encountered along their route. A successful strategy that De Soto used time and time again was to follow the natives' trails from outlying ceremonial centers and villages to the chiefdom's main center. Along the way, they sacked the storage granaries, which the hungry soldiers often found stocked with maize, beans, dried plums, and walnuts.[2] The Spaniards routinely burned the villages, killed the men, enslaved the women, and attempted to make hostages of the chiefs. The combat was often desperate, but the military prowess of Spanish cavalry, footmen, and their savage war dogs had always proved more than a match for any Native American militia. In the army's wake lay a sprawl of destruction across the Southeast, the survivors left deprived of their leadership, their houses, and their stores of food.[3]

The Spaniards spent the winter of 1541–1542 camped beside the Arkansas River in what is now east-central Arkansas. Their North American campaign happened to coincide with a period of unusually cold weather that archaeologists call the "Little Ice Age." The climate shift spared the armor-clad Spaniards the South's typically hot and humid summers, but during the winter months they were subjected to heavy snows and bitter cold.[4] In the spring, the army moved down the Arkansas River and encountered large chiefdoms near the confluence of the Arkansas and Mississippi rivers. The Spaniards kept the upper hand by forming an alliance with one of these chiefs, Guachoya, who was eager to wage war against a neighboring chiefdom. While at the chiefdom of Guachoya, De Soto's fading hopes of finding and subjugating a gold-rich kingdom were revived by intelligence he was receiving about the Province of Quigualtam, which lay across the Mississippi River and only three days journey downstream. Chief Guachoya himself called Chief Quigualtam "the greatest lord of that region."[5]

This news came at an inopportune time for De Soto, as his army was seriously weakened by the rigors of the three-year campaign. To make matters worse, De Soto's health was failing him. In his growing delirium, he concocted an ambitious scheme which, if successful, would solve all of his problems. He would bluff Chief Quigualtam into surrendering and take over the duped chief's province. With the Quigualtam granaries at his disposal, De Soto would rest and recuperate there during the coming summer and winter while some of his best men rode the Mississippi River to the Gulf in an attempt to gather supplies at Spanish settlements in the Caribbean or Mexico.[6] The Gentleman of Elvas, one of the chroniclers of the expedition, summarized De Soto's situation that spring:

> The governor's grief was intense on seeing the small prospect he had for reaching the sea; and worse, according to the way in which his men and horses were diminishing, they could not be maintained in the land without succor. With that thought, he fell sick, but before he took to his bed, he sent an Indian to tell the cacique of Quigualtam that he was the son of the sun and that wherever he went all obeyed him and did him service. He requested him to choose his friendship and come there where he was, for he would be very glad to see him; and in token of love and obedience that he should bring him something that was most esteemed in that land.[7]

Clearly, De Soto's illness had not dulled his haughtiness. The Gentleman of Elvas duly records Chief Quigualtam's astonishing answer and the conquistador's rage upon receiving it:

> [The cacique] answered him saying that with respect to what he [the governor] said about being the son of the sun, let him dry up the great river and he would

believe him. With respect to the rest [that the governor said], he was not accustomed to visit any one. On the contrary, all of whom he had knowledge visited him and served him and obeyed him and paid him tribute, either by force or by their own volition. Consequently, if he [the governor] wished to see him, let him cross there. If he came in peace he would welcome him with special good will; if he came in war, he would wait for him in the town where he was, for not for him or any other would he move one foot backward.

When the Indian came back with this reply, the governor was already in bed, badly racked with fever. He was very angry that he was not in condition to cross the river forthwith and go in quest of him [the cacique] to see whether he could not lessen that arrogant demeanor.[8]

Hernando de Soto died on May 21, 1542, with Chief Quigualtam's taunts ringing in his ears. His successor, Luis Moscoso de Alvarado, led the tattered army away from the Mississippi River and Quigualtam, following a southwesterly route that the men hoped would lead them to Spanish settlements in Mexico. Along the way, they sustained themselves in the usual manner by raiding the maize granaries of the tribes they encountered and running roughshod over any natives that dared to try and halt their progress. By October, however, the Spaniards were deep into what is now southeastern Texas and for the first time found themselves among Indians who lived by hunting and gathering instead of farming. Afraid to journey on into unknown lands without maize granaries to raid, the dejected soldiers turned back toward the Mississippi River. The return trip was an unpleasant one because they had to re-cross the territories of the people who had only recently experienced their brutality.[9]

Upon reaching the Mississippi River, the army found many natives destitute because of the Spaniards' raids on their villages and granaries the previous year. They finally settled in for the winter of 1542–1543 at the chiefdom of Aminoya, on the west bank of the Mississippi River some seventy-five miles north of Guachoya.[10] Moscoso's men drove out the town's inhabitants and helped themselves to the people's stores of maize and dried fruit. Realizing that there was only one way out of the land in which they found themselves, the soldiers spent the winter building seven boats to carry them down the great river to the Gulf of Mexico. During the winter months, chiefs of several nearby tribes met in desperation to consider pooling their forces in an all-out effort to kill the invaders or at least drive them away for good. Through the torture of captured Indians, Moscoso learned of the confederacy being formed and thwarted it by intimidating the Indians with more acts of cruelty, which included cutting off messengers' hands and noses before sending them back to warn their chiefs not to attempt an attack.[11]

Meanwhile, Chief Quigualtam waited. He had no doubt been quite pleased to hear from his scouts that the army of bearded aliens had scurried away toward the west rather than face his wrath. And now the chief was perhaps interested to learn from his contacts along the Mississippi River that the bearded ones had returned and were encamped upriver at Aminoya. Chief Quigualtam was well aware that the Spaniards were busy building boats in preparation to enter his province, and it is highly probable that the chief's ears were full of the long list of atrocities committed by the bearded invaders. So, while the Spaniards were cobbling together their makeshift vessels during the early months of 1543, the men of Quigualtam were making their own preparations for the coming contest.[12]

THE FLIGHT DOWNRIVER

On July 2, 1543, the Mississippi River was on the rise and its current swift. General Moscoso and about 350 soldiers in seven boats, with some twenty-five to thirty Indian captives, paddled their ragged little flotilla out into the main channel to begin the long journey to the sea. In canoes lashed to the seven boats were twenty-six horses and a few hogs.[13] The Indians of Aminoya who watched the departure of the bearded ones also saw the last of their maize and other stored food carried off in the invaders' boats. According to the one of the expedition's chroniclers, the Aminoyans were in a "pitiful condition" and had been reduced to begging the soldiers for food in order to survive the winter.[14] Also watching the embarkation that day were about five hundred Indian slaves whom the Spaniards were obliged to abandon for lack of transport. These hapless castaways included men, women, and children, some of whom had been with the soldiers almost the entire journey and spoke Spanish.[15] What the surrounding tribes did with these people is not known. They were probably viewed in the same light as the bearded ones and treated accordingly. Later that day, the Spaniards passed Guachoya, where the chief and a squadron of canoes awaited them, but refrained from attacking. Instead, Chief Guachoya sent emissaries in canoes out to catch up with Moscoso and ask him if the Spaniards would like to join with them and attack Quigualtam. Moscoso suspected treachery and politely declined the offer. So with Guachoya and his canoes receding in the distance, the Spaniards entered Chief Quigualtam's domain (Figure 2).[16]

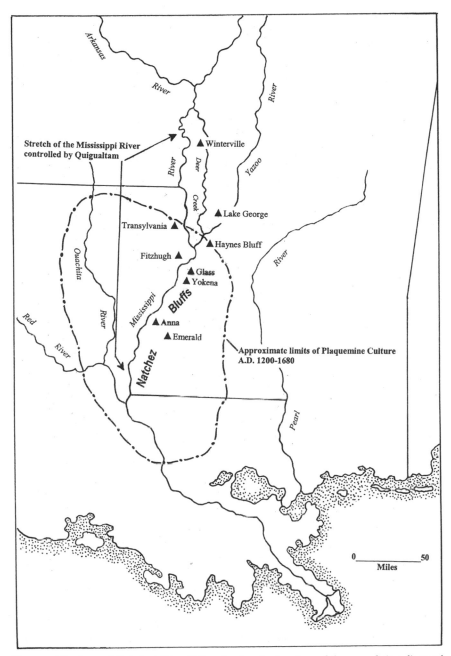

Figure 2. The Lower Mississippi River Valley showing the locations of the mound sites discussed in the text, the approximate limits of the Plaquemine Culture, and the stretch of the Mississippi River controlled by Quigualtam. (Based upon Brown 1998, 657–59; Hudson 1994, Figure 1; Jeter and Williams 1989: Figures 18–21; Worth in Clayton et al. 1993, 245.)

That first night the flotilla tied up at a wooded landing site, and the travelers slept in their boats. Under way the next morning, they came to an Indian town on the east bank. Upon finding the town deserted, Moscoso assumed that the native inhabitants had fled rather than face his army. More likely, most of the people had accompanied the town's fighting-age men, who had left to join Chief Quigualtam's gathering forces. The soldiers succeeded in capturing a woman who told them that the town belonged to a chief named Huhasene, a vassal of Quigualtam. She added that Quigualtam was waiting for them with many men. Meanwhile, a cavalry unit reconnoitering downstream a short distance located Huhasene's granaries, and the flotilla moved down to tie up and take as much maize as the boats could carry. With the local Indians showing fear and with well-stocked granaries close at hand, Moscoso and his men were probably just beginning to relax when the vanguard of Chief Quigualtam's armada of war canoes came into view upriver.

The native fleet formed up opposite the little Spanish flotilla, and Moscoso dispatched two canoes with crossbowmen to scatter the Indians.[17] To the Quigualtam boatmen watching the crossbowmen paddling toward them, one important fact was immediately obvious: Their adversaries were no match for them on the water. Mounted on their powerful warhorses, the Spaniards may have seemed invincible on land, but out on the Mississippi River it was clear that they posed little threat to these descendants of generations of riverfolk. Moscoso watched as the native canoes withdrew effortlessly before his men were able to even draw within crossbow range. Whether cruising downstream or back paddling upstream, the Quigualtam boatmen were perfectly at ease on the great river. Hurriedly, Moscoso and his men shoved off from Huhasene, with the Quigualtam armada cautiously following their progress. Along the shore, Quigualtam runners kept apace with the Spaniards' boats. Downriver, a group of Quigualtam people gathered at a town atop a bluff on the east bank. Seizing the offensive, Moscoso sent soldiers in canoes from each of his boats to attack the town. With the town's fighting-age men away in Quigualtam's canoe force, the natives retreated and allowed the invaders to burn the village. Moving further downstream, Moscoso selected a landing site beside a broad plain. Here, the army could rest on dry land, and the Indians could not approach them on foot without warning. No attack came; the warriors were content to wait until the bearded ones were back on the river. It was to be the army's last night's sleep for many nights to come.[18]

When the Spaniards cast off into the dawn mist on July 4, 1543, Quigualtam's full fleet of war canoes gathered ominously behind them. Biedma counted "forty or fifty very large and swift canoes of Indians, among which there was a canoe that carried eighty Indian warriors." Elvas reports "one hundred canoes, some of which held sixty or seventy Indians, and those of the principal men with their awnings, and they [the principal Indians] with white and colored plumes of feathers." Garcilaso says, "Among the many canoes that were found to be following the Spaniards at dawn . . . some extraordinarily large ones were seen that caused their [the Spaniards'] amazement. Those that were flagships and others similar to them were so large that they had as many as twenty-five oars per side, and in addition to the oarsmen, they carried twenty-five or thirty warriors, stationed in their order from bow to stern."[19] These native canoes that were capable of transporting from seventy to one hundred men were dugouts, fashioned from enormous logs of bald cypress. The Quigualtam armada drew up out of crossbow range, and the Spaniards watched as a small canoe with three Indians emerged from the group and approached Moscoso's boat. One of the Indians came aboard and addressed Moscoso on Chief Quigualtam's behalf, informing the general through interpreters that his chief had only friendly intentions toward the Spaniards. The emissary also asked Moscoso not to believe what he had heard about Quigualtam from the Indians of Guachoya, for they had revolted against his chief and were now their enemies. Moscoso responded with uncharacteristic politeness, although he realized that the messengers' real purpose was to get a close look at the Spaniards' numbers and weaponry. Perhaps it was the impressive sight of the native armada spread across the great river in the distance that kept the Spanish general from sending the emissaries back without their hands and noses.[20]

Upon the return of the messengers' canoe to the main body of the Quigualtam fleet, the big war canoes began to maneuver and close in on the Spaniards' position. As they plied their paddles, the native oarsmen called out in unison to the bearded ones, ridiculing the invaders and promising annihilation. To Moscoso's alarm, some of the enemy canoes were moving downriver to outflank and hem the Spaniards in at the landing. As the soldiers scrambled to cast off to try and gain the main channel ahead of the Indians, Moscoso sent twenty-five men in several canoes to help clear the way for the Spaniards' boats. The Quigualtam warriors' reaction to this counterattack was swift and efficient: The native war canoes in the vanguard divided and encircled the on-coming Spaniards. This was a battle maneuver the boatmen had no doubt executed hundreds of times, and as soon as the trap was sprung, the Indians raised a great battle cry and closed in on the astonished soldiers. A lifetime of training was brought to bear on the hapless twenty-five men as designated Indian oarsmen laid aside their paddles and leapt into the river, some to take hold and steady their own craft for their comrades, while others swam to the Spaniards' canoes and quickly overturned them. Under the weight of their armor, most of the bearded ones sank like stones, while others clinging desperately to their overturned canoes were dispatched by the warriors with clubs and paddles. A few lucky soldiers managed to survive the melee by swimming to one of their comrade's boats.[21]

Luys Hernández de Biedma, who chronicled the expedition as an official representative of the Spanish Crown, was in command of one of Moscoso's boats that day:

> The second day that we were going down river, there came forth to us about forty or fifty very large and swift canoes of Indian warriors, and they began to shoot arrows at us and pursue us, shooting more arrows at us. It seemed to some of those in our ships that it was cowardly not to attack them, and they took four or five small canoes of those that we were towing and went toward the canoes of the Indians, who, as soon as they saw them, encircled them as best they could and would not let them leave from among them. They upset the canoes in the water, and thus they killed this day twelve very honorable men, because we could not aid them, since the current of the river was so great and we had few oars in our ships.[22]

The doomed counterattack allowed Moscoso's boats to gain the current, and the chase was on. The rest of the day, the harried Spaniards struggled to keep their sluggish boats moving in some kind of order. The Quigualtam war canoes did turnabout cruising along beside their helpless quarry, with ranks of bowmen firing from their standing positions between the seated oarsmen. The oarsmen also had bows and arrows and would lay aside their paddles on command to increase their vessel's firepower. Elvas tells us that Spaniards only had one crossbow per boat and were unable to inflict any significant damage on their attackers. Those soldiers without body armor had no choice but to cower behind the gunwales. Luckily, the Spaniards had brought along a number of woven cane mats from Aminoya for bedding. In desperation, the men rigged these mats in such a way as to partially screen themselves from the fusillade of arrows. It seems that at any time, the Quigualtam fleet could have overwhelmed the Spaniards' boats, but the warriors were more than happy just to toy with the bearded aliens, relishing the chase and taking delight in their enemy's fear. As they rowed along in relentless pursuit, the native boatmen sang songs to set the rhythm of their oar strokes and frequently chanted out the name of their great chief "Quigualtam." The Spaniards never learned for certain whether or not the chief was personally leading his armada, but it is likely that he was with his men for what would have been one of his greatest triumphs.

When night fell and plunged the river into darkness, Moscoso ordered his men to continue to paddle, for the Indians were showing no signs of calling off their attack. The exhausted men were hoping that the river's current would soon carry them beyond Quigualtam's territory. Sometime in the night, the Spaniards became aware that the river behind them had fallen silent. Cautiously, they slowed their paddling and listened. Just as they began to believe that their tormentors had abandoned the chase, the war canoes came gliding silently in upon them and the blackness was shattered by war cries. With sudden fury, the attack resumed, and Moscoso and his men huddled behind their mat screens and paddled for their lives.[23]

The relentless attacks continued until noon the next day, when the warrior fleet slowed and there was a break in the action. According to Elvas, Chief Quigualtam's men turned their war canoes around at this point and headed back upriver, while the forces of a second chiefdom took up the pursuit: "They followed us that night and the next day, until noon, when we had now reached the land others whom they advised to treat us in the same way; and so they did. Those of Quigualtam returned to their own lands, and the others in fifty canoes continued to fight us for a whole day and night."[24]

However, both Biedma and Garcilaso indicate that it was indeed Quigualtam's people who pursued the Spaniards the entire way. Biedma wrote: "[After the initial skirmish] the Indians came following us down river, until we reached the sea."[25] Garcilaso wrote: "It was believed that they [Quigualtam] had followed and pursued our Spaniards four hundred leagues down the river with the continuous fighting and assaults they gave them day and night. In their songs and at other times in their shouts and outcries, they always called the name of their captain-general Quigualtanqui and never of any other cacique, as if they were saying that that great prince was the only one who was waging all that war."[26]

After almost twenty-four hours on the water chasing the Spaniards, Chief Quigualtam's warriors had probably had enough excitement to last them a lifetime. For many years to come, these men would tell and re-tell the story of their stunning victory over the bearded aliens who had caused other chiefdoms so much strife. If Elvas is to be believed, and a fresh warrior armada appeared around noon on July 5 to relieve the Quigualtam men, the new force apparently represented a chiefdom that was subject to Chief Quigualtam's authority. Obviously, word of the Spaniards' presence on the river had quickly reached fighting-age men from settlements throughout Quigualtam's realm. Even before the Spaniards embarked from Aminoya, Quigualtam's southern contingent had been gathering their weapons and decorating their war canoes in anticipation of the bearded aliens' arrival in their bailiwick.

The war canoes harassed the Spaniards the rest of the day and again through the night, finally leaving off around 10:00 A.M. the next morning, probably some distance south of the present day city of Natchez.[27] Even after this native fleet had turned back, other villages downstream, perhaps outside of Quigualtam's realm, were unable to resist sending out a few canoes to take swipes at the bearded ones who were so formidable on land but so helpless on the great river. Although their dignity had suffered greatly, most of the Spanish soldiers who began the fearful journey downriver made it to the sea shaken but still alive.[28]

With that, Moscoso and his bedraggled remnant of an army passed out of the Lower Mississippi Valley and our story. The narratives of Biedma, Elvas, and Garcilaso provide us with a brilliant, but narrow, window on the people of the Lower Mississippi Valley during the few days that the Spaniards were in their midst. But was Quigualtam a Natchezan chiefdom? Two lines of evidence seem to support this conclusion: geography and linguistics. Geographically, the stretch of the Mississippi River under Quigualtam's control extends well into the area of the prehistoric Plaquemine culture, which has been securely linked with the historic Natchez (Figure 2). According to the most recent interpretation of the route traveled by the De Soto army, archaeologist Charles Hudson believes that Chief Quigualtam's armada first encountered Moscoso's flotilla a short distance south of the mouth of the Arkansas River, and the southern chiefdom enjoined the attack near the mouth of the Yazoo River. The attacks apparently persisted until the Spaniards had passed the Natchez area.[29]

Because De Soto and his men never went to Chief Quigaultam's residence, the location of Quigualtam's primary ceremonial center remains a mystery. Over the past seventy-five years, archaeologists have identified numerous mound groups in the Lower Mississippi Valley that were probably occupied around the De Soto timeline, and a few might serve as candidates for Quigualtam. Of these, four sites have dominant mounds built to heights of over forty feet and are certainly large enough to seem worthy of such a powerful chief: Winterville and Lake George in Lower Yazoo Basin, and Anna and Emerald in the Natchez Bluffs (Figure 2).[30] According to LMS archaeological findings, both Winterville and Lake George were in full flower during the thirteenth and fourteenth centuries but seem to have been in serious decline or completely abandoned by 1500.[31] Nevertheless, Arkansas archaeologist Marvin Jeter notes that the terminal occupation at Winterville is not dated and that the site's artifact assemblage indicates occupation during the time of the De Soto expedition.[32]

Whether or not Winterville was Chief Quigualtam's home, his war armada may have used the Deer Creek outflow a few miles north of Winterville to enter the Mississippi River (Figure 2). Charles Hudson's reconstruction of the locations and events during the Spaniards' trip down the Mississippi River places the head of the Deer Creek outflow north of Huhasene.[33] This would agree with Elvas' account of Quigualtam's war canoes making their first appearance upriver from the Spaniards while the soldiers were raiding the Huhasene granaries.[34] The vanguard of Quigualtam's fleet could have waited in hiding at the Deer Creek outlet and allowed the Spaniards' boats to pass downriver on July 2 before entering the Mississippi in order to position the armada upstream from the enemy.

Farther south in the Natchez Bluffs, the Anna and Emerald sites must also be considered as candidates for Quigualtam's residence; both sites were occupied during the A.D. 1200–1600 period. According to LMS investigations, Anna was probably constructed earlier than Emerald and the periods of occupation for the two mound centers overlapped.[35] Emerald's dates of occupation apparently coincide with the De Soto timeline, although the mound center's location seems to be too far to the south if the expedition's embarkation point was in southeastern Arkansas. Emerald as Quigualtam takes on more credence in LMS archaeologist Jeffrey Brain's interpretation of the Moscoso-Quigualtam confrontation. Brain argues that the Spaniards' embarkation point was in northeastern Louisiana and that Quigualtam's force made its appearance in the vicinity of present-day Vicksburg.[36]

Several somewhat smaller, but nonetheless impressive, mound centers in the Lower Mississippi Valley appear to have been occupied around De Soto's time and should also be mentioned. On the west side of the Mississippi River, in the Tensas River Basin, the Transylvania and Fitzhugh mound sites are large ceremonial centers with dominant mounds that reach about thirty feet in height.[37] Likewise, in the northern part of the Natchez Bluffs, the Haynes Bluff, Glass, and Yokena mound sites contain dominant mounds of thirty feet or more in height.[38] If none of these secondary centers was Quigualtam's headquarters, then perhaps the people who built these mound centers were part of his chiefdom. For now, the Quigualtam mystery points up the difficulty in achieving a clean interface between archaeology and history in the Lower Mississippi Valley.

Along with geography, there is some tentative linguistic evidence for classifying Quigualtam as Natchezan. The Natchez language is now considered to have been a language isolate; that is, it was a separate language from the languages spoken by neighboring Lower Mississippi Valley tribes such as the Tunica, Choctaw, and Chickasaw.[39] Our information about the Natchez language comes from interviews with Natchez Indian descendants carried out during the late 1800s and early 1900s. Scholars including Albert Gatschet, Albert Pike, D. G. Brinton, Albert Gallatin, Mary Haas, and John R. Swanton searched out Natchez speakers and collected words and stories.[40] Using Natchez language word lists, Swanton identified Quigualtam as possibly being Natchezan. Marvin D. Jeter has also pointed out that a number of chiefdom names recorded by the De Soto expedition in eastern and southeastern Arkansas were also identified by Swanton as possibly being Natchezan, including Aminoya, Guachoya, Anilco, and Utiangue/Autiamque.[41] If this was the case, the Spaniards may have been virtually surrounded by Natchezan-speaking peoples once the expedition reached the confluence of the Arkansas and Mississippi rivers.

QUIGUALTAM'S WARRIOR BOATMEN

The extraordinary performance of the Quigualtam warriors suggests a long-established warrior tradition oriented toward fighting on the Mississippi River. Indeed, the Quigualtam force was apparently typical of the armadas representing other major chiefdoms along the Mississippi River in the mid-sixteenth century. When the De Soto army first came to the Mississippi River in May 1541, a fleet of two hundred canoes commanded by a chief named Aquixo converged on the place where the Spaniards were busy building rafts. The discipline and skill displayed by the Aquixo boatmen that day impressed even the militaristic Spaniards. As the lead boats of the armada approached the riverbank to parlay, De Soto attempted to lure the Aquixo chiefs ashore in order to capture them. Elvas described what happened when the chiefs began to suspect a trap: "Upon seeing that the governor and his men were on their guard, they began to withdraw from land. With loud cries, the crossbowmen who were ready, shot at them and struck five or six. They withdrew in splendid order; no one abandoned his paddle even though the one near him fell."[42]

To say the least, the Spaniards were similarly impressed with the Quigualtam navy. Had they known more about the challenges of maneuvering large craft on the Mississippi River, Moscoso and his men might have held their foes in even higher esteem. The following excerpts from John M. Barry's book *Rising Tide: The Great Mississippi Flood of 1927 and How It Changed America* may help readers who are not familiar with this river to understand some of the factors with which the Natchezan boatmen had to contend: "The Mississippi never lies at rest. It roils. It follows no set course. Its waters and currents are not uniform. Rather, it moves south in layers and whorls, like an uncoiling rope made up of a multitude of discrete fibers, each one separately and together capable of snapping like a whip. It never has one current, one velocity." "The river's sinuosity itself generates enormous force. The Mississippi snakes seaward in a continual series of S curves that sometimes approach 180 degrees. The collision of river and earth at these bends creates tremendous turbulence: currents can drive straight down to the bottom of the river, sucking at whatever lies on the surface." "For the last 450 miles of the Mississippi's flow, the riverbed lies below sea level—15 feet below sea level at Vicksburg, well over 170 feet below sea level at New Orleans. For these 450 miles the water on the bottom has no reason to flow at all. But the water above it does. This creates a tumbling effect as water spills over itself, like an enormous ever-breaking wave."[43] In July 1543, the Mississippi River was experiencing an unusual mid-summer flood, which would have made it an even more complex surface upon which to maneuver.[44]

The men who operated Quigualtam's colossal war canoes were not professional soldiers, but rather they were members of a militia force.[45] Upon receiving the call to arms from Chief Quigualtam, they had left their villages and farms and assembled to present the bearded invaders with as imposing a show of force as they could muster. And a show of force was probably the most important element in the game of warfare among the chiefdoms of the Lower Mississippi Valley. Although there are a couple of sixteenth-century accounts of pitched battles among Southeastern tribes, petty raids and ambushes, with little loss of life, were much more common.[46] Therefore, the river chiefdoms such as Aquixo, Guachoya, and Quigualtam probably used their flamboyant warrior fleets not to sail into battle but to maintain a state of detent. One can imagine two such fleets drawing within shouting distance so that boat crews could chant outlandish boasts, and each side might regale the other with songs about the heroic acts of their leaders— exactly as the Quigualtam boatmen had done when they approached Moscoso's flotilla. If such confrontations escalated to bow and arrow attacks, the boat crews were protected by tightly woven cane shields, which, according to Rodrigo Rangel, were "so strong and so tightly sewn that a crossbow would scarcely pierce them."[47]

Reading the Quigualtam accounts from the De Soto chronicles, the sudden appearance of the Indian war canoes is deceptive and belies the days or possibly weeks of preparation to assemble such a force comprised of militia. An example from a previous encounter indicates that Chief Quigualtam may have taken up to two weeks to assemble his warrior armada. On May 8, 1541, De Soto and his men completely surprised the town of Quizquiz when the army emerged from its trek across uninhabited land in what is now north-central Mississippi and entered the Mississippi River Valley for the first time. Here the Spaniards came upon a number of heavily populated river chiefdoms and, to their relief, copious maize granaries. Fourteen days later, on May 22, Chief Aquixo arrived with his two hundred war canoes at De Soto's camp on the east bank of the Mississippi River.[48]

In order to have his armada on the river and ready for action just one day after Moscoso and his men set out from Aminoya, Chief Quigualtam had to have anticipated the coming of the Spaniards. While the soldiers at Aminoya were completing work on their boats, Quigualtam's warrior boatmen were already preparing for action. As mentioned above, it is likely that, before emerging into the main channel of the Mississippi, the Quigualtam armada lay ready and hidden until Moscoso's boats drifted downriver.

Two of the battle tactics employed by the Quigualtam warriors bespeak considerable training and teamwork. The first was the concerted action of the phalanx of war canoes to divide into two arms and encircle an approaching enemy. This maneuver was made even more effective by Quigualtam's men having positioned themselves upstream from their foes. In this way, the warriors used the current to their advantage as the Spaniards labored to paddle upstream to make an attack. Such naval maneuvers were probably an important part of the militaristic showmanship calculated to impress an opposing chiefdom or, as the bearded invaders discovered too late, could be executed with lethal effect on a weaker opponent. The second tactic is the extraordinary teamwork displayed by Indian rowers who dove into the river as the battle closed to steady the gunwales of their own canoes for the standing archers, while others swam to the Spaniards' canoes and capsized them. All of this seems to indicate that river-oriented chiefdoms incorporated a long-standing and effective militia tradition that prepared men for the precision teamwork required to handle a 100-foot-long war canoe on the precarious and capricious Mississippi River.

THE DARK AGE OF SICKNESS AND DEATH

For nearly thirty years before the De Soto expedition penetrated the interior of the Southeast, Spanish ships had reconnoitered along the Gulf Coast from Florida to Texas. Among the earliest encounters between Indians and Europeans was Juan Ponce de León's landing in southern Florida in 1513.[49] Alvarez de Pineda's voyage along the Gulf Coast in 1519 had little contact with the coastal tribes; however, the expedition led by Panfilo de Narváez in 1528 made direct contact with Indians in the Florida panhandle and around Mobile Bay. Some members of the Narváez expedition were even abandoned to fend for themselves among the natives. In 1559–1561, Tristán de Luna y Arellano led expeditions among the tribes living up the valleys of the Alabama and Tombigbee rivers.[50] During the sixteenth century, Spaniards also pushed into the interior of the Southeast from the southern Atlantic seacoast.[51]

These face-to-face meetings between Indians, Europeans, and Africans set in motion the transmission from hand to hand, village to village, and chiefdom to chiefdom of devastating diseases that would have catastrophic consequences; the Southeastern Indians had no natural immunities against the germs being introduced from foreign continents. The De Soto expedition, numbering close to seven hundred people, had the longest sustained contact with the Southeastern Indians—for four long years, the interior tribes of the Southeast were exposed to infection from the Spaniards.[52] Patricia Galloway has noted the possibility that diseases may also have been spread among the Indians by the herd of pigs that accompanied the expedition.[53] Epidemics affecting the Southeastern Indians during this period are poorly documented but may have included influenza, malaria, smallpox, measles, typhus, and mumps.[54] The hierarchical ranking of lineages within the populous chiefdoms broke down as both elites and commoners succumbed to the sicknesses. All told, the century following the De Soto expedition must have been a dark age for the Native inhabitants of the Lower Mississippi Valley.[55]

However, we cannot lay all of the blame for the decimation of the Southeastern Indian populations at the feet of the Spanish conquistadors. The mound-building civilizations of Cahokia and Moundville that arose around A.D. 1000 had completely collapsed before the beginning of the sixteenth century, possibly because of overuse and exhaustion of available farmland.[56] Patricia Galloway has also pointed out the possible relationship between the decline of the Mississippian chiefdoms around the beginning of the sixteenth century and the onset of the Little Ice Age, which began around A.D. 1300 and lasted into the nineteenth century. The adverse affect of the colder climate on agriculture in Europe has been well-documented, and the drop in temperatures probably had a similar impact on the annual maize harvests, especially in the Middle Mississippi Valley.[57]

In the Lower Mississippi Valley, the archaeology indicates a decline in population in the sixteenth century, especially in the Yazoo Basin. At around this same time a significant shift in settlement patterning away from the Mississippi River and toward the eastern part of the Yazoo Basin has been noted by Jeffrey P. Brain.[58] These demographic changes seem especially momentous when we consider the people's ancient connection to the Mississippi River. Brain suggests that exposure to diseases and intertribal warfare may have pushed the population into the interior. The Natchez Bluffs seem to have been somewhat sheltered from the forces bringing about the population loss in the Yazoo Basin. LMS archaeology indicates that activity at the Anna mounds had decreased considerably by the beginning of the sixteenth century. After Anna, Emerald Mound became the focus of the people of the Natchez Bluffs. As we will see in Chapter Two, one of the smaller Mississippi Period mound centers in the Natchez Bluffs, known to archaeologists as the Fatherland site, was destined to play a central role in the eighteenth-century history of the Natchez Indians, when it was known as "the Grand Village of the Natchez Indians."[59]

Despite the enormous investment in time and energy by the Natchezan people in the construction and maintenance of Emerald Mound, its builders eventually abandoned this ceremonial earthwork. The absence of European trade artifacts at Emerald indicates that the site had ceased to function as a ceremonial center by the mid-1600s.[60] The reasons for this event have thus far eluded archaeologists and historians. Karl G. Lorenz suggests that Emerald's demise may have been caused by a combination of "cycling" or fluctuation in the size and complexity of Southeastern chiefdoms due to internal competition for leadership, and external pressures from European encroachment.[61] Whatever the causes, by the end of the 1600s the population in the Natchez Bluffs was considerably reduced, and the remnants of the Emerald chiefdom gathered in several small settlement districts near the modern city of Natchez.

The decline of the Lower Mississippi Valley's indigenous population opened up the region to tribal migrations of displaced Mississippian peoples from the north. The Diaspora included groups such as the Koroa, Tiou, Tunica, and Grigra, who were refugees from the upheaval of societies accompanying collapse of chiefdoms throughout the Mississippi River Valley.[62] By the close of the seventeenth century, elements of the Koroa, Tiou, and Grigra, all possibly Tunican-speaking groups, had found residence among the Natchez Indians.[63] Despite the quickening chaos around them, the people of the Natchez Bluffs managed to hold fast to their ancient homeland.

The northern part of the old Natchezan region, around the mouth of the Arkansas River, fell to the Acansa, also known as the Arkansas or Quapaw. Like most of the groups migrating into the region, the Acansa's origins are uncertain; however, they are considered to be a relatively late arrival on the scene.[64] The Chakchiuma, a Muskogean-speaking tribe in the northern Yazoo Basin, was very likely a remnant of the Mississippian chiefdoms associated with the Tombigbee River Valley farther east.[65] In the lower Yazoo Basin, three small Tunican-speaking groups held sway: the Yazoo, a Koroa group, and the Tunica themselves.[66]

According to Jeffrey P. Brain, the ancestors of the Tunica were living in the northern Yazoo Basin in the sixteenth century and are represented by the chiefdom of Quizquiz, which the De Soto expedition encountered in 1541. By the beginning of the eighteenth century, the Tunica had relocated to the Lower Yazoo River with the Koroa and Yazoo. After that, they moved farther south to the rugged area of the southern Natchez Bluffs known as the "Tunica Hills," opposite the mouth of the Red River. By 1790, the Tunica had migrated up the Red River to join the Avoyel in the vicinity of Marksville, Louisiana.[67] Marvin D. Jeter believes that the ancestral Tunicans may have moved down the valley from as far north as the Ozark Mountains of eastern Arkansas.[68]

Not far below the mouth of the Yazoo River, on the west side of the Mississippi River, the Taensa, a Natchez-speaking tribe, occupied several villages and a ceremonial mound center.[69] The Taensa, along with the Avoyel, a Natchez-speaking group located on the Red River about fifty miles from the Mississippi, probably constitute the remnants of the Natchezan people in the Tensas Basin.[70] Jeter has suggested that the Taensa's northern range in prehistoric times may have extended up into east central Arkansas, where he labels them "Northern Natchezans."[71]

Two large and far-ranging Muskogean-speaking tribes, the Chickasaw and Choctaw, were spread over an immense area that encompassed southwestern Tennessee, eastern Mississippi, and western Alabama. Like the Chakchiuma in the northern Yazoo Basin, the Chickasaw and Choctaw were the seventeenth-century descendants of the prehistoric chiefdoms of the region Patricia Galloway calls the "Tombigbee/Mobile Valleys."[72] Other important Muskogean groups on the lower Mississippi below the Natchez included the Houma, Bayogoula, and Quinipissa.[73] The Chitimacha, possibly of the Tunican language family, occupied the bayou lowlands between the lower Mississippi River and Atchafalaya Bay.[74]

All of these groups subsisted on a blend of hunting, fishing, gathering, and maize-beans-squash agriculture. The cultivation, consumption, and, importantly, long-term storage of maize, which had been especially prominent in De Soto's time, was just as robust in the late seventeenth century. The plentiful springtime supplies of maize documented among the Lower Mississippi Valley tribes by the La Salle expedition attest to the continued importance of storage granaries in these societies.[75]

When Europeans returned to the Lower Mississippi Valley a little over a century after De Soto, they came to stay. The expeditions of Marquette and Jolliet, La Salle and Tonti, and the corps of missionaries, soldiers, and entrepreneurs who followed behind them, found a place that was drastically different from the ostentatious world of Quigualtam, Guachoya, Aquixo, and their legions of warrior boatmen. The Natchez Indians, a small remnant of those sixteenth-century river empires, were about to play a brief and tragic part in shaping world history through their association with the agents and armies of two European superpowers: England and France.

Chapter Two

EUROPEAN RECONNAISSANCE,
1682–1715

→ →　　　　　　　　　　　　　　　　　　　　　← ←

BY THE END OF THE SEVENTEENTH CENTURY, the native peoples of the Lower Mississippi Valley (Figure 3) had become unknowing subjects of an overlapping patchwork of competing political, economic, and religious empires. Europe's superpowers weren't timid when they staked their claims to North America: France's Louisiana colony encompassed the Mississippi River Valley from the Illinois country down to the Gulf of Mexico, and England's vast Carolina Province cross-cut Louisiana as it stretched from the Atlantic to the Pacific between 36 degrees and 31 degrees longitude. Superimposed upon these two opposing interests lay the spiritual jurisdiction of the Roman Catholic Church.[1] Spain remained on the periphery of the French-English struggle for the Mississippi region in the late seventeenth and early eighteenth centuries, maintaining mission settlements in Florida and the Rio Grande Valley.[2]

Of course, the Natchez Indians and other Mississippi tribes were not privy to the plans being made for them in the schemes that were bandied about in the palaces of London and Paris and in the halls of the Vatican. One of the schemers was René-Robert Cavelier de La Salle, who naively assured the French Crown in 1677 that the Indians of the Mississippi Valley would "readily adapt themselves to us and imitate our way of life as soon as they taste the advantages of our friendship and of the commodities we bring them, insomuch that these countries will infallibly furnish, within a few years, a great many new subjects to the Church and the King."[3]

Five years later, La Salle put his ambitious plan into action. His historic expedition down the Mississippi River to the Gulf of Mexico was an inevitable outgrowth of France's seventeenth-century colonial activities in Canada, known as "New France." In 1673, the Jolliet-Marquette expedition had descended the Mississippi as far south as the Acansa villages near the mouth of the Arkansas River, and it was only a matter of time before someone would follow through

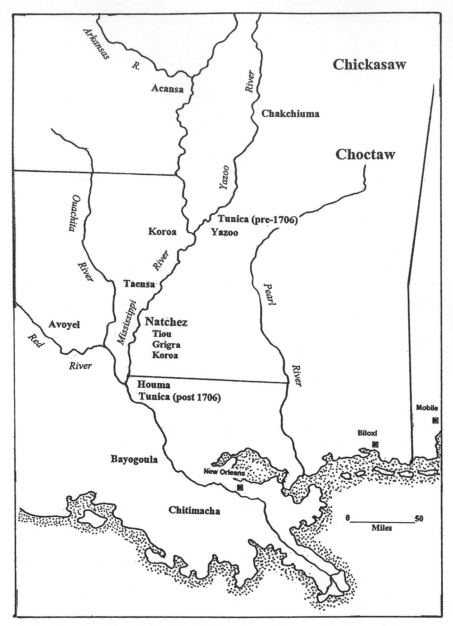

Figure 3. Location of Lower Mississippi Valley tribes, c. 1682–1735. (Based upon Galloway 1995, Figure 8.1; Swanton 1911, Plate 1.)

and reach the sea. La Salle's party, comprised of twenty-seven Mahican Indians (including seven women and two small children) and twenty-four Frenchmen, set out from the southern end of Lake Michigan in December 1681. In contrast to the cypress dugout canoes in use for centuries by Indians in the Lower Mississippi Valley, La Salle's party traveled in lightweight elm- and birch-bark canoes.[4]

Although La Salle's untimely death in 1687 precluded any memoirs he may have intended, narratives of the Mississippi expedition exist in various forms by two members of his party: Henri de Tonti and Nicolas de la Salle (no relation to the commander). Tonti needs little introduction. He was second in command of the expedition and had assisted La Salle with explorations in the Great Lakes area. Known for his skills as a backwoodsman and for his iron hand—he lost his right hand fighting the Spanish in Sicily—Tonti continued to be a force in the Lower Mississippi Valley for two decades.[5] Nicolas de la Salle was an official record keeper for La Salle's expedition. He later served as a naval officer and participated in the establishment of France's Louisiana colony.[6]

Following the Illinois River down to the Mississippi, the La Salle expedition reached the mouth of the Arkansas River and the villages of the Acansa by the second week of March 1682. At the Acansa, La Salle bought a young Mosopelea slave boy, whom he later traded to the Taensa.[7] Continuing southward, the party spent three or four days as guests of the Taensa, who lived some thirty-five to forty miles upriver from the Natchez, on the west side of the Mississippi (Figure 4). With the Taensa were some captive Koroa Indians, and Tonti and one of the Mahican Indians purchased two Koroa boys as slaves.[8] Departing the Taensa, the expedition spent the night of March 25 on an island in the river a few miles upstream from where a large contingent of Natchez men awaited them at a riverside camp.[9] The expedition's historic first glimpse of the Natchez Indians is recorded by Tonti: "The morning of the 26th, being on the water two leagues [six miles] from our camp, we perceived a dugout canoe crossing the river. We gave chase to it; my canoe, which traveled the best, distanced all the others, and as I was about to come up with the dugout I was surprised to see the whole shore lined with savages, bow and arrow in hand."[10]

The lone Indian boatman was probably a sentry who had spotted the French expedition and alerted his tribesmen. Tonti's intent was not to harm the Indian but to make the acquaintance of his chief. Outnumbered, Tonti and company broke off their pursuit, and La Salle and his men landed their canoes on the opposite bank. When tensions had cooled down a bit, Tonti crossed the river to present the calumet to the natives. His narrative continues: "As soon as I set foot

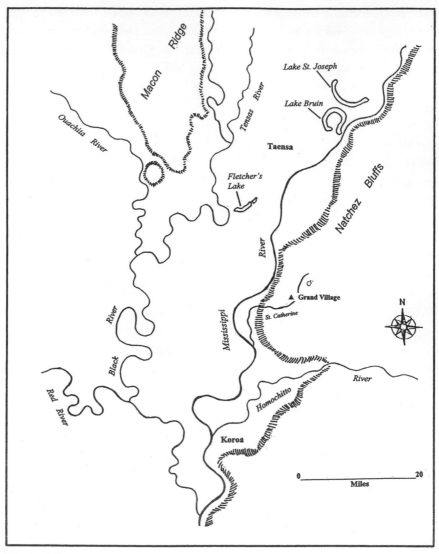

Figure 4. Fletcher's Lake, Lake St. Joseph, and the approximate locations of the Taensa and Koroa at the time of the La Salle expedition.

to earth on the other side where the savages were they sat down. I made them smoke the peace calumet, and gave a knife to an old man who appeared to me to be the chief. He put it promptly inside of his blanket as if he had committed a theft. Joining my hands I imitated him, because that signifies in their manner that people are friends."[11]

Assured for the time being of the strangers' peaceful intentions, the Natchez allowed La Salle and his men to cross the river and join Tonti. Although Tonti took one of the Natchez men on the riverbank to be a chief, the Frenchmen learned that the tribe's paramount chief was waiting for them at his village some distance in from the river. Later that day or the next (the narratives are vague on this point), La Salle and a small company of men, escorted by Natchez Indians, set out to meet the tribe's leader.[12]

The written accounts become confusing and contradictory once La Salle departs the riverbank to journey inland on his diplomatic duty. Unfortunately for historians, both Tonti and Nicolas remained at the riverside camp while their commander went to the chief's village. Tonti says that La Salle spent just one night as a guest of the Natchez chief;[13] however, Nicolas' journal, which is considered a more accurate itinerary of the trip, indicates that La Salle spent three days with the Natchez chief.[14] All of the accounts seem to agree that the chief's home village was called Nahy or Natché and that it was located three leagues (nine miles) from where the expedition landed. Chiefs from other Natchez villages were apparently invited to come and meet La Salle, but only one, the chief of the nearby Koroa tribe, seems to have responded to the invitation.[15]

Following his parlay with the Natchez chief, La Salle returned to the riverside camp and he and his men floated six to ten leagues (18 to 30 miles) down the Mississippi River, where they visited the Koroa village on a bluff next to the river. Here the Frenchmen were treated to a calumet ceremony and a welcoming feast, which was attended by Natchez Indians who had traveled downriver on foot. Two days later (Tonti says it was Easter Sunday), the expedition shoved off to continue its southward voyage.[16] Several days downriver, in the vicinity of the modern city of New Orleans, La Salle and his party were attacked by a tribe called the Quinipissa, who were allied with the Natchez and Koroa.[17] On the expedition's return voyage back up the Mississippi River, the Quinipissa again assaulted the Frenchmen and sent messengers upriver to implore the Natchez and Koroa to do the same.[18] When La Salle's group arrived back at the Koroa village, hungry and tired from paddling upriver, the chief invited them up to the village for a meal. While they were eating, many young warriors gathered menacingly about brandishing their weapons. Tonti estimated the number of warriors at one thousand; Nicolas describes an even more threatening scenario: "Halfway through our meal, we suddenly saw ourselves surrounded by about two thousand men daubed with red and black, tomahawks in hand and bows and arrows. They appeared to have ill intentions."[19]

Ominously, the French recognized some Quinipissa warriors among the hostile faces. To make matters worse, one of the Koroa slaves whom the expedition had acquired from the Taensa described to his countrymen how the French had been killing their allies, the Quinipissa. Upon being shown two Quinipissa scalps, which members of the expedition carried as grisly souvenirs from their skirmish downstream, Nicolas says that some of the Koroas "rubbed them with plaintive cries."[20] Although the situation was tense, La Salle and his men brazened it out and departed on the advice of the Koroa chief, who suggested the Frenchmen move on upriver to the Natchez.[21] Upon reaching the Natchez landing, the expedition found the riverbank deserted. Unsure of their welcome among these allies of the Koroa and Quinipissa, the Frenchmen encamped on the west bank of the river. To threaten away any Natchez who may have been contemplating an attack, Nicolas says that the French "shrieked as the Indians do as if to kill." The expedition didn't linger in Natchez country but moved out the next morning to ascend the river to the friendlier Taensa.[22]

CORRELATING HISTORY AND ARCHAEOLOGY

In all likelihood, the Nahy or Natché village visited by La Salle was the ceremonial mound center that the colonial French would later come to know as the Grand Village of the Natchez (Figure 4).[23] John R. Swanton is probably correct in surmising that the Natchez themselves referred to the chief's village as Nahy or Natché.[24] Although the Grand Village sits only one league (3 miles) inland from the Mississippi River and La Salle's informants all agree that the distance in to the chief's village was three leagues, we have no way of knowing where along the river the Frenchmen originally landed. Swanton's suggestion that La Salle's riverside camp was in the vicinity of Hutchins Landing near the mouth of St. Catherine Creek is a good fit distance-wise; Hutchins Landing is about 9 miles southeast of the Grand Village.[25] Importantly, archaeological investigations at the Grand Village turned up innumerable European trade items, including silver and brass bells, iron hoes and hatchet heads, brass kettles and pans, glass wine bottles and trade beads, elegant faience (tin-glazed ceramic) pitchers and bowls, and gun parts, all of which confirm the site's occupation during the time of French contact.[26]

Two other Natchez-area mound sites, Emerald Mound and Foster Mound, have been suggested as alternative locations for the village of the Natchez chief in 1682.[27] However, archaeological investigations at these sites have failed to find any artifactual evidence of European contact.[28] Even though La Salle's was probably the first European expedition since De Soto's to meet the Natchez Indians face to face, the Mississippi tribes had long felt the effects of European presence in the region. William C. Foster has pointed out the presence of European and North African plants in the Lower Mississippi Valley at the time of the La Salle expedition, including domesticated apple, peach, pear, plum, pomegranate, and watermelon. Just how and when these plants reached the region remains a mystery; Foster speculates that some or all of them may have been introduced from Spanish missions in northern Mexico during the late 1500s.[29] By the 1670s, English traders from the Carolina colony were distributing guns, iron hatchets and knives, and glass beads among the Mississippi Valley tribes. In 1673, Father Jacques Marquette and Louis Joliet found English trade goods among the Acansa living near the mouth of the Arkansas River. Seventeenth-century European trade items were also traveling down the Mississippi Valley from France's early settlements in Canada and passing into the interior Southeast from Spanish settlements in Florida.[30] Unfortunately, we don't know what European items La Salle may have seen at the main Natchez village, but members of his expedition saw copper and brass objects, guns, and even a Spanish sword in the main Taensa village, and copper springs of possible English origin at the Koroa village.[31] Since most of these exotic items would have flowed directly to the chiefly residences, any ceremonial centers occupied during the late seventeenth century would be expected to contain some European trade artifacts.

Scholars have debated the origins of the calumet ceremony, and some have suggested that the custom may have been introduced to the Lower Mississippi Valley tribes by the French.[32] If so, the French often misunderstood the ritual's meaning to the Native Americans. The calumet ceremony provided a way for two strangers to establish a fictive kinship as a basis for further negotiations. However, while the Native Americans usually saw the ceremony as temporary and fleetingly binding only to those few who were present, the Europeans often took the ritual to be permanent and binding to not only the chief but to all of his people.[33] At times, these different perceptions led to disastrous results. And as will be seen in later accounts, both the French and the Indians also occasionally used the calumet ceremony as a cunning ruse to trap and overcome opponents.

The Clark Bayou and Beasley archaeological sites beside Lake St. Joseph, an ox-bow lake in Tensas Parish, Louisiana, have been identified as possible locations for the historic Taensa villages. LMS surface investigations at both sites yielded Natchezan pottery fragments and a few stone tools; however, the absence of European trade items makes the association of these sites with the historic Taensa questionable.[34] Mississippi archaeologist Joseph V. Frank suggests that an alternative location for the Taensa villages might be in the vicinity of Fletchers

Lake in Concordia Parish, about 21 miles southwest of Lake St. Joseph (Figure 4). Frank's argument is based upon Fletchers Lake's proximity to the historic "Texas Road," an important east-west running trail that was probably used in prehistoric times.[35] At least three archaeological sites have been identified near Fletchers Lake, although none are associated with European trade items.[36] For now, the exact location of the Taensa villages remains a mystery.

Tonti's memoirs include two more voyages he made down the Mississippi River. In 1686 and again in 1690 he tried in vain to link up with La Salle, who had sailed from France in 1684 to establish a colony at the mouth of the Mississippi. In one of history's most famous navigational blunders, La Salle overshot his objective and landed somewhere on the Texas coast, where he and his colony eventually perished.[37] Tonti's 1686 and 1690 Mississippi River descents provide little new information on the Natchez Indians, which is unfortunate. As will be seen below, the period between 1682 and the arrival of Iberville and the French missionaries in 1700 were critical years of transition for the Natchez, as they were pulled beneath the overlapping shadows of both England and France.

Probably by 1686 and certainly by 1690, other Frenchmen had followed in La Salle's wake seeking trade and adventure among the Lower Mississippi Valley tribes. When Tonti passed through the Natchez area in 1686, his stop at a Natchez (or more likely Koroa) village did nothing to endear the native people to the French cause: "Having left the Taensa the first of April, after having navigated for 16 leagues, we arrived at the village of the Nachés, where the chief awaited me on the bank with the calumet. It is a nation which can furnish fifteen hundred fighting men. I did not sleep there. I contented myself with complaining that they had wished to kill us treacherously four years before, to which they answered nothing."[38]

Although Tonti's memoirs indicate that this incident took place at a Natchez village, John R. Swanton has pointed out that Tonti probably landed at the Koroa's riverside village, the Natchez villages all being situated some distance away from the river. Tonti's accusation of treachery "four years before," is obviously a reference to the Koroa-Quinipissa incident.[39]

THE INDIAN SLAVE TRADE

The hostility that La Salle and his men experienced with the Quinipissa and Koroa might simply be written off as cautious aggression on the part of the native inhabitants; however, there was another important factor that was driving the spread of mistrust and unrest among the Lower Mississippi tribes: the Indian slave trade. To be sure, the Natchez were caught up in this dark business and to understand their behavior it is necessary to trace the path by which the slave trade reached their homeland.

Long before La Salle's voyage, the presence of Europeans around the periphery of the Southeast had a tremendous effect on the interior tribes through the realignment of trade relationships and alliances, with the subsequent domino effect rippling into the interior. However, it was the intense pressure from English-instigated slave raids that had the greatest impact on the people of the Natchezan region in the closing decades of the seventeenth century. The English-Indian slave trade began around 1670, when colonial proprietors in Virginia and Carolina enlisted neighboring tribes to supply deerskins, furs, and border protection. Captives taken in the inevitable conflicts that arose from these alliances became a source of profit as enterprising traders found ready buyers through the slave markets in Charles Town and Port Royal. Soon, the Westo and other tribes in the Virginia-Carolina region were actively supplying the English with Indian slaves, who were being exchanged throughout the network of British colonies along the eastern seaboard and the Caribbean Islands for other goods and African slaves.[40]

As the Carolina slave raids spread further inland in search of new victims, the Westo penetrated the Lower Mississippi Valley, eventually bringing the Chickasaw into the cycle of violence. At about the same time, English traders reached the Illinois country and made their way south to contact the Chickasaw, arming them with guns and supplying them with other European goods.[41] Dr. Henry Woodward, who had helped put the Westo in the slave-catching business, was also contacting the Chickasaw around 1688.[42] As English contacts in the region spread, tribes were obliged to do business with the traders, for to do otherwise was to risk being targeted by slave-catchers.[43]

In the Chickasaw of northeastern Mississippi, the Carolina traders found a potent slave-catching force with the wherewithal to go marauding among the numerous smaller tribes in the Lower Mississippi Valley. The Chickasaw recognized two paths to tribal leadership, that of hereditary chief through an elite lineage, and big-man leaders whose authority was based upon individual ability and charisma instead of the inheritance of power through a lineage.[44] Chiefs of individual Chickasaw towns could be either hereditary chiefs or big-men; however, "war chiefs" who took control in times of aggression were big-men.[45] The English slave trade provided an unprecedented opportunity for Chickasaw big-men, as war chiefs, to enjoy positions of power for extended periods of time.

Prior to European contact, hereditary chiefs maintained their power by controlling the people's access to desired trade items; that is, chiefdoms interacted with each other through the communication between their elite lineages. The coming of the French and English with their trade emphasis on animal skins and slaves undermined the power of the hereditary chiefs. Instead of the European traders restricting their communication to the leaders of the elite lineages, the French and English were happy to deal with any tribal member with the entrepreneurial skills to provide these two raw materials. Big-man leaders could fill this lucrative niche.[46] Alliances were mercurial. One Chickasaw big-man could lead a small raiding party for quick profits or assemble a force of several hundred men for a slave raid to capture an entire village. Small refugee tribes such as the Koroa, who were attached to the Natchez, found safety in numbers to be their best defense against the Chickasaw slave-catchers. Indeed, fear of English and Chickasaw slavers may have induced the Quinipissa to show hostility toward La Salle's party and hurriedly fall back on the protection of the Natchez-Koroa.

Slave-catching escalated during 1690s and on into the early eighteenth century. In 1698, the English slave trader Thomas Welch began his long and profitable business association with the Chickasaw.[47] Three of the tribes heavily victimized by the Chickasaw were the Acansa, Tunica, and Taensa. Alan Gallay estimates that as many as three thousand people may have been taken from the Lower Mississippi Valley and sold east to Carolina, Virginia, and on to other English ports.[48] Of course, the French also participated in the Indian slave trade (recall that La Salle and Tonti acquired Indian children as slaves during their 1682 expedition), though apparently never on a scale to match the English. In the early eighteenth century, before French women began arriving at the Louisiana colony in numbers, Canadian voyageurs routinely captured Indian women and sold them as concubines to the soldiers at Biloxi and Mobile.[49] The voyageurs' slave-trading activities in the Lower Mississippi Valley exacerbated intertribal relationships and hindered the development of the Louisiana colony.[50] The Louisiana census of 1708 includes eighty Indian slaves; however, French colonial leaders were anxious to mimic the English and begin trading their Indian slaves for Africans, who were considered to be better workers and were less likely to escape.[51]

Plenty of evidence suggests that the Natchez Indians participated in slave raids against some of the smaller tribes in the region. In 1704, the Seminarian missionary Henri Roulleaux de la Vente wrote that "the English give presents to [the Natchez] and excite them to make war in order to obtain slaves by it."[52] In that same year, the Natchez and Houma were encouraged by the French to attack the Atakapa, a small tribe living along the Gulf Coast in southwest Louisiana, as punishment for the murder of a Frenchman.[53] For the Natchez and Houma, the incentive to carry out a French vendetta was obviously the opportunity to obtain slaves to sell to either the French or English. Being slave-catchers themselves, the Natchez were not targeted by slave raids.

When the War of the Spanish Succession, also known as Queen Anne's War, erupted in 1702, French and English agents in New England and Canada found it expedient to mobilize Indian tribes to do most of the fighting. In Carolina, English and Scottish traders who had already established partnerships with big-man chiefs were seen as crucial point men for raising an English-led Indian fighting force in the South. In 1708, Thomas Welch assisted Thomas Nairne, the author of Carolina's Indian policy, with a historic Mississippi expedition to assemble a confederation of tribes to throw against the French and Spanish settlements on the Gulf Coast. While Nairne consulted with Chickasaw and Choctaw chiefs on the Tombigbee River, Welch swung over to the Mississippi River and visited the Yazoo, Taensa, and Natchez. In Nairne's grandiose scheme, the Natchez and other Mississippi tribes would be enticed to move closer to Carolina, where they could be employed in the fur and slave trades, while harrying England's foes in the region.[54] Although Nairne's Indian army never materialized, the French in Louisiana certainly believed that the English were capable of assembling such a force. In 1710 and again in 1712, the French at Mobile were alarmed by rumors of thousands of English-led Indians preparing to attack.[55]

Eventually, the work of the Carolina slave traders got in the way of England's diplomatic goals in the Lower Mississippi Valley. Parties dispatched from Charleston to carry gifts and messages of goodwill from the English colonial proprietors to the Mississippi tribes often succumbed to the temptation to combine diplomacy with slave-catching, undermining England's efforts to win allies.[56] English slave traders such as Thomas Welch were initially viewed as useful adjuncts to efforts to counteract French encroachment in the Lower Mississippi Valley; however, the slave-catching business gradually turned many of Britain's powerful Indian allies against the Carolina colony.[57] Traders were increasingly being accused of failing to pay promised bounties to Indian slave-catchers, and all too often slave raids were carried out against "free" Indian settlements that were viewed as friendly to the Carolina colony. Attempts by colonial administrators to license and regulate the Indian slave trade failed, as one tribe after another grew dissatisfied with the traders operating among them. The situation exploded in 1715 with the Yamasee tribe's massacre of the slave traders at Port Royal, which incited attacks on traders by neighboring Creek and Cherokee tribes. Although some enslavement among the Southeastern Indians continued during the eighteenth century, wholesale slave-catching ended with the Yamasee War.[58]

EARLY MISSIONARIES CONTACT THE NATCHEZ

If the Catholic missionaries descending into the Mississippi Valley after La Salle were aware of the potential danger posed by the intertribal raiding and warfare wrought by the Indian slave trade, they hid their fears and trusted in voyageurs such as Tonti to deliver them safely to their new parishes. Although only a small number of missionaries visited the Natchez during the French colonial period, and only one made a serious attempt to missionize the tribe, these men of God impacted Natchez history in significant ways, mostly to the detriment of the tribe. For this reason, it is important to provide some background into the missionaries' presence in the Natchezan homeland.

Zenobius Membré, La Salle's chaplain, was the first Catholic missionary to visit the Lower Mississippi Valley after the ignominious departure of De Soto's army. Aside from taking note of his robed appearance, Father Membré likely made little impression on the Mississippi tribes. Being attached to the expedition, he directed his mission toward La Salle and his men, instead of toward the native people they encountered along their way.

Membré was a member of the Order of Franciscan Observants Recollects, who were active among the Spanish and French colonial outposts in Mexico, Canada, and Florida during the seventeenth century.[59] The Recollects' association with La Salle helped to awaken the Catholic Church to the potential for new missions among the native people of the Lower Mississippi Valley. In 1684, two Recollect priests, Membré and Anastase Douay, sailed from France with La Salle bound for Mississippi Gulf Coast, where the explorer planned to found a French colony at the mouth of the Mississippi River.[60] The next year, the bishop of Quebec appointed Recollect Father Hyacinth Le Febvre as superior of the Louisiana mission.[61] However, this auspicious beginning was short-lived; the Recollects lost their chance to missionize the Mississippi River tribes when La Salle's colonial venture failed.[62]

A better choice for the Louisiana mission might have been the Society of Jesus, better known as the Jesuits. Jesuit missionaries had arrived in New France (Canada) in the early decades of the seventeenth century and were firmly established in missions throughout the Great Lakes region by 1670. The Jesuit priests

were every bit as hardy and capable of thriving in the wilderness as the adventur-
ous *coureurs de bois* who were enjoying a prosperous fur trade business with the
colony's Indian tribes. In fact, the Jesuits were finding time in their mission work
to get involved in the fur trade themselves and were even branching out into
copper mining. Soon, La Salle and other secular entrepreneurs pursuing New
France's Indian fur trade were finding it difficult to compete with the industrious
missionaries.[63]

Although the Jesuits felt that the Louisiana mission should fall to them,
their successes among the Great Lakes tribes and their gains in the fur trade had
made some members of the Catholic Church hierarchy wary of their growing
independence. In May 1698, the bishop of Quebec awarded the Louisiana mission to a rival order, the Society of Foreign Missions (called Seminarians).[64] The
Jesuits protested the decision, but the Church stood firm, and by the fall of that
year three Seminarian priests, Antoine Davion, Jean-François Buisson de Saint-
Cosme, and François Jolliet de Montigny, left Canada to descend the Mississippi
with Tonti and a group of voyageurs to found their order's new dominion.
J.-B. La Source, a lay adult and possibly a servant of one of the priests, traveled
with the group and contributed some information about the Mississippi tribes.[65]
Davion selected the Tunica and settled with them on the Lower Yazoo River.[66]
De Montigny, who had been named vicar-general of the Louisiana mission by
the bishop of Quebec, wrote in January 1699: "For the present, I reside among
the Taensa, but am to go shortly to the Natchez."[67] Saint-Cosme traveled as
far as the Tamaroa Indian village on the Mississippi River near the mouths of
the Missouri and Illinois rivers, where he set about founding a mission for the
Illinois-speaking tribes in the area.[68] Saint-Cosme eventually moved his mission
to the Natchez Indians, and we will take up his story in a later section.

The missionaries found the Lower Mississippi River tribes to be severely
weakened by diseases—the unfortunate result of increased French-Canadian
traffic on the river. Saint-Cosme reported that the Acansa were suffering from
smallpox, and La Source wrote that the Tunica were "dying in great numbers."[69]
In fact, De Montigny and other Frenchmen making the voyage south that year
were themselves sick with fever and no doubt shared their malady with the tribes
they contacted.[70] Perhaps fortunately for the Natchez, the priests did not venture below the Taensa that winter. Even so, the Natchez may have already been
impacted by disease; La Source wrote that the missionaries received reports from
downstream of human sacrifices upon the death of a Natchez chief.[71]

Accompanying the missionaries were French servants who helped carry their
belongings, cooked meals, and assisted with preparing shelter. De Montigny,

being vicar-general, could afford two attendants, while Davion apparently arrived at the Tunica mission with only one man.[72] The Seminarians benefited from the Mississippi River tribes' willingness to accommodate travelers and provide safe haven for homeless groups, which seems to have been a common practice throughout the region. However, difficulties began to arise once their voyageur escort departed, leaving the priests and their retinue to make their way among the Indian people. The language gap made the communication of simple amenities and basic necessities, such as friendship, hunger, and the need for shelter, laborious and fraught with potentially dangerous misunderstandings. Before they could hope to communicate the much more complex ideas about religion, the priests faced many hours of arduous language study. There was also the ever present element of danger—two Frenchmen had been killed by the Natchez in 1690, and four more had died at the hands of the Chitimacha in 1695.[73]

Other hardships experienced by Davion and De Montigny came as a result of meager monetary support for their missions from their order's office in Quebec. Likewise, the Society of Foreign Missions issued directives to its missionaries forbidding their entering into secular business arrangements, which precluded hiring the occasional services of Canadian voyageurs passing up and down the Mississippi River.[74] Even though the Tunica and Taensa permitted the missionaries to live alongside them, without compensation the Indians contributed little to the priests' sustenance. Davion, who remained with the Tunica off and on for twenty years, persevered by growing his own vegetables, keeping chickens, and restricting himself to one meal every twenty-four hours.[75]

In the summer of 1699, De Montigny visited the Natchez and described the encounter:

> The 12th [of June] we reached the Natchez, or, as others call them, the Challaouelles, who are almost twenty leagues from the Taensas. They were warring at that time with almost all the nations which are on the Mississippi . . . and out of consideration for us, although they were at war with the Taensas, they gave those [Taensa] who were with us a very good reception. We told the chief that the black robes, like ourselves, were not warriors, that we had not come to see them in that spirit, and that on the contrary we exhorted every one to peace, they would know it well one day when I should know their language, which is the same as that of the Taensas and then, after having made them some little presents, we separated very well satisfied with each other.[76]

As mentioned above, the intertribal "warring" observed by De Montigny can be attributed largely to slave-raiding. The vicar apparently spent some time at the

Grand Village, where he observed the communal cultivation of the Great Sun's maize field by the inhabitants of the local settlement district and was impressed by the courteous respect shown by the people for their chief.[77] According to Swanton, De Montigny's visit to the Natchez in the summer of 1699 coincided with the death of one of the Natchez chiefs.[78] De Montigny visited the Natchez again in the spring of 1700 and managed to baptize 185 children.[79]

Inevitably, native practices ran afoul of European sensibilities, and the priests reacted imprudently, sometimes to the point of obstructing important tribal ceremonies and rituals. Naturally, such behavior tried the patience of their hosts. While in residence with the Taensa, De Montigny disrupted the funeral of a chief by preventing the customary human sacrifices of those who were selected to accompany their leader into the next life. When lightening destroyed the tribe's sacred temple building a short time later, some tribal leaders blamed the disaster on the priest's interference with a long-held and sacred tradition. Faced with a situation that may have been irreconcilable, the vicar hastily gathered his servants and belongings and hitched a ride downstream to the Natchez with Iberville's 1700 Mississippi River expedition.[80]

Iberville viewed the Natchez as the strongest tribe on the Mississippi River, and having a missionary priest in residence there would help to bind the tribe to the French.[81] However, De Montigny remained with the Natchez for less than two months before giving up his Louisiana mission and returning to France.[82] The cause of the vicar's rather abrupt change of heart is not known; however, his intolerance with native customs, as evidenced by the Taensa incident, probably withered his welcome among his new hosts. He was also aware of Iberville's impending return to France and was apparently unable to resist the opportunity to escape his responsibilities in the American wilderness.

THE NATCHEZ IN IBERVILLE'S JOURNALS

Pierre LeMoyne d'Iberville's journals about his Lower Mississippi Valley explorations in 1699 and 1700 provide us with the earliest description of the Natchez Indians' main ceremonial center, the Grand Village, along with a list of the different settlement districts that comprised the Natchez tribe. Iberville was first and foremost a military man, and his appraisal of the Mississippi tribes usually had a strategic slant, but he was also an engaging journalist with a sharp eye for detail.[83]

Iberville was in the Lower Mississippi Valley as a result of renewed European interest in the area following the end of the War of the League of Augsburg, or

King William's War, in 1697. Louis XIV selected the famous naval commander to follow through on La Salle's initiative to found a French colony at the mouth of the Mississippi River.[84] The adventure took on a sense of urgency when the French Crown received word of a British expedition preparing to sail to America and take possession of the Mississippi River in order to secure Dr. Daniel Coxe's immense Carolina patent. Ironically, it was the writings of the French Recollect priest Louis Hennepin about La Salle's 1682 Mississippi River exploration that fueled England's resolve to mount such an expedition.[85] Compounding irony upon irony, Dr. Coxe organized a party of Huguenots—exiled French Protestants—to found England's Mississippi River colony. A truly international incident was in the making when word of the rush to the Gulf of Mexico reached the Spanish at Vera Cruz, who mistakenly thought that the British and French objective was Pensacola.[86]

Like so many other European forays into the American Southeast, fever and sickness arrived with Iberville's small fleet at the Mississippi Gulf Coast in early 1699. The commander's journal entry for January 2, 1699, did not bode well for the Native Americans who would soon be exposed to the French sailors: "We are becalmed. On all our ships we have a great many sick, several men being sick of the plague."[87] Upon reaching the Gulf Coast, Iberville found the Spanish hurriedly building fortifications to guard their Pensacola harbor.[88] Over the next several days, the little fleet warped westward along the coastline, taking depth soundings and making careful observations of important geographical features such as Mobile Bay and the string of barrier islands. As they skirted the shoreline, Iberville and his men were alert for any signs of native inhabitants. Although he was charged with establishing a French presence in the area, the commander was keenly interested in gaining the allegiance of the Mississippi tribes and persuading them to view the English as their mutual enemies. To attract attention, the frigates occasionally fired off a cannon as they moved along. Where he could discern a possible Indian presence, Iberville went ashore and carved pictures on trees of stick figures holding calumets.[89]

On February 14, the expedition made initial contact with the Biloxi tribe, to whom Iberville distributed an assortment of gifts, including axes, knives, shirts, tobacco, pipes, tinderboxes, and glass beads.[90] Continuing to probe to the west for the mouth of the Mississippi River, the French encountered a Bayogoula hunting party. Upon learning that the Bayogoula were one of the Mississippi River tribes and that a chief of the tribe was among the group, Iberville seized the opportunity for a diplomatic parley. After doing his best to mimic the Indians' personable greeting ritual—caressing each other's chest and face—the French commander brought forth a special calumet made of iron and shaped like a sailing ship, complete with a little flag emblazoned with the fleurs-de-lis. How the Bayogoula viewed the ensuing calumet ceremony is anyone's guess. For Iberville's part, his journal entry is naively optimistic, to say the least: "[I made] them understand that with this calumet I was uniting them to the French and that we were from now on one." Moreover, the commander's journal entry goes on to claim that sharing the calumet with the Bayogoula chief bound ten other Mississippi tribes to the French, including the Thecloël, whom readers will recognize as an alternate name for the Natchez Indians.[91]

Over the next two months, the French began to consolidate their base on the Mississippi Gulf Coast, later known as Fort Maurepas, and Iberville made a foray up the Mississippi River. The expedition only went as high as the Houma villages near the mouth of the Red River, where the commander received the following intelligence from a Taensa Indian:

> [From the Houma] landing to the village of the Theloel [is] three days travel. These eight villages together make only one, of which the Natchés are one; the others are named Pochougoula, Ousagoucoula, Cogoucoula, Yatanocha, Ymacacha, Thoucoue, Tougoula, Achougoucoula. All these villages together make only one nation, which is named Theloel. [The Taensa informant] describes this village for me as having three or four hundred huts, crowded with people.[92]

Unbeknownst to Iberville and his party in the spring of 1699, the Seminarian missionaries De Montigny and Davion were already settling in upriver with the Taensa and Tunica. (Iberville would not learn of the missionaries' presence in the Lower Mississippi Valley until his return to the Gulf Coast in January 1700.)[93] When De Montigny visited the Natchez in June 1699, he also noted the dual names for the same group: "[W]e reached the Natchez, or, as others call them, the Challaouelles [an alternate spelling of Iberville's "Theloel"]."[94] De Montigny implies here that the Natchez people called themselves by the name of their main ceremonial center and chiefly residence. After 1700, the name Theloel (probably pronounced something like "tay-lo-el") disappears from the colonial documents and the term "Natchez" comes into accepted use as the name of the entire tribe. The native word was probably pronounced something like "not-chee," with the French taking responsibility for the "chez" suffix.

John R. Swanton and others have attempted to discern the meanings of the Natchez village names and correlate them with village names recorded some twenty years later during the time of the French colony at Natchez. Only three villages named by Iberville's Taensa informant are similar to those documented from the later colonial period: Natchés, Tougoula, and Cogoucoula. As discussed above, Natchés is the residence of the chief, later known as the "Grand Village of the Natchez." Tougoula may refer to the village of the Tiou, a small refugee group adopted by the Natchez.[95] Swanton points out that the frequent use of the suffix "goula" or "coula" may indicate that the information Iberville received from the Taensa informant was communicated in the Mobilian trade language, a lingua franca based on the Muskhogean language of the Bayogoula and Houma.[96] One interpretation of Cogoucoula, given in Swanton, is "swan people," which could refer to the *village des canard natchez* or the Natchez duck village shown on a 1723 map of the Natchez area.[97]

Having received a good deal of useful information from his talkative Taensa informant about not only the Natchez but about other tribes and geographic details to be found upstream, Iberville decided to head back downriver and put off further exploration for another time.[98] The following year, while making preparations to build a fort on the lower Mississippi (later called "Fort Mississippi"), the French received information from Indian sources that the Natchez had murdered the priest De Montigny. Iberville quickly organized a punitive expedition to the Natchez, whom he called "the strongest of all the nations that are on the bank of the river."[99] The rumor of De Montigny's death, however, proved to be false. When Iberville's party met Tonti and a group of voyageurs coming downriver, Tonti assured the commander that the priest was alive, and moreover, "[the Natchez] are quite friendly to us and delighted to learn that we are on this river."[100]

Tonti's news changed the expedition's objectives from militaristic to diplomatic. Despite being weakened by sickness among his Canadians, Iberville set out with fifty-eight men in late February to ascend the Mississippi River.[101] In addition to providing important information about the Natchez, Iberville's voyage upriver in the spring of 1700 documents the quickening distress among the people of the Lower Mississippi Valley due to the growing European presence. At the Bayogoula village, the Indians told of English-led Chickasaw slave raids among the Mississippi tribes. Further upriver, they found the Houma to be ravaged by dysentery. Iberville understood that the Houma had been suffering from the sickness for five months and more than half of their people had died.[102]

At the Houma village was a contingent of about forty "Little Taensas," who were later documented as the Avoyel tribe.[103] There are some indications that the Avoyel were Natchez speakers and they may have once resided with the Natchez. In Iberville's time, the Avoyel lived some fifty miles up the Red River in what are now Rapides and Avoyelles parishes.[104] When Iberville asked the Little Taensas to guide him up the Red River to the Caddoan country (northeast Texas, eastern

Oklahoma, northwest Louisiana) he had heard about the previous year, they refused, saying the only route into the upper reaches of the Red River was from the "Big Taensa" villages further up the Mississippi.[105] A casual glimpse at a modern map of the region indicates that the Little Taensa were not being completely truthful to Iberville. Perhaps, after seeing the Houma villages wracked by lethal diarrhea after visits by French voyageurs, the Avoyel were a bit wary of bringing these foreigners to their home village.

On March 11, Iberville's party reached the Natchez landing, and it was apparent that the Natchez were also suffering from dysentery, although Iberville's journal doesn't give any indication that the malady was as widespread here as among the Houma. The fact that the chief was suffering from the sickness illustrates the vulnerability of the river tribes' leadership to the diseases carried by parties such as Iberville's. After all, it was often the tribal leaders who had the most direct contact with Europeans traveling the Mississippi River in those days and therefore stood the greatest risk of contracting an illness.

The next passage from Iberville's journal is our earliest description of the Grand Village, the Natchez Indians' main ceremonial mound center: "We repaired to his cabin, which is raised to a height of 10 feet on earth brought thither, and is 25 feet wide and 45 long. Near by are eight cabins. Before that of the chief's is the temple mound, which forms a round, a little oval, and bounds an open space about 250 paces wide and 300 long. A stream passes near, from which they draw their water."[106]

Iberville's concise description of the site will be instantly recognizable to anyone familiar with the Grand Village. (We will examine the layout of this important site in more detail later.) The chief gave Iberville a letter from De Montigny, who had been baptizing Natchez children and had only left three days earlier to return to the Taensa. The priest said the Natchez settlement districts comprised 400 huts strung out along the stream later known as "St. Catherine Creek" for a distance of twenty-four miles.[107]

The commander ran his military eye for ground over the Natchez area and left us with this impression:

From the river landing one climbs a hill, about 150 fathoms high, a sheer bluff covered with hardwood trees. Once on top of the hill one discovers a country of plains, prairies, full of little hills, with clumps of trees in some spots, many oak trees, and many roads criss-crossing, leading from one hamlet to another or to huts. Those who have rambled around for three or four leagues say they have found the same country everywhere, from the edge of the hill to the chief's village. According to what I have seen, it is a country of yellowish soil mixed with a little gravel as far out from his hut as the distance of a cannon shot, where the grey soil begins, which appears to me to be better. This countryside is very much like France.[108]

On the return trip downriver after visiting the Taensa, Iberville and De Montigny stopped at the Natchez, where they found the old chief near death and his people consumed with grief.[109] Later that spring, a Natchez chief accompanied De Montigny and Davion on a visit to Fort Maurepas. Davion brought word of a party of Englishmen at the Acansa villages distributing guns and ammunition.[110] After receiving gifts from Iberville, the Natchez chief returned back upriver with Davion, and De Montigny sailed with Iberville to France on May 28, 1700.

Before his departure, Iberville sent one of his ship's cabin boys to live with the Natchez and learn their language. While this might seem to be a cruel assignment for a teenage boy, the practice was commonplace in Canada and Louisiana, where French cabin boys were routinely farmed out to important tribes. These young Frenchman helped to promote goodwill between their hosts and the French, and the Indians sometimes reciprocated by placing their youths at French outposts. The Indians seemed to welcome the young Frenchmen into their midst and treated them with kindness. Patricia Galloway points out that the custom of exchanging young men between allied tribes might have already been in practice among the Mississippi tribes and was in keeping with the matrilineal system previously discussed. Sadly, almost nothing is known about this anonymous French youth; the young man apparently left no record of his linguistic mission among the Natchez.[111]

THE NATCHEZ SETTLEMENT DISTRICTS

If the behavior of the tribe's settlement leaders at the time of the La Salle expedition is any indication, the Natchez settlement districts were already outside the authority of the Grand Village chief by the 1680s. The La Salle narratives indicate that the chiefs or head men from the other Natchez settlement districts were contacted to come to the Grand Village to meet La Salle and his party, but only the Koroa chief responded to the invitation.[112] Nicolas de la Salle's journal entry for March 27/28 is brief but informative: "M. de La Salle went with seven men to [the Natchez village] three leagues from the river on some small hills. He stayed there three days. The chief informed La Salle that he had sent for some other chiefs to talk to him. When La Salle had not returned after two days,

Tonty sent another eight Frenchmen to look for him. They all returned without having spoken to the other chiefs who had still not arrived."[113]

Three days would seem to have allowed plenty of time for an assembly of tribal leaders, so the failure of the "other chiefs" to come and smoke the calumet with La Salle may be a telling statement about the Natchez Indians' political structure. Did the Grand Village chief lack the power to bring together the leaders of the outlying settlement districts? Were some of the settlement districts already allied with the English and opposed to French contact with the tribe? Although there are no definitive answers to these questions, some discussion of the Natchez tribe's complex leadership structure will help provide a context for understanding their behavior in response to subsequent French and English contact.

Iberville's Taensa informant in 1699 spoke of nine villages or settlement districts making up the Natchez group.[114] After 1700, most French colonial narratives recognize only five districts: Flour, Tiou, Grigra, Jenzenaque, and White Apple. As shown in Figure 5, these districts are all situated close to three main creeks: Coles Creek and Fairchilds Creek in the north and St. Catherine Creek in the south.[115] The Grand Village or "Natchez village" is often listed as a village or settlement district; however, its status as a ceremonial center with only a handful of houses differentiates it from the tribe's extended settlement districts composed of scattered family farms on which the majority of the Natchez population resided.

The Flour village was the settlement closest to the chief's residence. This settlement is shown on some early maps on the opposite side of St. Catherine Creek from the Grand Village. Although their ethnicity is uncertain, the Flour people are assumed to have been Natchezan. A 1720s map by Jean-François Dumont de Montigny labels this area *Village Sauvage* (village of the savages).[116] LMS archaeological investigations in this area during the 1970s turned up evidence of settlements that may represent Flour district houses.[117]

A detailed map of the Natchez area done in 1723 by Ignace-François Broutin shows a Natchez village called *Canard* (Duck) located about 1.5 miles east of the Grand Village, situated on a stream labeled *Riviere des canard*. This stream, identified as Rules Branch on today's maps, is also shown on an early eighteenth-century map by d'Anville as *R. aux Canards*.[118] It is puzzling that the European narratives fail to mention the Duck village. Perhaps colonial observers simply considered this settlement to be an extension of the Flour district.[119]

The Tiou and Grigra were Tunican-speaking refugee groups living with the Natchez in the early 1700s.[120] Tunican is distinguished from other Lower

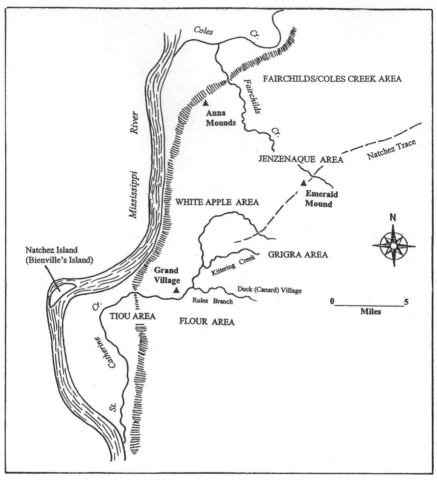

Figure 5. The Natchez Indian settlement districts in the early eighteenth century. (Based upon Brown 1985, Figure 3; Broutin 1723 map of the Natchez area.)

Mississippi Valley languages by the presence of the "r" sound, which is absent from the languages of the other tribes in the region.[121] In the late 1600s, the Tiou were living on the Yazoo River upstream from the Tunica. Following attacks by Chickasaw slave-catchers in 1700, the Tiou moved south to be closer to the French. Part of the tribe settled with the Natchez, and another group went to live with the Bayogoula.[122] The 1723 Broutin map places the Tiou's Natchez settlement area on St. Catherine Creek about three miles west of the Grand Village.[123] The pre-1700 location of the Grigra is uncertain; their Tunican connection implies that they came from further up the Mississippi River Valley.[124] The Grigra first appear in history around the time of the establishment of the

French colony at Natchez in 1716.[125] The 1723 Broutin map calls Kittering Creek the *Riviera des natchez grie*, and the Grigra settlement area is associated with a group of contact-period archaeological sites about four miles northeast of the Grand Village.[126]

The shared Tunican language has led some scholars to speculate that the Tiou and Grigra living with the Natchez in the early eighteenth-century may have in fact been the Koroa visited by La Salle and Tonti in the late 1600s.[127] By the end of the seventeenth century, the Koroa had left their riverside location south of the Natchez, and Swanton wrote that "were it not for the relations of [La Salle and Tonti] it would never be suspected that Koroa had lived there."[128] It is conceivable that they moved closer to the Natchez for protection. Most archaeologists consider the Koroa to have been a late arrival in the Lower Mississippi Valley. Marvin Jeter and Ives Goddard place them in southeastern Arkansas and along the Yazoo River in the 1690s.[129] In the early 1700s, a Koroa group was living on the Mississippi River near the confluence with the Yazoo River. This same group apparently moved up the Yazoo River in the 1720s, and Swanton mentions the possibility of Koroa settlements in the upper Tensas Basin around this time.[130]

The White Apple village is sometimes called White Earth or the Apple village and is presumably a translation of a Natchez village name that has since been lost. Jenzenaque, apparently a Natchez word, also appears in the colonial documents as the village of the Walnuts or Hickories. Jenzenaque does not resemble the Natchez language word for walnuts (yû ì xtal), but its suffix is similar to "a ì ca" the Natchez word for hickory. The ethnic affiliation of these two settlement districts is uncertain; they are assumed to have been Natchezan.[131] The White Apple and Jenzenaque settlement areas are associated with archaeological sites north of the Grigra area, along upper St. Catherine Creek and Fairchilds Creek.[132] Upper St. Catherine Creek is labeled *Riviera de la pomme* (River of the Apple) on the 1723 Broutin map. In the 1720s, a "grand square" apparently served as the center of the White Apple settlement district, but its exact location remains a mystery.[133]

The great Emerald Mound is located in the Jenzenaque area, and one 1720s account describes a chief's house atop a mound associated with Jenzenaque, but, as already mentioned, Emerald lacks the requisite European trade artifacts that would date the site's occupation to the French colonial period.[134] A sixth Natchez settlement district has recently been identified by LMS archaeologists in the Fairchilds Creek/Coles Creek area. Although the ethnicity of the residents of this settlement district is uncertain, archaeological findings (mainly shell-tempered pottery) indicate that this area was probably occupied by a northern refugee group.[135]

Archaeologist Marvin T. Smith has characterized the Natchez tribe in the late 1600s as a "coalescent" population composed of refugee groups, instead of a lingering Mississippi period chiefdom. Smith suggests that refugee populations set adrift by factors such as the effects of European diseases, the collapse of Mississippian chiefdoms, and the English-driven Indian slave trade led some displaced tribal groups to band together for mutual support.[136] Viewed in this way, the Natchez Indians of the late seventeenth century were a heterogeneous group composed of at least two linguistic elements: Natchezan and Tunican. Most archaeologists and historians agree that the Natchezan contingent of the tribe was a remnant population of the once powerful Anna-Emerald chiefdom.[137]

The leaders of the Natchez settlement districts for the most part remain shadowy figures throughout the early eighteenth-century history of the tribe. With few exceptions, these individuals cannot be connected with any certainty to the Sun lineage based at the Grand Village.[138] As subsequent history makes clear, even when a settlement district chief can be connected genealogically to the Sun lineage, his independent actions seem more characteristic of a big-man leader than a subordinate chief in a chiefdom organization.[139] As the French colonial narratives indicate, decisions affecting the whole group were made in councils composed of the settlement district chiefs and tribal elders.[140] All in all, the Natchez leadership structure at the turn of the eighteenth century appears to have been that of an uneasy coalition of big-men, some of whom may have been relatives of the titular chief in residence at the Grand Village.

To further complicate the picture, the Natchez tribe was divided into two opposing factions split along geographic rather than along linguistic lines.[141] The fissure was exacerbated, if not instigated, by the overriding competition between the French and English for dominance among the Mississippi tribes. The Natchez persevered during this volatile period because they had adopted a hybrid leadership structure that allowed them the flexibility to interact simultaneously with both the French and the English. The Flour and Tiou settlements near the Grand Village and relatively close to the Mississippi River comprised the tribe's pro-French faction. The remaining settlements, White Apple, Jenzenaque, and Griga, tended to align themselves with the English.[142] These three settlements were further inland and oriented toward the Natchez Trace, the important overland trail leading toward English Carolina. The Fairchilds Creek/Coles Creek settlement district is not specifically referenced in the French colonial documentation; however, the French may have considered this area a continuation of the

White Apple and Jenzenaque settlements. The northeastern periphery of the three pro-English settlements may have served as a meeting place for English traders arriving in the Natchez country from the Natchez Trace. We will touch on this subject again in Chapter Three, when we discuss the French occupation at Natchez. Certainly, the remoteness of the Fairchilds Creek/Coles Creek area would have allowed the English to exchange trade merchandise for Natchez deerskins without coming in contact with the French.[143]

To the French arriving from the Mississippi River, the Natchez appeared to be a single political entity under the control of the chief residing at the Grand Village. The Natchez chief, supported by the nearby Flour settlement district, provided the French with a familiar contact point for diplomatic relations. On the other hand, English traders arriving at the Natchez from the northeast via overland trails encountered big-man leaders at the White Apple, Jenzenaque, and Grigra settlements. To the English, the big-men representing these three settlements held authority much like the Chickasaw war chiefs discussed earlier. As Patricia Galloway has pointed out, under the new market parameters set by the French and English, hereditary tribal leaders such as the Natchez chief at the Grand Village lost power by losing control over the people's access to European trade materials; French and English muskets, iron hatchets and knives, and other coveted materials were available to any man who could deliver animal skins or slaves to the traders.[144]

THE GRAND VILLAGE OF THE NATCHEZ INDIANS

After 1700, the Natchez chief's mound center residence figures strongly in the final thirty years of the Natchezan story, so we will take a moment to examine the site's layout and archaeology (Figure 6). For an archaeological site as thoroughly documented as the Grand Village, Mound A, the northernmost mound, remains somewhat of a mystery. Colonial descriptions of the site only refer to two mounds, the chief's mound and the temple mound, and the archaeology demonstrates convincingly that Mound B was the chief's mound and Mound C the temple mound. Neitzel suggests that St. Catherine Creek may have started to erode the base of Mound A, causing its eventual abandonment prior to European contact. Apparently, any structure that may have once stood on Mound A was gone by 1700, and colonial visitors to the site simply did not recognize the significance of the earthwork. Because of Mound A's lack of relevance

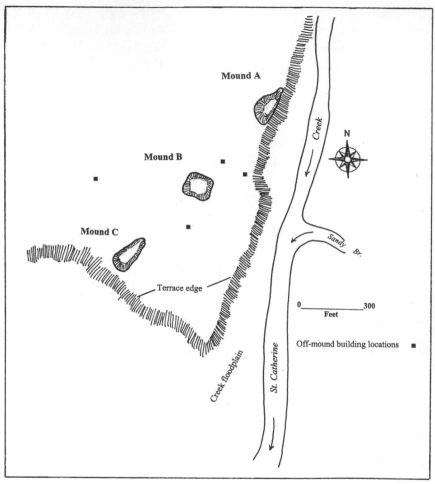

Figure 6. The Grand Village of the Natchez Indians (Fatherland Site), showing relationship of the mound center to St. Catherine Creek and building locations identified in archaeological investigations. (Based upon Neitzel 1983, Figure 3; Barnett 1984, Figure 1.)

to the known history of the Natchez Indians, Neitzel spent very little time excavating there and focused his work on Mounds B and C.[145]

Neitzel's Mound B excavations revealed that the earthwork was built up incrementally over a long period of time. The earliest structures associated with this mound were placed on the original ground surface. For unknown reasons that probably related to the tribe's spiritual belief system, these first structures were eventually dismantled and covered over with a low earthen platform, about 2.5 feet high, upon which two successive structures were built. After an indeterminate length of time, the mound's height was again raised about 2.5 feet and another structure erected. The third building episode added another four feet to the mound's height, and two successive structures occupied this surface for an unknown length of time. The final building episode added another two feet of fill dirt, upon which the last structure stood. Overall, Mound B was about eleven feet high.

Unfortunately, very little remained of the archaeological footprint of the last structure atop Mound B, which would have been the chief's house witnessed by Iberville and later European visitors to the site. The structures associated with Mound B were constructed with wall trenches; that is, narrow trenches about two feet deep were dug to form the outline the building's floor plan, and vertical posts were set into these trenches to form the walls. Due to erosion and other disturbance on the mound's summit, only about fifteen feet of the wall trench for the building's western wall was found. The fill dirt beneath this house floor contained the only historic period artifacts found in Mound B. These included two pistol barrels and a fragment of the bowl from a calumet made of catlinite, a reddish colored stone quarried in Minnesota and widely traded for making pipes and other ceremonial objects. The wall trenches representing the structures on Mound B's three prehistoric building levels and the pre-mound surface were somewhat better preserved. These buildings were single-room dwellings, square or rectangular in floor plan, with walls running about forty-five to fifty feet in length. Hard-packed dirt at the northeast and southeast corners of some of the house floors indicated possible entrances, and most of the interior fire hearths were placed near these corners. Although Neitzel speculated that placing the hearth near the entrance would allow the smoke to escape out through the door opening, experiments with fires inside a reconstructed Natchez house show that the fire draws air *in* through the corner opening and the smoke rises into the interior roof dome, where it bleeds out through the thatch. Experiments also indicate that smoke from regular interior fires would have helped to keep the roof thatch dry and free of varmints.[146]

Neitzel identified Mound C as the temple mound based upon the presence there of twenty-six human burials (twenty-five of which were excavated by Chambers in 1930), recalling French colonial accounts of burial activity in and around the temple building.[147] Atop Mound C, the archaeologist was surprised and elated to discover a significant portion of the wall trenches and post holes defining the footprint of the historic Natchez temple. Discoveries such as this are the "Holy Grail" of historical archaeology, where a building described in historical documents can be securely correlated to features found in the ground. The temple's floor plan reveals a two-room structure with a smaller northern room, or portico, adjoining a larger southern (or rear) enclosure, with the whole building measuring about sixty feet in length and forty-two feet in width. European trade items (iron wire rings) were found in association with the historic temple.

Mound C was also built in stages. Although no structural remains were found beneath Mound C, Neitzel found some cultural refuse indicating that the spot had been previously occupied. Unlike Mound B, the work on Mound C began with the construction of a flat-topped, earthen platform about four feet high that apparently had no standing structure on top. This platform was built in two separate construction episodes. Later, another two feet of fill dirt was added over this platform, and the mound's first temple was constructed on this building level. After an indeterminate length of time, this building was dismantled and replaced by another that was almost identical in floor plan. Both of these buildings closely resembled the historic temple with its two-room floor plan. Interior hearths were situated in the center of the rear enclosure and near its northwestern corner. In the final construction work on Mound C, the second temple was razed and a mantle of dirt approximately four feet thick was added to serve as the platform for the historic temple. An earthen ramp was incorporated into the mound's construction on the north side, sloping from the summit down to the plaza separating Mounds B and C.[148]

Iberville observed eight houses in addition to the structures on the mounds, and other colonial visitors to the Grand Village mention the presence of a few non-mound dwellings. Neitzel's 1972 excavations uncovered evidence of four building locations where one or more houses had been erected over time.[149] In 1983, a fifth building location came to light during excavations connected with an erosion-control project.[150]

SAINT-COSME WITH THE NATCHEZ INDIANS

When Davion and De Montigny took up their Lower Mississippi Valley missions, their fellow Seminarian, Jean-François Buisson de Saint-Cosme, settled at the Tamaroa village on the upper Mississippi River in the vicinity of the mouths of the Illinois and Missouri rivers.[151] However, as mentioned earlier, the Jesuits resented the Seminarians' intrusion into an area that they considered part of their dominion. Even though the bishop of Quebec supported Saint-Cosme's mission at the Tamaroa village, the Jesuits wasted little time in moving to supplant the Seminarian priest. A Jesuit missionary, Julian Binneteau, arrived at the Tamaroa village and, being skilled in the Illinois language of the Tamaroa, quickly upstaged Saint-Cosme. Binneteau and his successor, Pierre-François Pinet, were typical of the hardy, adaptable Jesuit missionaries who had become fixtures on the Great Lakes–area landscape. Adept at native languages and seasoned by life on the frontier, Binneteau and Pinet created an untenable situation for Saint-Cosme at the Tamaroa village. As luck would have it, De Montigny's defection back to France created the need for a replacement, and Saint-Cosme left the Tamaroa in the summer of 1700 to descend the great river and establish a new mission with the Natchez Indians.[152]

Saint-Cosme lived with the Natchez for six years and might have been our best source of information on the tribe, had he not died tragically in late 1706. As it is, only a few letters survive from Saint-Cosme's Natchez years to give us a glimpse into the world of the Natchez Indians during the first decade of the eighteenth century.[153] The priest's arrival at the Natchez is not recorded, but we can assume that Saint-Cosme, probably accompanied by a servant, traveled south in the company of voyageurs, who would have introduced him to the Indians. Fortunately for the priest, Iberville's anonymous cabin boy was already in residence, with a couple of months' Natchez language experience under his belt. Having this youth as a friend and helper must have eased the missionary's entry into the Natchez community and facilitated his study of their language. For their part, the Natchez apparently looked upon the black-robed missionaries as oracles, equating them with the shamans of their own tribe because of the marginal services they provided.[154]

Settling in a cabin near the Grand Village, Saint-Cosme managed to subsist on handouts from the Natchez, who shared their maize and fish. When he began to minister to his new charges, the missionary found the Natchez Indians' dispersed settlement pattern challenging. Where the Tamaroa had been conveniently settled in a nucleated village, the Natchez Indians' settlement districts were flung out over an area almost thirty miles wide. Without horse or cart, Saint-Cosme was obliged to cover his rambling parish on foot, accepting what food and sleeping accommodations that might be offered.[155] There is some evidence that missionaries occasionally suffered physical abuse from their Indian hosts, and Saint-Cosme's Natchez parishioners apparently were no exception. In a letter to the bishop of Quebec, the priest stated his need for servants who were big enough to stand up to antagonistic Natchez, adding "it is awkward for a missionary to have to punch an Indian."[156]

In the fall of 1700, Saint-Cosme received word that Davion lay ill among the Tunica, so the priest dutifully left his Natchez post to ascend the river and care for his friend and colleague. At Davion's Tunica residence on the lower Yazoo River, Saint-Cosme found the Jesuit missionary Jacques Gravier, who was on his way downriver to assist fellow Jesuit Paul Du Ru at the Houma village.[157] When Saint-Cosme returned to the Natchez, Gravier accompanied him, and from the Jesuit we learn that Saint-Cosme was disheartened by his initial impression of the Natchez: "The Nachés, Mr. de St. Cosme assured me, are far from being as docile as the Tounika. They practice polygamy, steal and are very vicious, the girls and women more than the men and boys, among whom there is much to reform before anything can be expected of them."[158]

Gravier's journal indicates that he spoke with the cabin boy, but, unfortunately, the priest didn't record his name. The youth may have witnessed the funeral ceremony of the Natchez chief, whom Iberville had found dying the previous March. From the cabin boy, Gravier learned that eight people were sacrificed to accompany the deceased leader.[159]

By the summer of 1701, Saint-Cosme was gaining fluency in the Natchez language. He was also getting to know the Taensa and was able to confirm the important fact that the Natchez and Taensa spoke the same language.[160] The priest also documents the drastic decline of the Taensa population, reduced by disease from eight or nine villages in 1682 to only forty cabins.[161] The Natchez appear not to have been as susceptible to the sicknesses the Europeans carried to the river tribes. Perhaps their dispersed settlement districts afforded them some protection.

After spending a year with the Natchez, Saint-Cosme's opinion of his parishioners had improved somewhat, but he was developing a low regard for his own countrymen. Despite the presence of a priest among the Natchez, visiting Canadians and Frenchmen made little effort to conceal their dalliances with native women. Saint-Cosme and other missionaries were beginning to recognize the order and tradition in the native society and could sense the disintegration of those values through ever-increasing European contact.[162] As the contact between these two drastically different cultures became more frequent, the potential for violence increased. By the beginning of the eighteenth century, a few deaths or disappearances of French voyageurs in the Lower Mississippi Valley had been attributed to Indians.[163]

The murder of one of Saint-Cosme's colleagues in 1702 underscored the growing potential for violence. The incident also nearly touched off a war that would have placed the Natchez at the very center of the conflict. In September of that year, the Seminarian priest Nicolas Foucault and two Frenchmen were on their way downriver from the Acansa villages to visit Davion, who had recently been appointed vicar general of the Louisiana mission. Along the Mississippi somewhere north of the mouth of the Yazoo River, the travelers fell ill (yet another reference to sickness) and hired four Koroa guides to take them on to

Davion's residence with the Tunica on the lower Yazoo River. While the expedition was encamped, these Koroa and some Yazoo accomplices murdered Foucault and his companions for the valuables they carried with them. Although the Koroa and Yazoo apparently waylaid Foucault for personal rather than political reasons, the incident happened to coincide with the outbreak of the War of Spanish Succession and a period of heightened enmity between England and France. The close ties between the Koroa, Yazoo, and the pro-English Chickasaw gave some in Louisiana the impression that the priest's murder may have been inspired by British agents.[164]

It is not known if Saint-Cosme remained at the Natchez, but shortly after Foucault's death, Davion abandoned his Tunica mission for a two-year residency at the Mobile outpost.[165] While in Mobile, Davion argued for a punitive expedition against the Koroa and Yazoo. Foucault's murderers remained unpunished, and the priest felt that retribution was necessary for the French to regain the respect of the Mississippi tribes.[166]

In late 1704, a combined force made up of Tunica warriors and around thirty Canadians under the command of Louis Juchereau de St. Denis rendezvoused at the Natchez in preparation for an attack on the Koroa and Yazoo.[167] We are left to wonder what part the Natchez Indians themselves were to play in this gathering drama. The Koroa were their former allies, and Koroa people may still have been living with the Natchez at the time. To make the situation even more awkward, some of the Natchez had recently been busy catching Indian slaves for the English.[168] While encamped at the Natchez, St. Denis called off the venture at the last minute, averting what was shaping up to be a war between pro-French and pro-English tribes. The journal of Jean-Baptiste Bénard de La Harpe simply records that "M. de Saint Denis changed his mind."[169] A decisive attack on the Koroa by the Acansa may have rendered St. Denis's campaign unnecessary.[170] The Natchez, who were in a position to benefit from their precarious dual allegiance with both France and England, were no doubt relieved to see the situation diffused.

PÉNICAUT AT THE NATCHEZ, 1704

André Pénicaut arrived in Louisiana with Iberville's second voyage in 1700 and remained in the colony until 1721. His importance to historians is summed up by his translator, Richebourg McWilliams: "No other Frenchman with an ability to write appears to have had so good an opportunity as Pénicaut had to witness the important events of the [first two decades of French Louisiana's history]. Pénicaut's trade of ship carpentry caused him to be picked as a member of historic expeditions. He was needed, he states, to repair boats used by exploring parties. He was needed, too, to serve as interpreter of Indian languages, for which he had an aptitude."[171] Lower Mississippi Valley scholars have learned to be cautious when using Pénicaut, particularly with regard to his dates. Nevertheless, Pénicaut's narrative is valuable for the ethnographic information it contains. Though this material is at times exaggerated, it remains a reliable first-hand account.[172]

In early 1704, because of the war's diversion of Louisiana's supply ships, Mobile's storehouses were running dangerously low on food for the colony. In order to lessen the drain on the limited supplies, about fifty of the men stationed there, including Pénicaut, volunteered to leave the post and live off what they could hunt and barter from the Mississippi tribes until the next supply ship arrived.[173] Pénicaut was familiar with the Natchez, having visited them with the Iberville and Le Sueur expeditions in 1700, so he talked about twenty of his comrades into going upriver to spend some time with the tribe, whom he considered to be "the most courteous and civil along the banks of the Missicipy."[174]

During his four years in Louisiana, Pénicaut had picked up a working knowledge of the Mobilian trade language, the lingua franca that was becoming more and more common throughout the Lower Mississippi Valley.[175] Doubtless by observing experienced Mississippi hands such as Bienville, Pénicaut had also acquired some sensitivity for Native American behavior and customs. He was apparently able to move freely among the Natchez, and he was allowed observe one of the tribe's most solemn and sacred events: the funeral ceremony of the tribe's highest-ranking female.

Although the Natchez Indians seem to have provided Pénicaut and his band of voyageurs with a friendly enough welcome, which seems to have been a courtesy common to most of the tribes along the Mississippi River, they did not extend the formality of the calumet ceremony. Instead of being received as chiefs or emissaries, Pénicaut and his friends arrived at the Natchez like any of the parties of voyageurs that came and went in those days. By this time, the Natchez were obviously accustomed to the easy-going backwoodsmen who stopped at their river landing to rest, repair their canoes, and swap trade items such as glass beads and metal tools for food and other amenities.

From Pénicaut's narrative, it is apparent that he and his party of young Frenchmen and Canadians were attracted to more than just the beauty of the Natchez countryside. He characterizes the Natchez women as "lustful and without restraint" and relates an amazing bit of Natchez folklore that we must take with a grain of salt: "[The Natchez girls'] fathers and their mothers and their religion teach them that, when they leave this world, they have to cross over a narrow and difficult plank before they can enter their Grand Village, where they claim they go after death, and that in the Grand Village will be only those who will have made merry indeed with the boys—they will pass easily across this plank."[176]

Whether or not this ribald folktale is based in truth, Pénicaut's narrative reflects the common reaction by the French to the behavior of Natchez women.[177] His writing also indicates that he was aware of the Natchez Indians' matrilineal kinship system ("they derive their nobility from the woman and not from the man.").[178] The Pénicaut narrative also gives us one of the earliest accounts of the two-tiered Natchez social organization comprised of nobility and commoners, and the tribe's rule or custom requiring all members of the nobility, including the members of the Sun family, to take their marriage partners from the commoner rank: "It should be observed that a grand chief, a noble, cannot marry any one except a plebian."[179]

Patricia Galloway and Jason Baird Jackson have suggested that the Natchez's two social ranks should be viewed as moieties, that is, the partitioning of a tribe into two groups, with one moiety being elder or of higher status than the other.[180] Although moieties have been documented for the Choctaw, Creek, Chickasaw, and other Southeastern tribes, their specific functions remain obscure and seem to differ from tribe to tribe. Some moieties were exogamous, as with the Choctaw, and others, such as with the Creek, were not.[181] Robert A. Brightman and Pamela S. Wallace, in writing about the Chickasaw, characterize that tribe's two moieties as being rivals that also complemented each other.[182] Tribal moieties are sometimes labeled "red" and "white" and are associated with war (red) and peace (white), although those terms should not be taken literally. A stickball game played by the Natchez in the 1720s between teams wearing red- and white-feathered headdresses may have been a competition between the tribes' two moieties.[183] Moieties within some tribes had connections, often obscure, with other tribes. The Choctaw Inholahta moiety was considered to be the younger brother of the Alabama tribe, and the Chitimacha tribe had a similar "brother" relationship with the Natchez.[184] These intertribal relationships hint at the possible existence of a moiety-based network that might explain some tribal alliances that the French simply viewed as political or economic, such as the longstanding bond between the Natchez and Chickasaw.

Pénicaut's party camped near the Grand Village and apparently had most of their interaction with the people of the Flour settlement district. The Frenchman notes the existence of eight other settlement districts but doesn't give any indication that he visited any of them. He wrote that these settlements (like other colonial visitors, he called them "villages") were under the authority of petty chiefs whom Pénicaut believed were subordinate to the "Grand Chief."[185] The sojourn of Pénicaut and his cohorts among the Natchez in the spring of 1704 happened to coincide with the death of the tribe's ranking female chief, the sister of the Great Sun and the mother of his successor.[186] Although we must be cautious in assigning prehistoric connections to the French accounts of Natchez mortuary rites, Pénicaut's description of the obsequies of the ranking Natchez female in that spring of 1704 may provide us with an extraordinary window into the Mississippian world that had all but vanished. The ceremonial activities described by Pénicaut are similar enough to the accounts of the only other well-documented Natchez chief's funeral, that of the Tattooed Serpent in 1725, to lend credibility to his reporting.[187] The documentation of these two eighteenth-century mortuary events among the Natchez has provided archaeologists with perhaps our best ethnographic example for interpreting human burials found at late prehistoric mound sites throughout the Southeast.[188]

The supply ship *Le Pélican* arrived from France not long before Pénicaut and his comrades returned to Mobile. As we might expect by now, the ship brought sickness as well as supplies to the Louisiana colony; *Le Pélican* happened to be carrying the yellow fever virus.[189] Pénicaut's narrative doesn't mention sickness among the Natchez people in that spring of 1704; however, he apparently did not visit the tribe's outlying settlement districts. He also leaves us to wonder if the female chief's death was the result of natural causes or European-borne disease.

SAINT-COSME'S LAST YEARS WITH THE NATCHEZ, 1705–1706

Curiously, Pénicaut mentions De Montigny, referring to the priest as having formerly resided with the Natchez; however, the tribe's current missionary, Saint-Cosme, is conspicuously absent from Pénicaut's Natchez narrative.[190] Perhaps Saint-Cosme was away at the time of Pénicaut's visit. But even if the priest had temporarily left his Natchez mission to travel to Mobile or elsewhere, it is difficult to imagine that Pénicaut would have been unaware of Saint-Cosme's house near the Grand Village. Also missing from this glimpse of the Natchez in 1704 is Iberville's cabin boy, whom Gravier had found dutifully living with the tribe in late 1700. With Iberville's departure from Louisiana to fight the War of Spanish Succession, this youth—by now a young man with considerable linguistic and frontier skills, may have thrown in with one of the voyageur parties coming and going in those days.

As has already been mentioned, Saint-Cosme didn't leave us much in the way of written observations about the Natchez, even though he spent considerable time with them. If he was absent during Pénicaut's early 1704 visit, then perhaps the missionary was on hand for St. Denis' rendezvous with the Tunica at the Natchez later that year. At any rate, the Natchez landing was becoming a busy place for all sorts of river traffic. In fact, one of Saint-Cosme's letters to his bishop indicates that a French family had taken up residence at the Natchez by 1705.[191] Unfortunately, like so many historical cul-de-sacs associated with the story of this tribe, we hear nothing more about this family, unless this is a reference to the Frenchman named La Vigne, who attempted to grow wheat at the Natchez prior to 1713.[192] From Pénicaut, we know that twenty-six French women arrived aboard *Le Pélican* in the summer of 1704 to find husbands among the Louisiana colonists, so it is reasonable to assume that at least one of these new families made their way upriver to set up housekeeping at the Natchez.[193]

As previously discussed, intertribal slave raids were causing havoc among the Mississippi tribes, undermining traditional alliances and trade relationships. According to John R. Swanton, it was slave-catching that led to the murder of Saint-Cosme in late 1706. The missionary and three voyageurs were encamped along the Mississippi River when they encountered a group of Chitimacha Indians, whose tribe had been especially hard hit by French-inspired slave-catchers.[194] Whether for revenge inspired by French slave traders or simply for whatever personal gain the Indians might have found among the missionary's possessions, the Chitimachas overpowered and killed Saint-Cosme and his companions. A little Indian slave belonging to the priest managed to escape and alerted the French to the tragedy. The loss of Saint-Cosme, an experienced missionary/frontiersman who had gained the confidence of perhaps the most important tribe on the Mississippi, was a severe blow to Louisiana, and Bienville's retribution was swift. In March of 1707, a combined force of French and Indians managed to capture a number of Chitimacha warriors, including one of the men who had murdered Saint-Cosme. The prisoners were taken to Mobile, where the guilty man was summarily scalped and beaten to death.[195] Another one of the murderers was apparently executed for the French by one of his own tribesmen.[196]

Considering his long tenure with the Natchez Indians and his importance as a reference on the tribe during the first decade of the eighteenth century, it is unfortunate that Saint-Cosme's reputation is marred by scandal. Readers delving into the literature of the Louisiana colony for the first time might be surprised, and perhaps a bit confused, to make the acquaintance of another Saint-Cosme—a Natchez Indian. This Saint-Cosme was a member of the elite Sun family and, as a young adult in 1729 and 1730, played a central role in the final confrontation between the Natchez tribe and the French (to be discussed in detail in Chapter Four). Saint-Cosme the Natchez chief would have been born around the time of the missionary Saint-Cosme's residence at the Natchez, leading some to speculate that he was fathered by the priest.[197]

The Jesuit missionary Charlevoix, who arrived in the Louisiana colony in late 1722, gives an alternative viewpoint. Charlevoix was obviously referring to the missionary Saint-Cosme when he wrote: "An ecclesiastic of Canada was [De Montigy's replacement] to the Natchez, where he resided a sufficient time, but made no proselytes, though he so far gained the good graces of the woman-chief, that out of respect to him, she called one of her sons by his name." There was little love lost between the Jesuits and Seminarians in Louisiana, so Charlevoix would have had no incentive to sugarcoat Saint-Cosme's reputation if he had any reason to believe otherwise.

As Charlevoix observed, Saint-Cosme was unable to interest the Natchez Indians in the Catholic faith.[198] The Christian optimism that began with La Salle and carried the Seminarian missionaries into the Lower Mississippi Valley was all but dead. Of the original group, only Davion persevered with at the Tunica. After Davion's departure from the scene in 1720, missionaries laboring in Louisiana gave up the goal of converting Indians and focused solely on the colonial population.

HARD TIMES FOR THE LOUISIANA COLONY

The War of Spanish Succession eventually cut off shipments of supplies to Louisiana as French trading vessels were redirected to military service. Between 1708 and 1711, no supply ships arrived at Mobile from France, and those few ships that put in from the Caribbean Islands often found the pitiful little colony too poor to purchase what goods they might have to offer.[199] During this period, the Louisiana colonists looked in desperation to their Indian neighbors. When their stores of flour ran out, the colonists were forced to subsist largely on Indian maize, usually prepared as "sagamité," a type of porridge made of ground corn. If one were lucky enough to have access to beans or meat, these were added to the dish.[200] Although corn was usually available among the Mississippi tribes, vagaries in rainfall amounts—too much in 1710 and 1711, and too little in 1712—continued to put this dependable food source in jeopardy. The flooding in 1710 and 1711 inundated many of the natural levees in the alluvial valley, preventing the Indians from farming these choice pieces of high ground.[201]

Following Saint-Cosme's death, the Natchez were without a permanent French presence for almost a decade and, in the face of increasing hardships besetting Bienville and the colonists at Mobile, the Natchez seem to have been forgotten. In a 1712 report on the state of the Louisiana colony, the Natchez are not even mentioned.[202] The scarcity of European trade goods in the Louisiana colony during the war years played to England's advantage as guns and other coveted merchandise continued to flow out of Carolina to the Mississippi tribes.[203] Bienville and other colonial officials recognized the diplomatic necessity of giving presents to maintain alliances with tribal chiefs but were sometimes forced to use trade merchandise earmarked for the Indians to purchase supplies from the Spanish at Pensacola.[204] With the French faltering in providing the glass beads, vermillion, blankets, knives, and guns that had become such an important part of the Indians' lives, the Natchez and other tribes were easily persuaded to attach themselves to the English. The chiefs and big men controlling factions that were involved in slave-catching and the procurement of deerskins had come to rely on European presents to maintain their positions of leadership by distributing these materials among their followers.[205]

Two tribes that remained loyal to the French during this period were the Tunica and Taensa. To distance themselves from English-led slave-catchers, both of these tribes abandoned their villages in 1706 and migrated far down the Mississippi River to be closer to their French allies.[206] Since La Salle's first contact with them, the Taensa had remained on good terms with the French, and Father Davion's long residence with the Tunica helped to keep that group in the French camp.[207] The Tunica's destination was the Houma village situated at the lucrative spot known as the "Portage of the Cross," opposite the mouth of the Red River. The Taensa went farther south and moved in with the Bayogoula on the west bank of the Mississippi River above Bayou Lafourche. These migrations proved disastrous for the Houma and Bayogoula, who were eventually displaced by their guests and forced to seek refuge elsewhere.[208]

A FRENCH TRADING POST AT THE NATCHEZ

With the end of the War of Spanish Succession, the struggling Louisiana colony was revived as part of a grandiose business venture, which happened to include plans for the establishment of a trading post at the Natchez Indians. The Natchez trading post was but a small part of an ambitious scheme devised by King Louis XIV and his minister of the navy, Jérôme Phélypeaux de Maurepas, Count de Ponchartrain.[209] In 1710, Pontchartrain appointed Antoine de Cadillac, sieur de La Mothe to be governor of Louisiana, not because the latter had any practical experience in the Mississippi Valley (he had none), but because Pontchartrain believed that La Mothe, who had spent almost thirty years in New France, could persuade the king's counselor and financial secretary, Antoine Crozat, to take over the development of Louisiana as a private, profit-making enterprise. The long war had seriously depleted France's treasury, and privatization of the country's colonial concerns seemed the most practical course for the near future. Crozat, who had become quite wealthy in overseas commerce, was convinced by La Mothe's glowing (and exaggerated) reports of gold and silver mines, valuable timber stands, and the wealth of animal skins to be had in Illinois and Louisiana. In September 1712, the king granted Crozat his Louisiana monopoly with a fifteen-year patent.[210]

Governor La Mothe finally arrived in Mobile in June 1713 (Bienville's title was lowered to "king's lieutenant"), accompanied by two of Crozat's picked employees, Marc-Antoine de La Loire des Ursins and Louis-Auguste de La Loire Flaucort, whose mission was to establish the aforementioned trading post for Crozat at the Natchez.[211] The trading post was located close to the Grand Village, where previous Frenchmen visiting the tribe had generally been made to feel welcome. The establishment consisted of a house for the La Loires and a warehouse for the storage of animal skins and trade items for the Indians.[212] Although the tribe's big-man leaders were profiting by their commerce in skins and slaves with the English and Chickasaw, they were apparently open (or at least ambivalent) to the placement of a French trading post in their midst.

Although no archaeological evidence of a prehistoric intertribal deerskin trade survives, an early French account hints at the dual roles that deerskins played in native society, being both utilitarian and ritualistic. Beyond the myriad everyday uses for leather, Iberville saw deerskins in a place of honor inside the Bayogoula temple and remarked that the Bayogoula considered well-tanned skins to be "one of their most prized possessions." Iberville was not impressed with the Bayogoulas' gift to him of twelve large deerskins, but he correctly recognized the gesture as a symbol of friendship and alliance.[213] When the European market for deerskins emerged, the Native Americans' ritual aspect of gift-giving to cement alliances became fused with international commerce. By the middle of the eighteenth century, deer hunting and hide preparation in the Southeast would make Indians a vital part of a profitable European industry, with deerskins being used to manufacture a variety of items, including saddles, book covers, and breeches.[214]

Before the coming of Crozat's trading post, the Natchez and other Mississippi tribes had found a limited market for deerskins among itinerate French voyageurs and English traders who paid them in trade items and carried their skins to Mobile or Charles Town.[215] In Mobile, soldiers and colonists supported themselves in part by buying deerskins from voyageurs coming in from the interior for about twenty sous (pennies) each and selling them to the Spanish in Pensacola or to the French trade boats for about twenty-five sous each.[216] This meant that the voyageur would likely have paid his Indian source in trade items amounting to around fifteen to eighteen sous per deerskin. An Indian would have to produce around twenty deerskins to purchase one French musket (360 sous). Likewise, powder and musket balls ran around ten sous per pound each, or another one to two deerskins.[217]

Even for an energetic man, the prospect of amassing twenty neatly tanned deerskins was a daunting task. Aside from the time spent out hunting, perhaps with a bow and arrow, the skinning and preparation of the hides was quite labor-intensive and was traditionally handled by women. Once the animal had been expertly skinned, the hide was stretched and laced onto a wooden frame, and all of the hair was scraped off. Next, the skin was coated with a mixture of water and the deer's own brains, which contain tannic acid to preserve the leather. Pounding and rubbing the skin until it was smooth and supple finished the process.[218] Besides guns, the deerskin trade infused the Indian societies with European-made items such as brass kettles, iron tools, and glass beads that rapidly replaced traditional clay pottery and other native-made items. While inter- and intra-tribal relationships deteriorated with the flood of European trade goods into the Mississippi Valley, the Indian deer hunters were forging what were to them new bonds of alliance with their English and French trading partners. For the traders' part, however, the exchange of European items for Indian deerskins was business pure and simple.[219]

This fledgling economy linking Indians, voyageurs, colonists, and outside purchasers was all but shattered upon Governor La Mothe's arrival in Louisiana. Crozat's monopoly cut off all individual colonial trade with French ships and with the Spanish at Pensacola. Now, the voyageurs and residents of Mobile were obliged to sell their animal skins to the company, and La Mothe abruptly lowered the price paid for deerskins from twenty-five sous to fifteen sous. As if that weren't bad enough, the governor insisted on inspecting the skins himself, rejecting as many as 50 percent for not measuring up to the quality he was used to seeing in Canada.[220]

Although there is no documentation, La Mothe's actions would have made it difficult for Crozat's new Natchez trading post to compete with English traders who continued to pay the accepted rate for skins. Of a more serious nature was the possibility that the sudden drop in prices being offered by the French for deerskins would jeopardize the alliance that the Indians felt had been forged by the ongoing exchange relationship.[221] Apparently, La Mothe was unsuccessful at manipulating the deerskin market in Crozat's favor and, by 1716, voyageurs at Mobile were once again receiving twenty sous per skin, and Indians doing business with the English were being offered a bonus of five sous per deerskin to trade with the French.[222]

However, the deerskin trade was only a minor part of Crozat's Louisiana business venture. A major goal was establishing trade relations with the Spanish in Mexico. Toward this end, a French expedition led by the Louisiana veteran St. Denis traveled up the Red River in 1714 to explore an overland route to Spain's mission settlements in east Texas. Another of La Mothe's goals was to investigate the voyageurs' reports of silver mines in the Illinois country. The governor led the Illinois expedition himself, setting out to ascend the Mississippi River in February 1714.[223] As it turned out, both expeditions impacted the Natchez Indians in unexpected ways.

André Pénicaut, who had remained in Louisiana since his Natchez visit in 1704, was a member of St. Denis' party.[224] In the spring of 1715, Pénicaut and six voyageurs left the expedition's Red River camp and made their way to the Natchez, where they planned to purchase corn meal and other supplies. At the Natchez, Pénicaut was surprised to find three Englishmen negotiating with a slave-raiding party composed of Natchez, Chickasaws, and Yazoos for the purchase of eleven captives taken in a raid on the Chaouacha, a small tribe living south of Lake Pontchartrain.[225]

The Carolina traders were led by a Welshman named Price Hughes, who was reconnoitering the Natchez country as part of a bold plan to found a colony of Welsh families on the Mississippi. Despite the presence of the La Loires and Crozat's trading post, Hughes asserted that the Natchez were England's allies.[226] By their geographic position on the great river and their ability to work with both French and English, the Natchez seemed to attract a parade of European dreamers who would draw the tribe into their empire-building conspiracies. When questioned by the La Loires as to his business at the Natchez, Hughes blithely replied that he was there to buy pelts.[227]

The La Loires confided in Pénicaut that Bienville had ordered them to capture Hughes, but they all agreed that the Welshman was too well-liked by the

Natchez to arrest him there. Instead, the Frenchmen followed Hughes as he made his way downriver, holding back while the little Carolina party stopped at the Tunica and was honored with a calumet ceremony. Below the Tunica, in the vicinity of Manchac, La Loire and his posse were finally able to take Hughes into custody and convey him to Bienville in Mobile.[228] Being under orders from La Mothe not to harm any British agents, Bienville questioned Hughes and released him, but not before confiscating the Welshman's written commission from the Governor of Carolina, which detailed the ambitious objective of settling five hundred Welsh families on the Mississippi in the fall of 1715.[229] Unfortunately for Hughes, his overland journey from Mobile to Charles Town happened to coincide with the Yamasee War. In April 1715, the Yamasee and a host of other tribes from Carolina to Alabama, fed up with being cheated and manipulated by slave traders, attacked English agents wherever they found them.[230] Price Hughes wandered into this maelstrom near the mouth of the Alabama River, where he encountered a group of Tohome Indians whose villages had frequently been targeted by slave catchers. Hughes' fate is summed up by Pénicaut in four words: "They broke his head."[231] With the deaths of Hughes and a host of other English traders, the era of the Southeastern Indian slave trade finally came to an end. However, decades of slave-catching and amity with the English would profoundly affect Natchez—French relations during the next fifteen years. When the Yamasee War temporarily threw the English out of favor among many tribes in the region, the Chickasaw remained friendly to Carolina.[232] Likewise, the Natchez, or at least a strong faction of the tribe, continued to prefer the English to the French as the more profitable of two evils. Meanwhile, Governor La Mothe's travels on the Mississippi River that year did little to endear the Indians to the French. Bienville summarized the situation in a January 2, 1716, letter to Pontchartrain:

[La Mothe told me] that the Natchez were a very docile nation. I replied to him that I knew these Natchez better than he did; that that was the nation that I distrusted more than any other because they had previously killed some Frenchmen and that I knew that they were very dissatisfied. And in fact on the journey that Mr. de Lamothe has just made to the Illinois he quarreled as he went up with all the nations that are along this river. All the villages received him as best they could [and] gave him presents of everything they might have. He made them no presents and promised the chiefs and headmen that he would bring them here to receive presents. He returned [downriver from Illinois] without stopping [and] passed straight on. That made a very bad impression. All the nations are talking about it with very great scorn to the shame of the French to the extent of threatening to kill some of them.[233]

The governor not only failed to give the customary presents to tribal leaders, he also made the diplomatic blunder of refusing to smoke the calumet with the tribes along the Mississippi, including the Natchez.[234] Given La Mothe's long experience with Indians in the Great Lakes area, it is hard to imagine why he would have behaved so imprudently. According to Bienville, La Mothe claimed to have been in too much of a hurry to accept the Natchez's hospitality.[235] Perhaps the governor made the mistake of believing that earlier calumet ceremonies involving Iberville and Bienville rendered the ritual unnecessary. Or maybe La Mothe, like Iberville, simply found smoking to be disgusting. As we will see, La Mothe's behavior would have serious repercussions for the La Loires, Bienville, and the Natchez Indians.

Chapter Three

EUROPEAN OCCUPATION,

1715–1729

ANDRÉ PÉNICAUT HAPPENED TO BE at the Natchez trading post again in late 1715 when an incident on a lonely stretch of the Mississippi River sparked the confrontation known as "the first Natchez war." According to Pénicaut, four voyageurs on their way from Mobile to the Illinois country stopped at the Natchez landing and hired four Natchez Indians to assist them in paddling. Some distance upriver, the Natchez allegedly waylaid their employers and helped themselves to the merchandise in their canoes. Bienville believed that the murders were in reprisal for Governor La Mothe's refusal to smoke the Natchez calumet, which the Natchez are thought to have interpreted as a declaration of war.[1] However, the timing of the confrontation between the voyageurs and the Natchez may have been coincidental, and the violence may have possibly been caused by the voyageurs themselves. Like so many other pivotal events in American history, we will never know what really happened on that winter day beside the great river.

At the time, Pénicaut was assisting the younger La Loire at Crozat's Natchez warehouse while the elder La Loire was away in Mobile. When he chanced to recognize the voyageurs' belongings in the possession of some Natchez Indians, Pénicaut told the young La Loire that he suspected foul play. Discretion being the better part of valor, Pénicaut and La Loire kept their suspicions quiet and took care to be on guard until the elder La Loire returned from Mobile with fourteen men.[2] The elder La Loire was under orders from La Mothe to continue on to the Illinois country with three canoes containing trade items, and his party spent two weeks at the Natchez gathering supplies for the journey. During this time, Pénicaut shared with the elder La Loire his misgivings about the fate of the four voyageurs and even claims to have received further warning of Natchez hostility from a "petty chief." However, he and the other Frenchmen were confident enough of the tribe's loyalty to the French to ask the Great Sun for the services of eight Natchez Indians to assist with the paddling.[3] Pénicaut was enlisted to accompany the elder La Loire to the Illinois country, and he described what transpired upon their departure:

> Before leaving, M. de la Loire had a good deal of trouble in persuading his young brother to stay to guard the warehouse of company supplies, for he saw the evident danger that he ran, which would have been still greater than we thought if God had not protected us. After embracing this young man, we left him at the Natchez greatly distressed over our having to leave him behind; and we went off with the eight savages the Grand Chief had given us to help us row up the river. When we got in our boats, that traitor of a Grand Chief instructed his savages, quite loud and in our presence, to do whatever we told them and not to approach the river bank if we should find any people on the bank signaling for us to come to them, for fear they might be people that would wish to do us harm or make an attempt upon our lives.[4]

Pénicaut wrote his Louisiana memoirs long after the events that he described, and his indictment of the Grand Chief or Great Sun as a "traitor" is based upon his interpretation of what happened during the next twenty-four hours.[5] In fact, the Great Sun's warning was probably genuine. As we've already seen, Pénicaut and most other Frenchmen mistakenly thought that the Great Sun held authority over the big-man leaders of the tribe's settlement districts. An incident later that day clearly indicates that the Natchez Indians were not unified behind one leader. One of the Natchez men who had hired on to help paddle the canoes upriver confided to Pénicaut that a Natchez chief named Le Barbu, The Bearded, was waiting a short distance upstream at a place called Le Petite Gouffre (the Little Gulf) with one hundred and fifty men.[6]

If the intelligence shared by the Indian informant was reliable, then Pénicaut and La Loire were risking ambush by an overwhelming force by continuing upriver. The Frenchmen called the eight Natchez men together and offered them presents and assurances of protection if they told the truth. All eight affirmed that The Bearded and his band of armed warriors were waiting upstream to attack the little flotilla. The confession of these men, who were supposedly hand-picked by the Great Sun, indicates that while The Bearded's plot might have been generally known among the Natchez, the tribe was not unanimous in its enmity toward the French.

The Bearded is the only Natchez settlement district leader who has been connected genealogically to the Great Sun's lineage, which makes his renegade behavior somewhat surprising. He was the Great Sun's maternal uncle, an especially close familial bond in a matrilineal society. He also controlled the Jenzenaque settlement district and was known to have supported English traders.[7] Although we can't know all of the factors affecting Natchez politics in that fall of 1715, several things might have contributed to The Bearded's hostility toward the French. Aside from Governor La Mothe's rejection of the Natchez calumet, the tribe's pro-English faction probably resented the La Loires' removal of Price Hughes, who represented a potentially lucrative and long-term trading partnership. At the same time, Crozat's company's attempt to drive down the prices offered for deerskins would have jeopardized the exchange relationship that represented (to the Natchez) friendship and goodwill. Andrew Albrecht has also suggested that The Bearded's aggression just might have been of a more personal nature; perhaps the chief sought revenge for some unrecorded atrocity on the part of the French.[8]

For Pénicaut and La Loire, no course remained except to turn around and head back downriver to safety. At the Natchez, young Le Loire abandoned the trading post, and the party of Frenchmen made their way downstream during the night.[9] Pénicaut's account of his heroic, single-handed rescue of young La Loire from the Natchez trading post is one of the more entertaining passages in his narrative; however, his mission's element of danger is probably exaggerated. Later testimony makes it clear that the Great Sun and the people of the nearby Flour settlement were not a part of The Bearded's plans to ambush the Frenchmen.

Around mid-morning, the group of nervous Frenchmen reached the Tunica landing, where they were welcomed by Father Davion, who was aware of the trouble upstream and was relieved to see his countrymen alive and well. While La Loire and his party were at the Tunica village, Pénicaut reports that a small group of Natchez Indians arrived and brazenly invited the Tunicas to join them in war against the French. Fortunately for the Frenchmen, the Tunica chief declined the invitation, and the La Loire party subsequently made its way to Mobile to raise the alarm about the Natchez hostilities.[10]

THE FIRST NATCHEZ WAR

While the La Loires were setting up Crozat's trading post, plans were under way to place a more substantial French outpost at the Natchez. In an effort to secure Louisiana's mineral resources from English encroachment, the French Council of the Navy proposed constructing forts at several strategic locations, including the Natchez and Yazoo tribes, and along the Wabash, Red, and Alabama rivers.[11] In 1715, Bienville received orders from the king to go and establish two of these forts, one at the Natchez and the other on the Wabash River near its junction with the Ohio. The Natchez fort was to be named "Rosalie" in honor of the Duchess of Pontchartrain, the wife of the king's minister of the navy, and the Wabash fort would be named "St. Jerome," after the minister himself.[12] The La Loires and Pénicaut arrived in Mobile with word of the Natchez hostilities in January 1716, just as Bienville was readying an expedition to ascend the Mississippi and carry out the king's directive.[13] The distressing news from upriver affected French objectives in several ways. Obviously, there could be no Natchez outpost until peace was restored there. Even more important, the Natchez now threatened French travelers on the Mississippi River, disrupting the tenuous lifeline between New France and Louisiana. The deaths of the four voyageurs also obligated the French to exact revenge, for to allow the murderers to go unpunished would have sent the wrong signal to the other Mississippi tribes.

Bienville's business upriver was now transformed into a punitive military strike against a native force thought to number 800 warriors.[14] In 1715, the French garrison at Mobile totaled about 150 men, and Bienville wanted to take at least 80 men to move against the Natchez, but La Mothe would only allow Bienville to take a company of thirty-four soldiers, plus fifteen sailors. The outlook for success looked dire, for not only were the numbers heavily in favor of the Natchez, the quality of the French Louisiana military personnel left much to be desired. Bienville later referred to his men on the 1716 Natchez campaign as "little raw soldiers, two-thirds of whom are ill and without provisions." The garrison at the Mobile fort was plagued with desertions that winter, and at least twenty-four men had decamped to go and live with the Spanish at Pensacola. Bad food, poor living conditions, sickness, and meager pay all contributed to the French army's low morale.[15]

Captain Louis Poncereau de Richebourg participated in the Natchez campaign and wrote an account of what happened, which probably includes substantial input from Bienville. De Richebourg reports that the little army, traveling in eight dugout canoes, arrived at the Tunica settlement on April 23 and learned that the Natchez had killed another Frenchman.[16] In 1716, the Tunica were settled at the "Portage of the Cross," a familiar landing site on the Mississippi River opposite the mouth of the Red River.[17] Pénicaut was traveling with Bienville and had this to say about this latest hostility: "[A] Frenchman named Richard on his way downstream from the Illinois had been seized by the Natchez. After taking his merchandise, they brought him to their village, where they cut off his feet and his hands and then threw him in a mudhole."[18] Elements of the Natchez and Tunica were apparently in close communication, and Davion confided to Bienville that the Tunica shouldn't be trusted.

Leaving the Tunica, Bienville moved his force upriver and set up camp on an island known today as "Natchez Island" and labeled on some eighteenth-century maps as "I. Bienville" (Figure 5).[19] A familiar landmark on nineteenth- and twentieth-century maps of the Mississippi River, Natchez Island has become fused with the west bank and is no longer an island.[20] The choice of the island as a base of operations is odd given Bienville's years of experience in the region—after all, it was springtime, and the river could be expected to be on the rise. However, the Natchez outnumbered the French, and the island provided some measure of protection against a surprise attack. Bienville's strategy was not to confront the Natchez with force but to lure the tribe's ranking chiefs to his camp and take them hostage. He could then demand the deaths of those who had murdered the Frenchmen. The soldiers set to work erecting a crude palisade and sheds to be used for storage of their provisions and arms, a shelter for the soldiers, and a prison.

Traveling with the expedition was a Frenchman whom De Richebourg says "spoke [the Natchez] language perfectly." According to Bienville, the French employed two interpreters at Mobile who could speak some of the languages of the Mississippi tribes. It is possible that the interpreter on the 1716 expedition was the cabin boy sent by Iberville to the Natchez in 1700.[21] Bienville himself was fluent in the Mobilian trade language, so communication with the Natchez over the next several days was probably accomplished through a mixture of Natchez and Mobilian.

On April 27, three Natchez emissaries arrived bearing a calumet, which Bienville refused, saying that he would only smoke the calumet with the tribal chiefs. The next day, the three Natchez men left the island accompanied by Bienville's interpreter with instructions to bring back the chiefs.[22] After sunset, one of the Canadians was dispatched in a canoe to quietly go upriver above the Natchez and warn any Frenchmen coming down from the Illinois country about the tribe's hostility. A week passed without incident, then a party of six Canadian voyageurs landed at the island from upstream with an astonishing story. The group had been descending the river with a load of pelts, smoked meats, and bear's oil when they were taken captive by about twenty Natchez men and led to the village of The Bearded chief. There they were held for three days while a council of several Natchez chiefs from different villages deliberated on what to do.[23]

The Canadians had apparently been taken to The Bearded's Jenzenaque settlement district and their capture must have galvanized the tribe's pro-French faction, bringing about a crucial confrontation between tribal leaders. It seems that the tribe's pro-French leadership, which included The Bearded's maternal nephews, was able to convince the Jenzenaque chief of the need to reestablish friendly terms with Bienville. Tunica messengers had already informed the Natchez that the French wished to reopen the trading post and establish a greater presence in the area. Although the tribe's pro-English faction may have protested, the alternative seemed to be war, and the Chitimacha example was still in their minds. After the murder of Saint-Cosme in 1706, Bienville had encouraged several tribes to target the Chitimacha for relentless slave raids.[24] If the Natchez tribe was far from unified under one chief, the three-day conference at Jenzenaque shows that they could put aside (at least temporarily) their differences for the common good.

A few days later, a party of Natchez chiefs came to Bienville's island with their calumets. The scene, as described by De Richebourg, is eerily reminiscent of ancestral Quigualtam: "The 8th of May, at 10:00 o'clock in the morning, we saw 4 dugouts coming, in which were 8 men standing, who sang the calumet song, and 3 men in each dugout seated under parasols, 12 who paddled and 2 Frenchmen."[25]

When the chiefs disembarked and were in the midst of their calumet song, Bienville's men seized them and locked them in a makeshift jail.[26] Based upon fragmentary knowledge of the Natchez chiefs in 1716, the eight chiefs captured by Bienville are tentatively identified as

The Great Sun (ranking hereditary chief, residing at the Grand Village)

Tattooed Serpent (the Great Sun's younger brother, residing at the Grand Village)

Little Sun (younger brother of the Great Sun and Tattooed Serpent, residence unknown)

The Bearded (ranking chief of the Jenzenaque settlement district and maternal uncle of the three Sun brothers)

Old Flour Chief (ranking chief of the Flour settlement district and Master of Temple Ceremonies at the Grand Village, no known genealogical relationship to the Sun family)

Old Hair (ranking chief of the Apple or White Earth settlement district, no known genealogical relationship to the Sun family)

Yakstalchil (second ranking chief of the Flour settlement district, no known genealogical relationship to the Sun family)

Alahoflechia (ranking chief of the Grigra settlement district, no known genealogical relationship to the Sun family)[27]

To the captive chiefs, Bienville's abrupt demand for satisfaction for the deaths of the five voyageurs could only mean that they were about to be killed in retribution. According to Alan Gallay, the Mississippi River tribes viewed acts of aggression against an outside group—in this case, elements of the Natchez tribe had attacked French voyageurs—not as crimes between individuals but as crimes between groups. Therefore, in the Natchez way of thinking, the French now had the right to take vengeance on any member of the Natchez group, not necessarily the actual killers.[28]

That night, guards brought the three Sun brothers to Bienville's tent, where with the help of his interpreter he told them he wanted the Natchez to bring him the heads of the murderers and the heads of the chiefs who had given the order. According to De Richebourg, Bienville "wished their heads in order to recognize them by their tattoo marks." To leverage his point, Bienville reminded the chiefs about what had happened to the Chitimacha tribe after Saint-Cosme's murder and recounted a number of instances when he had punished tribes by making them deliver up the scalps and heads of guilty individuals. The next day, the three brothers agreed to Bienville's demands, and the Tattooed Serpent volunteered to go among his people and carry out the beheadings. However, Bienville refused to release such an important hostage, so the Little Sun was deputized to undertake the risky assignment alone. In the meantime, thirteen Canadians arrived at Bienville's island from upriver. Having been warned of the hostilities, they had slipped successfully past the Natchez landing without stopping and brought word that a Frenchman and two Illinois Indians had been captured.[29]

On May 14, the Little Sun returned to the island carrying three heads, two of which were recognized as murderers of the four Frenchmen. Failing to capture a third murderer, the Little Sun had beheaded the guilty man's brother. As mentioned above, the Natchez probably viewed the situation as a conflict between groups instead of individuals, making the brother a suitable substitute for French vengeance. To Bienville's way of thinking, however, an innocent man had been killed.[30] The Little Sun also brought in the Frenchman and two Illinois Indians whom the Canadians had reported captured a few days earlier. As De Richebourg put it, the Natchez chief "had delivered them from the frame where they had been attached to be burned." The captives had apparently been taken to one of the pro-English settlement districts where an element of the Natchez tribe obviously remained quite hostile to the French, despite the accord reached at the Jenzenaque conference of chiefs held a few days earlier. Unimpressed with the Little Sun's rescue of his countryman, Bienville had the chief manacled and returned to the island's makeshift prison.[31]

Around this time, according to De Richebourg, Bienville's island was covered by spring floodwaters to a depth of six inches above the highest land. Somehow, Bienville's men coped with these conditions instead of moving the encampment to higher ground. The commander himself relocated to an improvised shelter on a raised platform.[32] De Richebourg doesn't say whether the Indian hostages were given dry accommodations, but when the Tattooed Serpent became ill, Bienville moved the three Sun brothers into his quarters. The chiefs told Bienville that the recent troubles were due to the "war chiefs" of the three pro-English settlements, Jenzenaque, White Earth, and Grigra. Two of these war chiefs, The Bearded (Jenzenaque settlement) and Alahoflechia (Grigra settlement), were sitting in Bienville's jail, while the third, Oyelape, the second ranking chief of the White Earth or White Apple settlement district, remained at large. Old Hair, the ranking chief of White Apple, was apparently cleared of any wrong-doing.[33]

Bienville stubbornly kept his men and hostages on the flooded island throughout the month of May while demanding that the Natchez bring him the head of Oyelape. During this time, the commander received word through Tunica sources that the Natchez might be planning an all-out attack on the island to free their captive chiefs. If the tribe had indeed contemplated such a bold move, they apparently lacked the leadership to carry it out. On June 1, with Oyelape still not captured, Bienville realized that the stalemate had to be broken. De Richebourg wrote: "The number of sick, which increased every day in our little camp, determined M. de Bienville to terminate this little war."[34]

Bienville kept The Bearded, Alahoflechia, and two warriors in his jail and assembled the rest of the hostages, to whom he stated the terms of their release. These included the pledge to continue to pursue Oyelape and deliver his head to the French, an agreement to restore the merchandise pillaged from the trading post after the La Loires abandoned it, and a promise to help build a fort and lodging for a French occupation force. The chiefs agreed to Bienville's terms and gave their consent for the French to break the heads of the four men still being held in the jail. However, the Tattooed Serpent advised Bienville to make it appear as though The Bearded and Alahoflechia were being sent to Mobile for trial because he feared a possible revolt among the Natchez people if the two chiefs were openly executed.

Jacques Barbaza de Pailloux, one of Bienville's officers, took two soldiers and accompanied the freed hostages back to their respective settlements to announce the terms of peace to the Natchez people.[35] Over a period of four days, Pailloux supposedly witnessed these town meetings at each of the tribe's settlement districts. The punitive campaign was finally concluded on June 7, when Bienville and the Natchez chiefs smoked the calumet.[36] Five days later, some of Bienville's Canadians secretly executed The Bearded and Alahoflechia to avoid alarming their supporters among the Natchez. According to De Richebourg, The Bearded remained defiant to the end:

> The Bearded ceased for a moment singing his death song and sang that of war. He related his great deeds against different nations and the number of scalps he had carried away. He named the five Frenchmen whom he had caused to die, and said that he died with regret at not having killed more. The Tattooed Serpent, who was then the only one of his nation among us, listened attentively and said to M. de Bienville, "He is my brother, but I do no regret him. You are ridding us of a bad man."[37]

The Tattooed Serpent's remarks hint at the power struggle among settlement district chiefs that had fractured Natchez society in recent years. According to De Richebourg, the three Sun brothers told Bienville that the chiefs of the White Apple, Jenzenaque, and Grigra settlement districts had "assumed so much authority in their nation that they were more feared and obeyed than themselves [the Suns]."[38] By removing The Bearded and Alahoflechia, Bienville had eliminated two-thirds of the tribe's pro-English leadership. The Tattooed Serpent and his brothers could take heart that an expanded French presence at Natchez would return some measure of authority to the Sun lineage.

As the month of June wore on, the Mississippi River continued to flood the island camp, so Bienville and those of his men suffering from sickness moved downriver to the Tunicas and higher ground. The rest of the company assisted Pailloux with the construction of the fort on a prominent bluff overlooking the Natchez landing. According to the terms of the hostage release, the Natchez Indians supplied acacia wood posts and cypress bark, which served as a roofing material.[39] The acacia wood specified by Bienville was probably black locust (*Robinia pseudoacacia* L.), a durable Southern hardwood that is often used for fence posts.[40] The preparation of the poles would have necessitated stripping away the bark to prevent the wood from being attacked by borers. On July 1, Pailloux reported to Bienville that "three-quarters of the piles for our fort were brought in place; that there were savages at work making trenches, and that there would be need of six skillful soldiers to show the savages how to plant the piles straight and of equal height."[41]

Fort Rosalie, completed on August 3, 1716, was a simple four-cornered, wooden palisade measuring approximately 150 feet by 90 feet, with a guardhouse, barracks, magazine, and storehouse. On August 25, the Natchez, joined by the

Yazoo and Ofogoula tribes, danced at the fort and the calumet ceremony was repeated. De Richebourg optimistically wrote that "all these people were come to dance at [Bienville's fort] in order to show him their joy at having Frenchmen established among them."[42] Rather than being overjoyed at the presence of Frenchmen, the Natchez were probably relieved to have averted war. Having satisfied Bienville's demands, they could continue, at least for a time, to enjoy their precarious dual associations with the French and the English.

THE INDIAN VERSUS INDIAN STRATEGY

Beinville's use of a hostage situation to coerce the Natchez Indians into punishing their own tribal members for crimes against the French was a variation on a common European strategy in colonial North America. This strategy often took the form of instigating inter-tribal warfare, as in the so-called "French and Indian Wars," which were largely fought by Indian armies led by British and French commanders. Bienville apparently believed, as did most European officers who instigated inter-tribal wars, that the warring tribes would see their way clear to stop fighting each other when peace was concluded between France and England.[43]

When tribes were set against each other in these wars, the incentive for the Indians was usually access to European trade merchandise, either in direct payment for mercenary services or through the sale of slaves captured in raids. By 1716, Bienville had employed this strategy successfully on several occasions, notably in ongoing wars against the Chitimacha and Alabama.[44] In 1706, Bienville adopted a scalps-for-guns policy that he said had been used effectively in Canada, promising to give a firearm to any Indian who brought in the scalp of a member of a tribe that had harmed Frenchmen or were allied to the English.[45] Of course, the effect of these policies was to create a heightened state of unrest in the Lower Mississippi Valley. Sounding patronizingly paternal in 1709, Bienville wrote to Pontchartrain: "All our Indians are very much attached to us and behave well except in the wars that they are carrying on with each other. They are betraying each other every day and I am taking pains to restore them to peace."[46]

Most of Bienville's machinations among the Mississippi tribes involved setting tribes against tribes. With the first Natchez war, he took the Indian versus Indian strategy *inside* the tribal unit and caused individuals to be hunted down and killed by members of their own group. That the Natchez consented to kill their fellow tribesmen is an indication of the importance that the people placed upon obtaining the release of their chiefs. Although we have no way of knowing what repercussions followed from the executions carried out by the Little Sun and his accomplices, in all likelihood, these beheadings would have obligated the families of the three men to avenge their kinsmen. For example, a Chitimacha man who acted on behalf of the French and killed a fellow tribesman implicated in the Saint-Cosme murder triggered a vendetta that lasted more than a decade.[47] Although Bienville had demanded the heads of both chiefs and warriors involved with the murder of the Frenchmen, the Little Sun returned with only the heads of three men of lower tribal rank. Considering that the tribe held a strong taboo against the violent death of a chief, it is not surprising that they repeatedly excused themselves from bringing in Oyelape's head by pleading that he had escaped.[48]

The failure of the Natchez to try and rescue their chiefs is puzzling. With their superior numbers and skill in handling dugout canoes on the Mississippi River, it would seem that the Natchez could have overrun the flooded island and rather easily defeated Bienville's demoralized little army. However, the Natchez people may have feared that such a bold move might prove fatal for the captive chiefs. Indeed, by capturing most of the tribe's highest-ranking members, Bienville may have inadvertently disabled the Natchez in much the same way as Maya kingdoms are known to have been affected when their leaders were taken captive. In one stroke, all of the rules of succession and delegation of authority may have been suspended, and new leaders could not legitimately take control while the current leader's fate was in limbo.[49] Unfortunately, we will never know what was discussed around the council fires in the Natchez settlement districts during the twenty-four days that their chiefs were held hostage, but the episode was undoubtedly a stressful period for the tribe. After the first Natchez war, one colonial administrator justified Bienville's heavy-handed manner of dealing with the Natchez by saying "to succeed with [Indians] it is necessary to treat them with extreme severity without, however, doing them any injustice."[50]

THE NATCHEZ TRADING POST REOPENS

The Natchez trading post was reestablished around the time that work was completed on Fort Rosalie. By the terms of Bienville's treaty, the Natchez were obliged to return or replace the animal skins and merchandise that were taken when the trading post was abandoned in late 1715. Instead of reopening the trading post near the Grand Village, the new trading post, or commissary, as it is labeled on some maps, was placed near Fort Rosalie, making the fort the new center of commerce between the Indians and the French.[51] The La Loires were back in charge of the Natchez trading post by 1718 or 1719 and may have been on hand in 1716 to reopen the business.[52]

Although the Natchez had been participating to some extent in the European deerskin and bearskin trade for many years, this activity increased dramatically in the years between 1716 and 1729. In 1726, Bienville would estimate that the Indians of Louisiana could supply fifty thousand deerskins annually for the French market.[53] To maintain access to coveted trade goods such as guns, woolen blankets, glass beads, iron pots, and many other European products, Indian families devoted more and more time to chasing and skinning deer and other animals.[54] In adapting to the deerskin trade economy, the daily labor of the native residents of the Lower Mississippi Valley was redirected from providing for their own families and extended kinship groups to supplying the raw material for the European leather industry.

According to Gregory Waselkov, the deerskin business was conducted on a credit basis. For the Natchez and other Mississippi tribes, the seasonal round began in the summer when French traders supplied the native hunters with merchandise. Gunpowder and bullets were especially critical commodities, since the Indians could not produce these things themselves. After hunting and dressing hides during the fall and winter, the Indians presented their animal skins to the company trading post in the spring. The skins were then transported to Mobile or New Orleans and sold for shipment to Europe. With the proceeds from the sale, the traders purchased new merchandise for distribution to the Indian hunters.[55] The French probably captured most Natchez tribe's deerskin business through the local trading post; however, the English quickly reestablished their trade relationships with the Chickasaw, and it is reasonable to assume that some Natchez deerskins were also going to Carolina by 1720.[56] Rather than risk the ire of the French at Fort Rosalie, English deerskin traders could have arrived with packhorses on the tribe's northeastern periphery, perhaps in the relatively remote Fairchilds Creek/Coles Creek settlement area, to exchange their merchandise for deerskins.[57]

Bienville remained in command of Fort Rosalie during the French garrison's first winter at the Natchez.[58] Although we don't have any accounts of his activities during this period, it is safe to say that part of the commander's time was spent maintaining discipline in the Natchez garrison. If the French soldiers at Mobile felt isolated and discontent, the men at Fort Rosalie must have thought that they were stationed at the end of the world. They knew that if and when a supply ship appeared at Mobile Bay, it could be months before the ration of flour, meat, and brandy reached them at the Natchez outpost, if the shipments even made it that far.[59] Therefore, the soldiers at Fort Rosalie soon found it necessary to make acquaintances among the Natchez Indians in order to barter for food. Indeed, catering to the French garrison quickly became another facet of the Indian families' new European-driven cottage industry. Deer meat, either fresh or dried and pounded into pemmican, was traded to the French soldiers along with fish and corn meal.[60]

Despite the growing availability of European trade merchandise brought about by the presence of a French fort at the Natchez, the White Apple, Jenzenaque, and Grigra settlement districts remained stubbornly pro-English. This stance was no doubt fueled by the executions of The Bearded and Ahaloflechia, but the pro-English faction showed no open enmity toward the French during the first years of the occupation. Chief Oyelape remained a fugitive under the terms of Bienville's hostage settlement, although there is no evidence to suggest that he was being actively pursued. If Oyelape left the Natchez area, he probably found refuge among former slave-catching partners such as the Yazoo or Chickasaw.

THE COMPANY OF THE WEST AND THE NATCHEZ INDIANS

The rescue of France's struggling Louisiana colony by Scotsman John Law while Frenchmen in the colony labored to fend off strategic advances by the Carolina English has to rank as one of history's greatest ironies. Although it is doubtful that Law himself ever gave much consideration to the Natchez Indians, his Company of the West had a devastating impact on the tribe. Under the company's regime, hundreds of would-be tobacco planters, their families, and servants would soon be flocking to the Natchez colony. Unlike Bienville, Pénicaut, and most of those who had come before, these new inhabitants would have no idea how to interact with the Natchez, nor would most of them be inclined to learn the sounds and gestures that would help the Indians recognize them as friends.

After being shunned in Scotland for his radical banking ideas, Law happened to wind up in France during a time of change and opportunity. Upon the death of Louis the XIV in late 1715, a regency of noblemen headed by the Duke of Orléans (for whom New Orleans is named) assumed control of the country's affairs and found Law's prescription for economic prosperity irresistible. In the spring of 1716, Law opened a private bank in Paris and began introducing the

French to the concept of paper money. Law's bank positioned him to move into the business of foreign trade, with profit-seeking tentacles reaching out around the world and eventually extending into the Lower Mississippi Valley.[61]

In the meantime, the regency's Council of the Navy equipped and dispatched two frigates carrying supplies to the Louisiana colony. These two ships and a ship outfitted by Crozat all reached Mobile in March 1717.[62] Unfortunately for the Fort Rosalie garrison, most of these supplies remained in Mobile, including desperately needed flour and medicine.[63] The supply ships also delivered a motley crew of criminals and vagrants who comprised the first wave of immigrants selected by the Council to increase the colonial population. Although it seems ludicrous, Crozat and the regency set about filling the ranks of the colonial army with homeless children and soldiers convicted of desertion.[64]

Having failed to produce any profitable exports for Crozat, Governor La Mothe was recalled in 1716 and replaced the following year by Sieur de Lépinay.[65] Natchez chiefs were among the leaders of more than twenty tribes who traveled to Dauphin Island to meet the new governor, dance the calumet, and receive presents.[66] However, Governor Lépinay, like his predecessor, lacked the necessary frontier experience to advance France's standing among the Mississippi tribes. Although he knew enough to distribute gifts to the chiefs when they came to present the calumet, the new governor failed to grasp the importance of continued gift-giving in maintaining a good relationship with the tribal chiefs. Lépinay seems to have been adequately supplied with merchandise from France to be used as "presents for the Indians," but he did not send any of this material to the Natchez outpost during his first eight months in office.[67] Bienville understood the role of gifts in Indian diplomacy and might have been of considerable assistance in these matters, but under Lépinay he lacked the authority to dispense presents to the tribes.[68]

In August 1717, Crozat, weary of throwing good money after bad with no hope of profits in sight, relinquished his monopoly to John Law's Company of the West, setting in motion France's last enthusiastic push to colonize the Lower Mississippi Valley.[69] Through the Duke of Orléans and the regency, Law expanded his company's trade monopoly to include both New France (Canada) and Louisiana. The Company of the West was attracted by the thriving Canadian fur trade and by the speculation that profitable mines could be opened in the Illinois country. In the company's ambitious advertising campaign to convince entrepreneurs to invest their time and money in developing Louisiana, the Lower Mississippi Valley was touted as an agricultural El Dorado where, among other things, Indians would be clamoring to farm silkworms in the native mulberry trees.[70]

By 1718, Law's Company of the West and its growing number of nobleman shareholders had granted extensive Louisiana concessions (plantations) to 116 upper middle-class Frenchmen. However, the company's ambitious advertising campaign about the good life to be had in the Mississippi country failed to attract the respectable yeoman families necessary to work the land. So, like Crozat in previous years, the company, with the help of the French government, shanghaied into indentured servitude more than six hundred vagrants, orphans, smugglers, prostitutes, and thieves to begin the business of populating the colony. All over France, the local constabulary scrambled to take advantage of this windfall by cleaning out the jails and rounding up the homeless from the town streets.[71]

Among the enlightened gentlemen concessionaires aboard the company's ships sailing to Louisiana in the summer of 1718 was an extraordinary naturalist and memoirist named Antione-Simon Le Page du Pratz. Du Pratz was to become an ardent champion of the Natchez Indians, documenting in considerable detail the tribe's last years.[72] Shortly after arriving at Dauphin Island in August 1718, Du Pratz purchased a young Chitimacha slave woman.[73] Owing to the long war with the Chitimachas that followed Saint-Cosme's murder, female slaves from that tribe were plentiful among the French in Louisiana. In fact, when hostilities ceased between the French and the Chitimacha in 1718, Pénicaut, who was present at the calumet dance, noted that the French refused to release any of the Chitimacha women being held in slavery.[74]

Du Pratz also attended this calumet ceremony, and his slave girl provided him with a detailed translation of the speech by the Chitimacha orator.[75] By coincidence, Du Pratz's slave was the daughter of a Chitimacha noble who had aided the French by executing one of his tribesmen implicated in the Saint-Cosme affair. The resulting vendetta on the part of the dead tribesman's relatives forced the girl's father to seek refuge among the Natchez, where he had relatives of his own. Patricia Galloway has mentioned the possibility that one of these relatives may have been the wife of a Natchez Sun.[76] According to the Chitimachas' origin mythology, they once lived with the Natchez Indians, and John R. Swanton has noted that the Natchez referred to the Chitimacha as "brothers."[77] Although the connection between the Natchez and the Chitimacha has yet to be defined, Du Pratz's slave girl has illuminated a small Chitimacha contingent living with the Natchez, further emphasizing the tribe's heterogeneity. Du Pratz and his retinue eventually settled near the newly established town of New Orleans, where he staked out a Company of the West concession for himself.[78]

In the process of settling in on his farm, Du Pratz began hearing glowing accounts about the Natchez area from other concessionaires and from his

Chitimacha slave, who was anxious to go there to be near her relatives. Eventually, the colony's *commissaire-ordonnateur* Marc-Antoine Hubert, who shared administrative power with Governor Lépinay, convinced Du Pratz to assist him in moving to the Natchez country where he planned to establish a plantation.[79] Before leaving New Orleans, Du Pratz purchased two Negro slaves, a man and his wife, to augment his workforce and hired some voyageurs to serve as paddlers. As the little band traveled upriver in a large dugout canoe, Du Pratz shot a nineteen-foot-long alligator basking on the riverbank and noted that one of the voyageurs claimed to have once killed one measuring twenty-two feet in length.[80]

COLONIAL ENCROACHMENT

Du Pratz and his party reached the Natchez landing on January 5, 1720.[81] They were among the first of hundreds of Europeans and Africans who settled in the Natchez colony over the next decade. Compared to the fleeting encounters by La Salle, Iberville, the missionaries, and Pénicaut, the information about the Natchez Indians gathered by Du Pratz and others during the colonial years of the 1720s is quite detailed. However, the Natchez Indians documented in these narratives were rapidly evolving away from whatever their prehistoric society had been like in an effort to cope with the European invasion of the previous forty years.

By the time that Du Pratz and his retinue arrived at the Natchez, a colonial community was already in existence, with the first-comers staking out the high ground for their farms. According to Pénicaut, sixty soldiers were garrisoned at the fort, but many of these men probably had their accommodations outside the palisade walls.[82] Before leaving New Orleans, Du Pratz had been deputized to secure two large concessions or plantations at the Natchez, one (later called "St. Catherine") for Hubert and the other (later called "Terre Blanch" or "White Earth") for the Company of the West. Through La Loire, Du Pratz secured the services of an interpreter and began exploring the area. Before selecting the sites for the larger concerns, he purchased for himself a Natchez Indian's cabin and around six acres of cleared land beside the trail leading from the fort to the Grand Village.

The Indian from whom Du Pratz purchased his farm had his own house on an adjacent plot of land. When Du Pratz attempted to purchase the Indian's house and land to increase his holdings, the latter refused, saying that he preferred to live near his new neighbor and serve as his hunter and fisherman.[83] This Natchez man was probably typical of a growing number of his tribesmen who were finding employment by providing services for the burgeoning French population. Unfortunately, we know little about the nature of Du Pratz's land transactions with the Natchez Indians. Du Pratz apparently purchased his farm from an individual instead of from a settlement district or lineage, and he apparently believed that this man had the legal right to convey ownership of a specific piece of property. For the Indian's part, Patricia Galloway has suggested that the land was probably only conveyed to Du Pratz as a usufruct.[84] The Natchez had a long tradition of providing living space to those who would come and settle near them—elements of the Koroa, Tiou, Grigra, and Chitimacha tribes have been documented thus far—and there is no reason to think that the Natchez viewed the French any differently. If anything, the trade goods provided by the French made them quite desirable neighbors. However, the different viewpoints on property ownership were a potential source of trouble.

After securing his own place, Du Pratz and his guide made a walking tour into the St. Catherine Creek valley to the east of the fort, where two sites were selected for the plantations of Hubert and the Company of the West.[85] The historian/soldier Jean-François Benjamin Dumont de Montigny, who was stationed at Fort Rosalie in the late 1720s, points out an important difference between land acquisition at the Natchez in comparison to other Company of the Indies operations:

> The establishments which were made among the [Natchez Indians] were not formed at all in the same manner as in all the other cantons of the province, where, to have a habitation after having chosen such land as one wished, it sufficed to present one's request to the council which never failed to sign it after having put in certain clauses; this act took the place of a contract of sale and title in order to possess legally the lands which had been ceded. On the contrary, those who had first established themselves among the Natchez, purchased the land they wished to occupy from the savages of the place themselves, who by this traffic were bound to the French, were attached to them, and became their friends.[86]

The Natchez lands were probably already cleared to a certain extent by the Indians, reducing the amount of work necessary to begin farming operations. Although Dumont doesn't mention the French concessions near the Yazoo and Acansa tribes, these lands may have also been purchased from the native occupants.[87]

Figure 7 shows the approximate locations of the plantations acquired by Du Pratz in relationship to the Grand Village and Fort Rosalie. Obviously, Du Pratz saw no need to place the plantations near the fort for protection and was

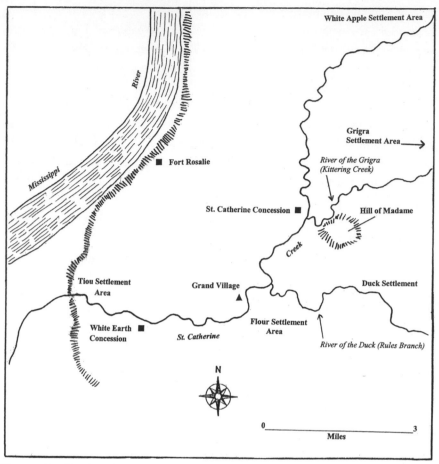

Labels within the figure:

White Apple Settlement Area

River

Grigra
Settlement Area →

Mississippi

Fort Rosalie

River of the Grigra
(Kittering Creek)

St. Catherine Concession

Hill of Madame

Creek

Tiou Settlement
Area

Grand Village

Duck Settlement

White Earth
Concession

St. Catherine

Flour Settlement
Area

River of the Duck (Rules Branch)

N

0 — 3
Miles

Figure 7. Fort Rosalie and French concessions. (Based upon Broutin 1723 map of the Natchez area.)

apparently unaware of the anti-French sentiment among the people of the White Apple, Jenzenaque, and Grigra settlement districts when he staked out Hubert's concession in that vicinity. As we will see, this plantation became a convenient target for harassment by the residents of the three pro-English settlements during the next few years. The concession earmarked for the Company of the West was better situated, being closer to the pro-French people of the Flour and Tiou settlement districts. Already on St. Catherine Creek by 1720 was the plantation of Jean Houssaye (sometimes given as Houassin). According to Pénicaut, the Houssaye plantation was established close to the Grand Village in 1718, and Pénicaut later purchased this farm for himself.[88]

In early 1720, Hubert and his family, with sixty indentured servants from France, arrived to take possession of his Natchez concession. Traveling with

Hubert's party was Montplaisir de La Gauchay, an expert in tobacco cultivation from Clerac, who brought thirty indentured servants to the White Earth Concession to establish the company's tobacco plantation.[89] By the summer of 1719, the Company of the West had acquired a monopoly on virtually all of France's foreign trade and had renamed itself the "Company of the Indies." Among the monopolies purchased by the company in 1718 was the right to control France's tobacco trade, a crop for which the Natchez country was touted as being ideal.[90]

Du Pratz observed that most of the European inhabitants at the Natchez were concentrating on growing tobacco in 1720.[91] Of course, tobacco was already being cultivated by Native Americans, and the Natchez Indians, seeing the commercial value placed on the plant by the French, began to grow the crop in their settlement districts.[92] For his plantation, Hubert was determined to grow wheat. Although wheat cultivation had been attempted without success at Biloxi and Mobile, the Natchez area had gained a reputation for fertility and previous experiments with wheat in the bluff hills had been promising.[93]

Because of Hubert's status as *commissaire-ordonnateur*, the tribe's chiefs honored their new neighbor with a calumet ceremony at his plantation. At the end of the ceremony, the chiefs asked Hubert to reverse Bienville's indictment of Oyelape, the chief of the White Apple settlement who had been in hiding since the summer of 1716 (see above). Hubert subsequently wrote to Bienville and secured Oyelape's pardon. Upon hearing the news, Pénicaut wrote: "The Natchez were so delighted that the noble Grand Chief proclaimed a festival of dancing in the nine villages, which lasted one week."[94]

Here, Pénicaut repeats his 1704 statement that the Natchez tribe comprised nine villages, whereas only five (six if one counts the Grand Village) are usually named after 1716. He also writes that delegations from the Yazoo, Chakchiuma, Acansas, Choctaw, and Chickasaw brought calumets to Hubert, who reciprocated by giving them "substantial presents."[95] In 1721, Hubert sold his concession to Faucon du Manoir, director-general of the St. Catherine Land Company. Du Manior and around one hundred employees arrived in Natchez in late 1721 and began expanding on Hubert's operation, which included a water mill on St. Catherine Creek and a blacksmith's forge.[96]

In 1720, after a phenomenal period of growth, the Company of the Indies collapsed as shareholders attempted to claim their profits from too few assets. The news of the company's downfall reached Louisiana in June 1721, causing colonists to fear that the recent level of support from the home country would disappear, bringing a return to the hard times experienced during the War of

Spanish Succession.[97] According to Du Pratz, some of the company's concessions, such as the one at the Acansa, were abandoned and their indentured servants freed. Although thousands of investors were financially ruined, including several hundred residents of Biloxi and New Orleans, Law's bankruptcy seems to have had little effect on the Natchez colony.[98] The company's Louisiana enterprise was temporarily taken over by the French regency and restored to a reorganized Company of the Indies in 1723.[99]

At about the time of the collapse of the Company of the Indies, its Natchez plantation, White Earth, was acquired by a business partnership made up of Sieur Le Blanc, French secretary of state; Marquis Dasfeld, count of Belle-Isle; and Gerard Michel de La Jonchere, treasurer general of the Military Order of Saint Louis. In addition to White Earth, they also established two plantations near New Orleans.[100] After reorganization, the Company of the Indies expressed an interest in once again establishing its own concession at the Natchez; however, certain events that I will discuss later precluded those plans.[101]

CHARLEVOIX'S NATCHEZ VISIT

The Jesuit priest and noted historian Pierre F. X. de Charlevoix arrived at the Natchez on December 15, 1721, and spent eleven days in the colony. He was on a mission for the French regency to explore the interior of New France and search for a route to the Pacific Ocean, known in those days simply as the "Western Sea." Upon reaching the confluence of the Missouri and Mississippi Rivers at the onset of winter, Charlevoix decided to descend the Mississippi and return to explore the Missouri during warmer weather.[102] He later made use of the narratives of Tonti, Pénicaut, Gravier, and other writers to supplement his own journal and compile his *Histoire et description generale de la Nouvelle France*.[103] Although Charlevoix's stay at the Natchez was brief, his first-hand observations are valuable. Unfortunately, the priest remained in the vicinity of Fort Rosalie and didn't venture out to the Natchez settlement districts.

Before Charlevoix's departure from the Natchez outpost, several colonial residents and their Indian companions asked the priest to marry them "in the face of the church." These couples had already received civil marriage contracts from the post commandant and principal clerk. At first, Charlevoix refused to authorize what he called "this concubinage," but he finally relented, rationalizing: "In short, the evil being done, the question was only how to remedy it, which I did."[104] Although seemingly a minor event in Charlevoix's narrative, the priest's wedding service for the couples further documents the intermingling of colonists and Indians at the Natchez that would later have disastrous consequences.

In the year following Charlevoix's visit, Father Maximin, a Carmelite priest, arrived at the Natchez post. Because he died shortly after establishing himself at the Natchez, little is known about Father Maximin's mission. His service was apparently directed toward the burgeoning French population instead of the Natchez Indians.[105] In 1723, missionaries of the Capuchin Order came to the Lower Mississippi Valley to share the Louisiana mission with the Jesuits, both under the auspices of the Company of the Indies.[106] By this time, Father Davion, the last of the Seminarians in the region, was finishing his mission with the Tunica.[107] After Maximin, the Natchez post was without a resident priest until the arrival in 1726 of the Capuchin Father Philibert de Vianden.[108] Like Maximin, Philibert had come to serve the colonists and not to missionize the Natchez.

AFRICANS AT THE NATCHEZ

From the very beginning, the French in Louisiana expected to use slave labor for the backbreaking work of clearing land and tilling the soil. Attempts to use Indian slaves captured by tribes allied to the French were usually fruitless—the native workers simply walked into the forest they knew so intimately and disappeared. In 1706, Bienville expressed the sentiments of the entire colony when he wrote to France asking for African slaves. Two years later, Mobile opened a slave-trading agreement with Santo Domingo, in which two Indian slaves were to be exchanged for one African.[109] By 1711, there were twenty African slaves in Louisiana, but the black population remained low until the Company of the West brought to bear its vast resources and trade fleet. According to the French concessionaire Jean-Baptiste Bérnard de La Harpe, over six hundred African slaves arrived in Louisiana in 1719 and 1720, and over thirteen hundred Africans were brought to the colony in 1721.[110] Hundreds of enslaved people died of scurvy during the notorious Middle Passage, and La Harpe relates the following grisly story of the frigate *Charles*:

> April 20, 1721. The frigate *Néréide*, commanded by M. de Chaboiseau, arrived with 294 Negroes from Angola, the remainder of 350. It brought news that the frigate *Charles*, commanded by M. Grys and M. Clinet and loaded with Negroes, had been burned more than fifty leagues from the coast. The majority of the crew had perished; those who had been saved suffered greatly from thirst and hunger, having been reduced to loading their launch with a few Negroes for their subsistence.[111]

For the most part, the enslaved people comprising these company shipments came from the Kingdom of Juida, in what is now Guinea on the West African coast.[112] Historian Allan Kulikoff has pointed out that the people sold to European slavers in coastal countries such as Juida were gathered from all over West Africa.[113] Most likely, the people crowded into the company's slave transports on the Juida coast would have spoken different languages, held different religious beliefs, and grown up in a variety of social organizations. Slave shipments to Louisiana were temporarily halted during 1722 while the Company of the Indies was being reorganized. In late 1723, two shipments of African slaves arrived at New Orleans, most having embarked from the frightful slave depot on the French-owned Gorée Island off the coast of Dakar, Senegal.[114]

Only a small number of these Africans were taken upriver to the Natchez colony, traveling north with concessionaires such as Hubert and Montplaisir. As has already been mentioned, Du Pratz brought a young African couple when he moved from New Orleans to Natchez. Not long after arriving at the Natchez, the couple ran away, and they were apparently making their way downriver when they were captured by Tunica and turned over to the French. The couple was eventually returned to Du Pratz; however, the man subsequently died of what Du Pratz called a "defluxion on the breast, which he caught by running away into the woods, where his youth and want of experience made him believe he might live without the toils of slavery."[115]

By 1725, the Natchez concessionaires were growing wheat, indigo, tobacco, and cotton, employing a large labor force made up of indentured servants and African slaves.[116] As the indentured servants from France paid off their debts and gained freedom, Africans took their places in the fields. Very little is known about the early contact between Africans and Natchez Indians; however, the two groups probably found more in common culturally than either group found with the Europeans. One area where Africans and Native Americans seemed to find common ground was in the realm of folklore, and stories blending African and Indian elements have been well documented.[117]

THE SECOND NATCHEZ WAR

Writing on "what gives occasions to wars in Louisiana," Le Page du Pratz believed that wars and disputes with the Indians were largely caused by the French colonists having "too familiar intercourse with them."[118] Nowhere was the fraternization between French and Indians more prevalent than at the Natchez, where the natives and Europeans were in daily contact. As mentioned earlier, the infrequency of supply shipments upriver from New Orleans forced the soldiers and other colonial inhabitants to turn to the Indians, who supplied corn, fish, and meat in exchange for trade items. As time went by, most of the garrison found living quarters outside the fort, many of them taking up residence with Natchez women. The historian Marcel Giraud put it succinctly: "The whole [Natchez] community was too closely interwoven, the intermingling too intimate."[119]

The food services the Indians provided for the colonists probably operated much the same as the deerskin trade, in which the French paid the Indians in advance with trade merchandise, creating a debt that the Indians then paid off after hunting, fishing, or gathering corn. This was evidently the case in the fall of 1722, when a dispute between a French sergeant named La Fontaine and a Natchez man over a debt of corn erupted in violence. As the two argued and fought, more French soldiers arrived and fired on the Indian and some of his companions. When the smoke cleared, at least one Natchez Indian was dead and others were wounded. The Natchez seethed as the French soldier received only a reprimand for his conduct. Du Pratz, La Harpe, and other sources cite this incident as the cause of the brief confrontation known as the second Natchez war.[120] However, the altercation may have only been coincidental to the hostilities. Dumont relates the Natchez Indians' behavior in 1722, in part, to the 1720–1724 war between the Chickasaw and Choctaw, in which the Choctaw were backed by the French.[121] The Chickasaw conflict was engineered by Bienville to pit the Choctaw and Chickasaw against each other so as to prevent these two large tribes from forming an alliance that could threaten French interests in the Lower Mississippi Valley.[122] The longstanding Natchez-Chickasaw connection has already been discussed, and a significant faction among the Natchez tribe would have favored the Chickasaw in this conflict. The strong amity between the two tribes probably prevented the French from convincing the Natchez to attack the Chickasaw.[123]

Dumont also indicates that M. de Guenot, the inspector of the St. Catherine concession, may have contributed to the aggressive behavior on the part of the Natchez that fall: "Perhaps . . . the Sieur Guenote brought on himself the misfortune which befell him; at least it was suspected that he would not have been attacked if he had not caused some discontent on the part of the Natchez savages established at the Apple Village."[124] The reader will recall that the Apple Village, or White Apple settlement district, which was situated close to the St. Catherine concession, was the home of Chief Oyelape and a hotbed of pro-English/Chickasaw sympathy.

A narrative of the hostilities written by four of the officers of the St. Catherine concession gives a daily account of the confrontation, beginning in the late afternoon of October 21, 1722, when a group of Natchez Indians ambushed Guenot as he was returning on horseback to the concession from Fort Rosalie. He was struck by gunfire, but he managed to stay on his horse and reached the concession to sound the alarm. The next day, hostilities escalated when a nervous Frenchman fired upon some Indians who were seen talking to a group of African slaves. The Indians returned fire with the Africans apparently caught in the middle and an African man named Du Bougou was shot and killed.[125]

Off and on for the next seven days, Natchez Indians, most of whom were apparently from the nearby White Apple settlement district, sniped at the St. Catherine concession from concealed positions among the trees on a piece of high ground called the "Hill of Madame" on the east side of St. Catherine Creek (Figure 7).[126] At night, parties of Indians also raged around the other farms in the colony, shooting livestock and burning some houses, including that of Le Page du Pratz.[127] La Harpe estimated that as many as eighty Indians were involved in the uprising.[128]

In 1722, Fort Rosalie was manned by Captain M. de Barnaval and a garrison of eighteen men.[129] The military outpost would hardly have inspired confidence. After years of affable relations between the French and the Natchez Indians, maintenance of the palisade must have no longer seemed necessary. In January of that year, La Harpe described the structure as "composed only of bad, decayed posts, so that it admits of no defense."[130] The soldiers were probably all quartered outside the fort, which proved unfortunate for a trooper named La Rochelle, who was surprised in his house and killed during the second night of the uprising.[131]

The next day, Captain Barnaval prevailed upon the Tattooed Serpent to try and restore peace.[132] Here I will comment that the Tattooed Serpent, the younger brother of the Great Sun, is often referred to as the tribe's "War Chief," a title that evokes an image of combativeness.[133] In reality, it is the Tattooed Serpent who appears again and again in times of conflict between the French and the Natchez in the diplomatic role of peacemaker. (Recall the Tattooed Serpent's role as statesman in the First Natchez War.) Rather than being expected to lead the Natchez into war, the Tattooed Serpent's duty appears to have been that of the tribe's ranking negotiator, allowing the Great Sun to maintain a position of aloofness. Out of respect for his office, the warriors surrounding the St. Catherine concession allowed the Tattooed Serpent to pass through their ranks unharmed as he carried messages between Fort Rosalie and the besieged farm.[134]

On October 24 the Tattooed Serpent went to the residence of Chief Old Hair in the White Apple settlement district to seek a peaceful solution to the conflict. According to the narrative mentioned above, the Tattooed Serpent told Old Hair that the people of the Flour Village were prepared to take the part of the French if the men from his settlement district continued to harass the settlers.[135] Here again is a clear indication of the division of alliances within the Natchez group. If the narrative is correct, the tribe's pro-French and pro-English factions teetered briefly on the brink of civil war.

The standoff continued for three more days while the Tattooed Serpent relayed messages between the concession, the fort, and White Apple. He also made it a point to talk with the Indian snipers on the Hill of Madame. Although larger groups of Indians were seen prowling around the settlements, it seems that only about five Indians continued to hide in the trees around the concession and take potshots at the settlers.[136] Considering the tension and stress of the situation, it is remarkable that the Tattooed Serpent was not inadvertently fired upon as he walked back and forth between the two sides. He must have been dressed distinctively so as to be easily recognizable to the French. A glance at Figure 7 will give an indication of the distance this man walked, repeatedly covering the ground between the fort, the concession, and Old Hair's residence.

Having seen military service in the War of Spanish Succession, Du Pratz was deputized by Barnaval to lead a group of settlers to assist the French soldiers who had been sent from the fort to protect the St. Catherine concession.[137] While his detachment was on duty at the concession, emissaries from White Apple came bearing the calumet, which they presented to Du Pratz. Although he felt that the honor should have gone to Barnaval, he participated in the ceremony to avoid prolonging the hostilities. The Natchez emissaries assured Du Pratz that they intended to carry the calumet to the commandant as soon as they were assured of peace at the concession.[138]

In early November, the settlers at the St. Catherine concession received calumets from two other Natchez chiefs. According to the narrative by the St. Catherine officers, the chief of the Grigra settlement district brought the calumet from his village on November 1. This chief would have been the successor to Alahoflechia, who had been executed by Bienville in 1716. Following the usual custom, the chief expected to receive presents, and the settlers didn't disappoint him, presenting him with a shirt, gunpowder, and vermillion. Three days later, according to the narrative: "The Sun of the Flour Village, with the Woman Chief, came to sing the calumet. We gave them two shirts, two hats, a pound of powder, and a quarter pound of vermillion."[139] The Sun in this case may have been the chief of the Flour settlement district or, more likely, the Great Sun, whose Grand Village residence was contiguous with the Flour settlement. The "Woman Chief" was probably the Sun woman known as "Tattooed Arm," the daughter of the woman chief whose funeral was witnessed by Pénicaut, and the ranking female in the Natchez tribe.[140]

As soon as the hostilities ceased, the Tattooed Serpent and a party of his tribesmen carried the calumet to Bienville at New Orleans. The French commander delivered a typically stern lecture to his guests (recorded in the General Correspondence of Louisiana), in which he admonished the Natchez to behave themselves or risk his retribution. Bienville indicated that the killing of the Natchez Indian over the corn debt was done in self-defense: "[The French soldiers] would not have fired on [the Natchez Indians] at all if they had not seen thy people disposed to kill the French." Bienville also vented his displeasure over rumors that the "chief of the White Earth" had been visiting the Chakchiumas, a small tribe on the Yazoo River that was currently at war with the Choctaw. However, the French commander wisely tempered his harangue with the following presents that the Tattooed Serpent carried back to the Natchez:

Presents for the Indians of the nation of the Natchez given to the Tattooed Serpent by M. de Bienville's order. Seen.
One barrel of powder
Two hundred pounds of bullets
One hundred pounds of lead
Eight guns
Eight ells of limbourg
Ten hats
Twelve shirts
Two large kettles
Two pairs of stockings
Two pairs of shoes
Six powder-horns
Six axes
Six pickaxes
Five hundred gun-flints
One pound of iron wire
Two pounds of vermillion
Two dozen awls
Six dozen combs

Sixteen dozen horn-handled knives

One gross of worm screws

    The sixth of November 1722.[141]

Bienville's speech to the Tattooed Serpent doesn't indicate which of the two known White Earth or White Apple chiefs, Old Hair or Oyelape, was accused of being friendly to the Chakchiuma. As mentioned above, Bienville pardoned Oyelape in 1720, but the chief's name is conspicuously absent from the narratives of the 1722 uprising. On the other hand, Old Hair, the ranking White Earth chief, who had avoided indictment in the First Natchez War, was seen as the leader of the insurgency. According to the narrative of the hostilities, six Indians were either killed or wounded in the action.[142] On the French side, two soldiers and one African slave were killed, and several slaves and settlers were wounded.[143] Guenot, who was shot on the first day of the conflict, was taken to New Orleans, where he eventually succumbed to gangrene.[144]

Finally, there is a humorous postscript to the Second Natchez War. Dumont reports that when Bienville received word of the uprising at the Natchez, he sent troops from New Orleans in four canoes under the command of a Sieur Payon to check on the situation and take action if necessary. Upon their arrival, the Tattooed Serpent met the detachment bearing the calumet. According to Dumont, the Tattooed Serpent said that his tribe wished to have peace with the French and laid the blame for the recent hostilities on not only the White Apple settlement but also on the Jenzenaque and Grigra settlements. The war chief also made it clear that the Flour settlement had remained on the side of the French in the conflict. Payon agreed to accept the calumet but stated that the guilty settlements must reimburse the French for the expense incurred in treating those wounded during the uprising. The price for peace that they agreed upon that day must be unique in American history: the recompense would be paid in fowls, to be delivered to the river landing for transportation back downriver to New Orleans. While Payon and his men waited, word went out to the residents of the White Apple, Jenzenaque, and Grigra towns to bring to the river landing what Dumont only refers to as "a certain number of fowls." Although Dumont doesn't specifically say it, one must assume that these were live chickens. The subsequent chicken round-up must have caused quite a commotion on the Indians' farms as people ran about catching hens and roosters and carrying them through the countryside to the Frenchmen waiting beside the river.[145]

When one contemplates the lives of the Natchez Indians, chickens may seem incongruous in the imagined picture of an Indian farmstead; however, chickens were apparently quite common in all of the settlement districts.[146] No one knows when chickens were first brought to the Lower Mississippi Valley; they were documented among the Acansa by the La Salle expedition in 1682, and Iberville found them with the Bayogoula in 1699.[147] Chickens and other domestic animals and plants were probably introduced from Spanish settlements in the Rio Grande valley or the Caribbean Islands in the seventeenth century.[148]

THE THIRD NATCHEZ WAR

The causes of the third Natchez war that occurred in the fall of 1723 are more obscure than those of the 1722 conflict. Du Pratz indicates that the French attack on the Natchez was without provocation; however, Dumont blames the three renegade settlement districts for making attacks on the livestock belonging to the St. Catherine concession.[149] Although lingering resentments from the 1722 conflict probably fueled the troubles at the St. Catherine concession, the plantation managers apparently made no attempt to promote peace with the residents of nearby Natchez settlement districts. St. Catherine laborers reported to Bienville that Natchez Indians had been whipped and put in chains on the concession.[150]

Another source of friction was the European concept of property ownership and boundaries. The owners of the St. Catherine concession believed that they had legally purchased the property for their operation.[151] The Natchez Indians, on the other hand, probably had little regard for property lines, and a cow or horse grazing out of sight of the plantation would have presented a tempting target. While the Indians may have killed some of the St. Catherine farm animals for food, others may have been molested as a way of counting coup against the French.[152] Another motivation for harming the French livestock might have been the desire to get mane hair, tails, or horns for personal adornment. Whatever the reason, the killing of some farm animals hardly merited the severity of Bienville's retaliation.

The French commander left New Orleans on September 29, 1723, at the head of four boat-loads of company soldiers accompanied by Canadians in pirogues.[153] Along the way, they were joined by the Tunica chief and some of his warriors. At Fort Rosalie, they rendezvoused with parties of Yazoos and Choctaws, the latter led by the chief known as Red Shoe.[154] Red Shoe, who would later turn against the French, was from the western part of the Choctaw territory, which Patricia Galloway has suggested is possibly affiliated with the Natchez in the "Sixtowns" communities.[155] Bienville directed his men to cut up cloth to make armbands for the friendly Indians so that the French would not mistake them for Natchez. As an incentive, the word was passed that any Natchez Indians captured during the campaign could be kept as slaves.[156]

Upon arriving at the Natchez, Bienville met with the Tattooed Serpent, who assured the French commander of the innocence of his people at the Flour settlement and reminded Bienville that the chiefs at the Grand Village had lost control over the White Apple, Jenzenaque, and Griga settlements. The next day (Dumont says it was All Saints Day), the mob of French soldiers, settler vigilantes, and Indian mercenaries set out from the St. Catherine concession moving north to attack the White Apple settlement district.[157] Du Pratz, who had been placed in charge of the settlers, says that Bienville's force totaled seven hundred men.[158]

As previously discussed, the Natchez Indians' farmsteads were spread out within the settlement districts, which put the Indians at a disadvantage in a wartime situation. Although it is difficult to imagine that the people of the White Apple settlement were unaware of Bienville's arrival at the Natchez, the first household that the army encountered seemed genuinely surprised by the appearance of armed Frenchmen accompanied by Indians painted for war. Perhaps they knew about Bienville's coming but simply misunderstood his purpose. At any rate, three Natchez women caught pounding corn beside their cabin were abducted by settlers, the Natchez men in the cabin were killed and scalped, and the cabin was set afire.[159] Du Pratz himself tried to catch a Natchez Indian slave later that same day: "I took it upon myself to surround [twelve to fifteen Natchez Indians in three cabins] with my troop in order to take them from behind. They fled; I pursued them, but we would have needed the legs of deer to catch them. However, I approached so close that to run faster they threw away their clothing."[160] Those Natchez settlers who did manage to grab Indian women during the campaign probably didn't hold them for long. The natives knew the local countryside intimately and, at the first opportunity, would have returned to their waiting families.

At the sound of shooting, most of the White Apple residents were able to flee to safety. From a distance, they watched the mob set fire to their cabins and granaries. Eventually, Bienville and his force arrived at the ceremonial center that served as the political core of the White Apple settlement district. Dumont called it the "grand square of the village" but made no mention of a mound. This was probably Old Hair's residence, although the chief was lucky enough to avoid capture. To date, no archaeological sites in the White Apple area have been identified as possible locations for the grand square. As has already been noted, the Foster Mound site is in this vicinity, but no European trade materials have been found there to indicate occupation during the French colonial period. The nearby Thoroughbred site, discovered by Joseph Frank and investigated by the LMS in the early 1980s, has produced trade materials and may have been one of the Indian farmsteads in the White Apple area.[161]

After burning all of the cabins around the grand square, Bienville and his men returned to the St. Catherine concession for the night. The next morning, the commander divided his force into two groups. One group, under the command of Payon (recall the Frenchman who took the fowls back to New Orleans), returned to the White Apple area to burn more cabins and further harass the residents. The other half of the army, led by Bienville, set out across St. Catherine Creek to the northeast to invade the Grigra settlement district. Frank has also found a number of European contact-period archaeological sites in this area that have been excavated by the LMS. Because of the Grigra's supposed Tunican origins, having come to the Natchez from further north in the Mississippi River Valley, LMS archaeologist Ian W. Brown expected to find a high percentage of shell-tempered ceramics at these sites. Instead, most of the pottery fragments found in this area are the typical grog-tempered Natchezan varieties. Brown suggests that these sites may predate the Grigra presence and that the Grigra settlement locations are yet to be found.[162]

Having received word of Bienville's scorched-earth campaign, the Grigra had abandoned their homes and gone into hiding. Eventually, the mob found and burned the Grigra ceremonial center, which consisted of a temple and nearby cabins. (No mound is mentioned.) Torching Indian homes was hot work, and the thirsty Frenchmen began searching the area for a source of water when they happened upon an old woman who had failed to flee with the others. After questioning the woman, Bienville left her to one of his Indian slaves, who killed and scalped her on the spot.[163] With the old woman's dying screams, the Grigra vanished from history. Although they probably continued to live in the Natchez area, perhaps joining in with another settlement district, they are never mentioned again in the French colonial narratives.

Leaving the Grigra farms in smoking ruin, the marauding force moved northward into the Jenzenaque settlement district. Along the way, a Natchez Indian man was killed and scalped, and Red Shoe's Choctaws managed to capture four Natchez women, who defiantly told Bienville that fifty Natchez warriors were waiting at the Jenzenaque "village" to confront the attackers. Dumont tells us that the Tunica chief was the first to reach Jenzenaque, where the house of the local chief, identified by Dumont as the Little Sun, was situated atop a hill or possibly a mound. As the Frenchmen watched, the two chiefs leveled their muskets and fired at each other simultaneously. When the smoke cleared, the Little Sun lay dead and the Tunica chief was seriously wounded.[164]

As mentioned earlier, Emerald Mound is in the area usually associated with the Jenzenaque district. One wonders if the Little Sun killed in the showdown with the Tunica chief was the same Little Sun who was identified as the younger brother of the Great Sun and Tattooed Serpent in the 1716 conflict. If so, then he apparently assumed his position of leadership at the Jenzenaque settlement district after the execution of his uncle The Bearded.[165] This Sun affiliation with the Jenzenaque district is of interest because it may reveal the Natchez Sun family's connection to this area, perhaps as descendants of the elite lineage who caused Emerald Mound to be built.[166] A possible connection between the Grand Village and the Jenzenaque area was also noted in Ian Brown's analysis of the pottery from the Rice site, a historic Natchez Indian burial location three miles east of Emerald Mound.[167]

After razing the Jenzenaque temple and farmsteads, Bienville's force camped for the night and returned to the French settlements the following morning.[168] The two-day blitzkrieg had cost the Natchez dearly. According to one colonial account, sixty men, women, and children were killed or enslaved.[169] Back at Fort Rosalie, Bienville met with the Tattooed Serpent and threatened to attack the Grand Village and the Flour district for allegedly harboring refugees from the burned villages. As in the past, the Tattooed Serpent was able to convince the French commander to spare his home settlement district and ceremonial center. The negotiated terms of peace are extraordinary. The Tattooed Serpent was told to bring in the heads of six of his tribesmen, whose names were Tchietchiomota, Capine, Ouyou, Nalcoa, Outcital, and Yooua. Presumably, one of these men was Old Hair, the White Apple district chief. For their part, the French distributed brandy to the friendly Natchez chiefs; the Tattooed Serpent received five bottles for himself.[170]

Bienville also demanded the head of a free black man who was living with the Natchez Indians at the time. According to Dumont, the black man had elected to leave the French and may have been living in the Flour settlement district. He had developed his own following in the manner of a big-man chief and was accused of making seditious speeches against the French and leading attacks against friendly Indian tribes. Bienville feared that this man might teach the Natchez about French military maneuvers and tactics.[171] Dumont records that the heads of Old Hair and the black man were delivered to Fort Rosalie within three days.[172] It is not known if all of the executions demanded by Bienville were carried out. Only one head—apparently that of Old Hair—was carried to New Orleans as proof of victory.[173]

The execution of the African was probably inconsequential to the Natchez; however, the assassination of Old Hair was another matter. According to Du Pratz, the tribe had a strong taboo against killing a member of the Sun lineage.[74] Although Old Hair may not have been directly related to the Great Sun, the killing of a big-man chief by a member of his own tribe was unprecedented— recall that the tribe avoided killing Oyelape in 1716 by convincing Bienville that the chief had absconded. In Old Hair's case, the taboo may have been circumvented by having an outsider brought in to do the killing and beheading, but even if the deed was not carried out by a member of the tribe, the murder of a powerful leader such as Old Hair must have had serious repercussions.

By ridding themselves of Old Hair (who may not have been responsible for the St. Catherine attacks), the French handed over control of White Apple to the settlement's second-ranking chief. Although we cannot be certain, Old Hair's successor may have been Oyelape, who had kept a surprisingly low profile since his pardon by Bienville in 1720. Whoever succeeded Old Hair, he would have had little reason to regard the French as his friends.[75] The closing remarks of Dumont's narrative about the third Natchez war belie the hostility that must have permeated the tribe: "Then the commandant, seeing the war ended, left orders, as well to the commandant of the fort as to the great chief of the savages, and returned to the capital, after having reestablished peace and tranquility in these parts."[76]

THE TIOU INCIDENT

The Tiou, a Tunican-speaking refugee group attached to the Natchez, are not mentioned in the narratives of the Natchez wars. The Broutin map of 1723 locates their settlement well to the south of Fort Rosalie and apparently far enough from the 1722 and 1723 conflicts to avoid trouble from the French. However, their close proximity to the large White Earth concession led to a minor confrontation with the French when someone, ostensibly an Indian from the Tiou settlement, struck one of the concession's horses with a war club and then cut off the animal's tail. As previously discussed, striking an animal, or counting coup, was deemed an act of bravery, and the horse's tail served as proof of the encounter.[77]

The director of the White Earth concession at the time was Ignace-François Broutin, an engineer who created several very useful maps of the Lower Mississippi Valley and also happened to be the commander of Fort Rosalie.[78] As was customary when disputes arose between the Indians and the French, Broutin summoned the Tattooed Serpent. This elder statesman of the Natchez tribe had been a strong ally of the colonists for almost ten years at this time and may have been able to communicate in French. When Broutin told the story of the wounded mare, the Tattooed Serpent placed the blame on the Tiou tribe, whose chief, Bamboche, was summoned immediately. Upon hearing the charge against his people, Bamboche, whom Dumont says was a "rascal," denied the charge, citing as proof an iris-shaped bruise on the horse's flank. The Tiou chief told Broutin that none of his people used war clubs that would leave such a mark but that war clubs of this type were said to be commonly found in the Natchez villages. At this, according to Dumont, the Tattooed Serpent abruptly left the meeting, leaving Broutin to believe that an Indian uprising might be imminent. Putting his soldiers at White Earth on the alert, Broutin sent word to Dumont, who had been left in charge of the fort, to fire the cannon and alert the inhabitants of the colony of possible attack.

Whatever the Tattooed Serpent had in mind when he left the meeting with Broutin and Bamboche, it was not to wage war. Upon hearing the cannon fire at the Fort, the Tattooed Serpent quickly carried the calumet to Broutin at White Earth and then to Dumont at the fort. In reparation for the attack on the mare, the Tattooed Serpent ordered every Natchez household, including the Tiou, to give the White Earth concession a basket of corn weighing approximately twelve pounds.

The smoking gun in this drama was the iris-shaped bruise on the horse's flank, caused by a blow from an Indian war club. Apparently, this type of war club was a common item in the Natchez villages. Dumont illustrated what he called a "fleur de lys club," which is probably the weapon in question.[179] The fleur de lys club drawn by Dumont, patterned after the familiar emblem of French sovereignty, appears to be a spiked metal blade of European manufacture that was fitted to a wooden shaft.

THE FRENCH LOSE AN IMPORTANT ALLY

The Tattooed Serpent, or "Olabalkebiche" in the Natchez language, died during the night of June 1, 1725. By all accounts, his death was a peaceful one, although there is some indication that he may have succumbed to some type of sickness.[180] His age at death is not known. He may have assumed his office in 1699 or 1700, at the time of the deaths of high-ranking Natchez chiefs reported by missionaries.[181] If he was in his twenties at that time, then he would have been in his forties during the 1720s. Du Pratz estimated that the Tattooed Serpent's older brother, the Great Sun, was in his nineties in the 1720s, but this may be an exaggeration.[182] Certainly, the Tattooed Serpent's statesmanship, patience, and vision indicate that he was a mature individual, and the death of this high-ranking friend of the French proved to be an incalculable loss from a diplomatic standpoint. As has already been mentioned, the Tattooed Serpent was considered to be the tribe's "war chief," but all of his documented activities were in the role of peacemaker. At every conflict between the Natchez and the French, he was front and center, negotiating to restore friendship between his people and the foreigners who occupied his country.

Invariably, the price that the Natchez Indians had to pay for peace was high, and in the case of the assassination of Old Hair, even outrageous. (One might wonder, if the shoe were on the other foot, how the French would have reacted to a demand from a Natchez chief for Bienville's head.) Nevertheless, the Tattooed Serpent always acquiesced, realizing that to defy the French would lead to the destruction of his people. His remarkable commentary on the relationship between the French and the Natchez, told to Du Pratz not long after the third Natchez war, speaks to us from across the intervening centuries:

One day I stopped Tattooed Serpent who was passing without looking and without stopping. He was the brother of the Great Sun and great warchief of the Natchez, and to go to the fort he could not go otherwise than in front of my house. If he had taken another route it would have appeared to be an affectation and he was too prudent and too politically shrewd to act in that way.

Thus I called to him and said to him, "Formerly we were friends. Aren't we so any more?" He answered, "*Noco*, I don't know." I answered thus, "You used to come to my house. At present you just pass straight by. Have you forgotten the road, or is it that my house gives you sorrow? As far as I am concerned, my heart is always the same for you and for all of my friends. I do not know how to change. Why, therefore, do you change?" It took him some time to answer me, and I perceived that I had embarrassed him by what I had said to him. He had been summoned to the fort by the commandant. The commandant had also spoken to me and begged me to talk to Tattooed Serpent, seeing that the interpreter did not render him any good responses, and that it was appropriate to make an effort to discover if there was among the Natchez a remnant of resentment stemming from the recent conflict.

He finally broke his silence and said to me, "I am ashamed to have to be so long without seeing you, but I believed that you were angry with our nation. This is because of all the French who took part in the war." "You are wrong," I answered him, "to think in that way. Monsieur de Bienville, being our war chief, we have to obey him the same as you are obliged to obey your brother the Great Sun."

He said to me then, "I did not approve, as you know, the war that our people have made against the French to avenge the death of their relatives, because I made them carry the calumet of peace to the French. You know it, because you were the first to smoke it. Is it that the French have two hearts, a good one today and tomorrow a bad one? As far as my brother and I are concerned, we only have one heart and one word.

"Why," he continued in an angry manner, "why have the French come to our land? We have not gone to find them. They asked us for land because that of your country was too small for all the men who were there. We told them that they might take some land where they wished, that there was enough for them and for us, that it was good that the same sun shown on us, that we would walk on the same road, that we would give them of that which we had to live, that we would aid them to build and to make fields. We have done that. Isn't that true?

"What need did we have of the French? Before them, didn't we live better than we do now? Because we deprive ourselves of a part of our grain, of game and of fish that we killed to share with them. In what, therefore, did we have need of them? Was it for their guns? We used our bows and arrows which sufficed to make us live well. Was it for their white, blue, or red blankets? We did well enough with the skins of buffaloes which are warmer. Our wives worked on these coverlets of feathers for the winter and of the bark of myrtle trees for the summer. It wasn't so beautiful, but our wives were more hard working and less vain than they are now. Finally, before the arrival of the French, we lived like men who know how to do with what they have, whereas today we walk like slaves who do not do what they wish."[183]

The French narratives of the Tattooed Serpent's funeral, in addition to the ethnological information they contain, provide a snapshot of the Natchez leadership structure in mid-1725. Two of Bienville's former hostages from his 1716 campaign, the old Flour chief, who held the title of "master of ceremonies" for ritual events at the Grand Village, and Yakstalchil, the second-ranking chief of Flour village, are both mentioned. Saint-Cosme, the young Sun named for the tribe's former resident priest, was in attendance, as was the chief of the Apple settlement. One of the funeral narratives (Dumont) says that "many other chiefs" attended the obsequies, although we aren't told what other settlement districts were represented.

The chief of the Tiou settlement is named as the person who first warned French that the Tattooed Serpent's death might lead the Great Sun to commit suicide. The French apparently took this warning very seriously and disarmed the old chief before he could do himself injury. Although the narrative seems to indicate that the Natchez believed the Great Sun's life was threatened, it is hard to tell if the danger was real or part of an elaborate ritual to formally mourn the death of the chief's brother.[184]

Along with the chiefs in attendance, accounts of the Tattooed Serpent's funeral include a fascinating glimpse of a Natchez Indian man of the commoner rank whose name is recorded variously as Ette-actal, Taotal, Tactal, and Wideawake. He had apparently been known to the French for some time, having served as a hunter and possibly interpreter for Bienville. Ette-actal caught the attention of Frenchmen who were present at the Tattooed Serpent's funeral when he shamelessly talked his way out of being strangled as a sacrificial victim (and thus joining the Tattooed Serpent's entourage in the next life). He even managed to turn the situation to his advantage by strangling an elderly woman who had agreed to die in his stead, a deed that increased his tribal status to that of "honored man."[185] Although the French colonial narratives paint him as a scoundrel, Ette-actal appears at least two more times at critical junctures during the course of the Natchez story.

FALSE SENSE OF SECURITY: 1724–1729

At the end of the third Natchez war, Bienville attempted to settle all of the Natchez tribe in one village, probably the Flour settlement district, so that they could be more closely monitored.[186] The evidence is lacking as to how many refugee families from the Apple, Jenzenaque, and Grigra settlements complied with this directive. According to a document signed by Bienville at the conclusion of the war, the residents of the burned settlement districts had "retired to inaccessible country."[187] This probably meant that many of these people had moved further north to the Fairchilds Creek/Coles Creek area or beyond. It is also likely that some of the Natchez left the area at this time and settled with other groups that favored the English, such as the Chickasaw. As mentioned earlier, archaeological evidence from the Chickasaw homeland in northeastern Mississippi indicates a strong Natchezan presence there, perhaps beginning prior to European contact.[188] At least one of the hostile settlement districts, White Apple, was reestablished in its former location.[189]

One consequence of burning the three Natchez settlement districts was a shortage of Indian corn in 1723 and 1724. Most of the corn granaries in these districts had been either destroyed or emptied by Bienville's forces, and many of those left homeless by the campaign didn't replant their cornfields in the spring of 1724. Unfortunately for the French at Natchez, this shortage coincided with a time of flooding and heavy rainfall that severely hampered the Indian corn crop throughout the Lower Mississippi Valley. The arrival of African slave shipments in 1724 put an additional strain on food supplies.[190]

The people of the White Apple, Jenzenaqe, and Grigra settlements were in temporary disarray and dependent upon their tribesmen for help, and the residents of the Flour and Tiou settlements continued to support the French. With the death of the Tattooed Serpent, it fell to the Great Sun to keep that portion of his tribe still under his influence in the good graces of the European colony that had come to dominate every aspect of their lives. After all, he had grown accustomed to French brandy, and his people living close to the fort and concessions were equally accustomed to having relatively easy access to the brass, copper, iron, and glass trade goods that the soldiers and settlers waved in front of them. The Indians' desire for guns and other trade materials also continued to drive the flourishing deerskin business.[191] Although there are no figures for Natchez themselves, the Avoyel and Tunica tribes were each supplying the French with a thousand deerskins per year during the late 1720s.[192]

After 1725, the French at the Natchez increasingly took the local Indian population for granted as concessionaires focused on the profits that might come from the sale of the cash crops they were growing. At least seventeen Natchez concessionaires were operating plantations producing indigo, tobacco, and cotton, and the richness of the Natchez soil was being extolled in New Orleans and back in France.[193] Most of these concessions focused their energies on tobacco and were under pressure to produce a product comparable to the tobacco coming from Virginia, which the French public seemed to prefer.

Although tobacco seemed to thrive in the Natchez soil, transporting the harvested bundles of leaves to New Orleans for shipment to France proved to be quite difficult.[194] By 1729, with support from the Company of the Indies, many of the logistical problems involved in moving tobacco downriver were being addressed, and Natchez tobacco was a substantial part of the estimated 300,000 pounds of tobacco Louisiana planned to ship to France that year.[195] In fact, the tobacco market looked so promising that the Company of the Indies began formulating plans to establish a company-owned plantation at the Natchez.[196] Between 1726 and 1729, the French population doubled from two hundred to four hundred people, and the number of African slaves rose to two hundred and eighty.[197] The company also answered the colonists' pleas for slave labor to clear land and plant crops.[198] At least four shipments of Africans arrived in Louisiana during the 1726–1728 period.[199]

While the settler population at the Natchez continued to expand, the French military detachment at Fort Rosalie remained quite small. During the years from 1726 to 1729, only about thirty men were garrisoned at the outpost, with the company divided between the fort and the two large concessions. Despite the lessons learned in the 1722 war, most of the soldiers continued to find quarters outside the fort.[200] Capuchin Father Raphaël de Luxembourg saw Fort Rosalie in 1726 and left us this unflattering description:

> There is a fort on the first eminence with a garrison of about thirty men, if however, an enclosure of poor piles, half-rotten, that permit free entrance almost everywhere can be called a fort. There are several pieces of cannon but very useless because this would-be fort, being at a distance from the edges of eminence, cannot command any of the approaches, and if it were attacked, the enemy would be at the palisade before a shot could be fired at him.[201]

The fort's maintenance undoubtedly suffered from the frequent changes in the garrison's leadership. Nine commandants came and went during the fort's first thirteen years, with some of the commanding officers being more preoccupied with farming than with soldiering.[202] The Natchez situation reflected the state of the Louisiana army in the 1720s under the for-profit management of the Company of the Indies. When the company was first formed, its directors assured the concessionaires of adequate military protection for their plantations; however, following the collapse and reorganization of the company, cost-cutting to maximize profits overshadowed the need for a strong army in Louisiana. Perhaps the company's directors thought that the Indian wars were a thing of the past, because the troop strength throughout the colony had been reduced from sixteen companies (a company had fifty men) to just eight companies by 1726.[203]

The lack of attention to military preparedness at the Natchez would have dire consequences. The Natchez Indians' leadership was undergoing profound changes, and the colonists seemed to be oblivious to the ominous signs gathering around them. The Great Sun and the old Flour chief, the last pillars of French support among the Natchez tribe, died in 1728.[204] When the high chief's office devolved upon a new Great Sun who was immature and ineffectual in tribal politics, the reins of power were taken up by hostile dark horses—the unnamed chief of the White Apple settlement district (possibly Oyelape) and the new chief of the Flour settlement district. The new Flour chief may have been Yakstalchil, who was the second ranking chief of the Flour settlement in the 1720s and had suffered as Bienville's hostage in the first Natchez war.[205]

Chapter Four

THE REBELLION

$\rightarrow \rightarrow$ ──────────────────────────── $\leftarrow \leftarrow$

IN THE FALL OF 1729, the plantations at the Natchez were brimming with row upon row of shoulder-high tobacco plants. Of particular interest to the concessionaires were the plants being grown from seeds stolen from the English in Virginia, which the Company of the Indies hoped would please discriminating French smokers.[1] The White Earth or Belle-Isle concession was the Natchez colony's largest tobacco producer, with about 280 acres in cultivation.[2] The other big Natchez concession, St. Catherine, was enjoying a visit from one of its owners, Jean-Daniel Kolly, who had made the journey from New Orleans with his son to inspect his investment.[3] Although estimates vary somewhat, around four hundred Europeans and two hundred Africans were living in the Natchez area that year.[4] After a long struggle, the colony was on the verge of prosperity.

If anything placed a damper on the Natchez colonists' spirits that fall, it was the unpredictable and sometimes abusive behavior of their highest-ranking officer, Commandant Chépart.[5] Even though he had commanded at Fort Rosalie for less than a year, Chépart had already been reprimanded by his superiors at New Orleans for mistreating one of his officers. The offended officer happened to be the memoirist Dumont, who was stationed at Fort Rosalie when Chépart assumed command.[6] Instead of being replaced, Chépart had received a pardon from Governor Perier and was allowed to return to the Natchez post. It was an act the governor would soon have reason to regret.[7]

In addition to creating problems within his command, Chépart was apparently exercising poor judgement in the way that he behaved toward the Natchez. The two authorities on this situation, Du Pratz and Dumont, were both in New Orleans at the time and their accounts, which differ significantly, are probably based upon hearsay. Dumont's recent feud with Chépart almost certainly would have colored his portrayal of his former commander. At any rate, it seems that Chépart apparently desired to establish a plantation on land already occupied by some element of the Natchez group. In Dumont's account, the commander had either displaced, or planned to displace, the White Apple settlement's inhabitants and had plans to eventually occupy the Grand Village. On the other hand, Du Pratz wrote that Chépart had set his sights on the White Apple settlement for his future plantation. Both narratives indicate that the Natchez chiefs pretended to acquiesce while they planned a preemptive strike against the French. To buy them some additional time, the Indians pled that they needed to harvest their fall crops.[8]

If indeed Chépart did have his eye on usurping Natchez lands, a move to confiscate either of the two locations would not bode well for the French at the Natchez. Any attempt to take over the sacred Grand Village would likely enrage all of the settlement districts and alienate the tribe's pro-French element. If the target was White Apple, Chépart could hardly have selected a more sensitive faction of the tribe to bully. Du Pratz's narrative makes it clear that the White Apple people had defiantly reestablished their settlement at or near their old haunts with eighty cabins and were probably biding their time until the opportunity arose to exact vengeance for Bienville's 1723 attack.[9]

Aside from Chépart's activities, there were other factors affecting French and Indian relations at the Natchez, not the least of which was the late 1720s increase in the efforts of the English traders to gain the deerskin business and alliance of the neighboring Chickasaw and Choctaw tribes. In 1729, the French were becoming frustrated by the low exchange rate being offered by the English for the coveted items such as brandy, salt, brass kettles, knives, shirts, needles, and glass beads.[10] Although there is no proof that the English were actively seeking a stronger Natchez alliance, word of this favorable trade access to English goods no doubt reached the ears of many Natchez Indians as they grew increasingly weary of the French presence. However much they may have resented the presence of the French, the Natchez had become addicted to European merchandise, and they were dependent upon French or English gunsmiths to keep their muskets in working order.[11] They would not have turned on the French had they not been assured of receiving these items and services from the English.

The Natchez had other reasons to be discontent. The new French colonists flooding into the Natchez area were oblivious to the all-important communicative signs and gestures that had been part of the diplomatic repertoire employed by Iberville, Pénicaut, and the voyageurs. The majority of the French at the Natchez didn't know very much at all about the culture of the people in whose midst they had come to live. The for-credit way in which the Indians provided services for the French was another inevitable source of trouble. As described above, the usual business procedure was to advance trade goods to the Indians for services (deer-skins, meat, corn, etc.) that would be rendered at a later date. As a result of this arrangement, the Indians were chronically in debt to the French.

Importantly, the Natchez chiefs were probably aware of Bienville's recent departure from Louisiana and they had no reason to respect or fear his successor. Likewise, the Indians undoubtedly recognized the weakness of the French garrison that occupied their country. The contingent of about thirty soldiers was sometimes scattered miles apart, with some men being stationed at the fort while others were occasionally assigned to the concessions. This small garrison had not been able to keep the peace while the Tattooed Serpent and Great Sun were alive to use their influence in support of the colony. Now that the anti-French faction was gaining strength in the Natchez settlement districts, the little group of soldiers would hardly be noticed in the coming whirlwind.

THE MASSACRE

The arrival at the Natchez landing of the company's new galley, accompanied by an eighteen-oar longboat, must have been a reassuring sight for the colonists and soldiers. Both vessels were laden with supplies and would soon return to New Orleans carrying the concessionaires' bumper tobacco harvest.[12] The company's galley was probably similar to the vessel illustrated by Dumont in his circa 1725 map of the French settlements at the Natchez, which depicts a boat about fifty feet in length, equipped with a single mast for a sail and probably also fitted with oars. In colonial Louisiana, the term "galley" was used interchangeably with the French term "*batteau*," a general-purpose, flat-bottomed, shallow-draft vessel. *Batteaux* (the plural) were from thirty to fifty feet in length and were propelled by poles, oars, and a small sail.[13] Among those at the Natchez to celebrate the galley's arrival were M. du Codère, commandant of the Yazoo fort, and Father Paul du Poisson, a Jesuit priest en route downriver from his mission with the Acansa.[14] Father Philibert, the Capuchin priest in residence at the Natchez colony, was away at the time, so Du Poisson delayed his departure from Natchez to say Mass on the first Sunday of Advent.[15]

Not long before the appearance of the company's supply boats, rumors of unrest and hostile intentions among the Natchez began circulating through the settlement. Some of the more seasoned members of Chépart's staff and a few of the settlers had gotten wind of a possible uprising, either through talking with sympathetic Natchez informants or by observing a change in the Indians' behavior toward them. Du Pratz indicates that at least one French officer received a warning of the impending attack from a Natchez woman with whom he was romantically involved.[16] When these men communicated their suspicions to Chépart, the commander responded by placing them in irons.[17] Chépart's bizarre actions can only be interpreted as an effort to quash the rumors that stood to damage his already shaky reputation while Du Codère and Kolly were on hand. According to Broutin, the Natchez Indian Ette-actal, Bienville's former scout, also brought warnings of a possible uprising to the commander.[18]

On the morning of November 28, 1729, the commander awoke with a hangover, having spent the previous evening drinking brandy with some of his associates at one of the Natchez villages, probably the Flour. According to Du Pratz, whose informants included Tattooed Arm, the tribe's ranking female chief, Chépart had had second thoughts about the rumors he had heard and sent his interpreter to the young Great Sun to find out if the tribe held any hostile intentions.[19] The interpreter duly reported back to his commander that all was well.[20] Chépart, as many other Frenchmen, erroneously believed that the Great Sun was in control of his people when, in fact, the White Apple chief had emerged as the real leader. According to Du Pratz, "the Sun of the Apple village was a man of great abilities," and it was he who apparently engineered what was to come.[21]

Later that same morning, remembered by the French as the Eve of St. Andrew, the Great Sun and his entourage of Honored Men arrived at Fort Rosalie. To all outward appearances, the visit was friendly, and a member of the Natchez group carried the calumet. The Great Sun announced that his people were about to go hunting with the intention of sharing their deer meat with the French. The soldiers stood around at ease while thirty Natchez men entered Fort Rosalie with their muskets loaded. It all must have happened so easy and seemingly friendly that the Frenchmen never realized they were outnumbered. Unbeknownst to Chépart and his men at the fort, groups of Natchez men were quietly surrounding all of the settlers' homes that morning. In some instances, they came with chickens and corn to exchange for powder and bullets to use in the hunt they were about to undertake. In the lives of the Natchez colonists, moments such as this must have been fairly routine; the faces of the Indians calling on the Frenchmen and their families were familiar ones, and they obviously weren't painted for war. At every colonial residence, the Natchez took care to outnumber and outflank the unsuspecting Frenchmen.[22]

Back at Fort Rosalie, the Great Sun's calumet song reached its conclusion, and the Natchez surrounding Chépart and his staff suddenly raised their muskets and fired point-blank at the astonished soldiers. The crash of gunfire at the fort served as the signal to the rest of the Indians, and the carnage began.[23] Simultaneously at each plantation, white males were either gunned down or killed with war clubs. Women and children looked on in shock as their men were scalped and beheaded. Some may have tried in vain to run away. The unthinkable fear that had no doubt crossed the minds of all of the colonists in Louisiana had suddenly become a screaming reality. Pregnant women and mothers with very small children were also killed and other women and children were herded away as slaves. At the riverfront, the Natchez quickly seized the galley and oar boat and watched the landing to catch any fleeing colonists who might come that way.[24]

In a matter of just a few hours, Chépart, Kolly and son, La Loire, Du Poisson, Du Codère, and many others were all dead. Out of about 150 white men at the Natchez, only 20 managed to escape. Their stories—some of which are related by Swanton—tell of a few lucky individuals who were able to find refuge downstream among the Tunica or managed to commandeer canoes and reach New Orleans.[25] The following year, Father Philibert, who was fortuitously absent at the time of the massacre, tallied the French dead at 138 men, 35 women, and 56 children.[26] Based upon eyewitness accounts, the French estimated that only 12 Natchez Indians died in the fighting that day. Eight of the Natchez casualties occurred while they were attacking the home of La Loire des Ursins, where several Frenchmen had managed to mount a defense before being overwhelmed.[27] Echoing Bienville's longtime policy, the severed heads of the French soldiers and planters were collected for viewing by the Natchez chiefs. Blood vengeance for the 1716 and 1723 executions had finally been discharged—with interest. Two Frenchmen were spared, a carter named Mayeux and a tailor named Le Beau, the former employed to use his team of oxen and wagon to transport the French possessions to the various villages and the latter to adjust the European clothing to fit the new owners.[28]

The fate of the Africans in the colony was much different; their lives were spared if they did not join the whites in resisting the uprising. According to the stories of slaves who had managed to escape the massacre and reach New Orleans, some of the Africans had conferred with Indians before the attack and joined the rebellion when the massacre began.[29] The collusion between the Natchez and the Africans seems to underscore the affinity that these ethnic groups held for each other; however, Charlevoix speculated that the Indians' real reason for sparing the Africans was to sell them back into slavery to the English in Carolina. Some of the blacks may have anticipated this or simply were not aware of the plot, because several attempted to escape during the massacre.[30]

Most of the captive French women and children were apparently held together at the house of the ranking female chief, probably at the Grand Village or in the Flour settlement district.[31]

With the captives under guard and no white males left to kill, the Natchez ransacked the French concessions and storehouses. The former possessions of the French were hauled out of the houses and scattered throughout the settlements, as men, women, and children took what items that pleased them and discarded the rest. The supplies in the galley and oar boat were also confiscated. Then, in final retribution for Bienville's scorched-earth campaign six years earlier, the Indians set fire to the fort, commissary, boats, and houses, along with hundreds of acres of tobacco.[32] French brandy and butchered livestock were plentiful after the massacre, and the jubilant Natchez spent several days and nights eating, drinking, dancing, and recounting the victory.[33] At the smoking ruins of the fort and concessions, dogs and other scavengers pulled and chewed at the corpses of the victims.[34]

A party of Yazoo Indians, who had accompanied Commander Du Codère to the Natchez, apparently remained neutral during the fighting, although they did provide assistance to at least one of the escaping Frenchmen.[35] However, after participating in the Natchez tribe's revelries, they resolved to return to their own settlement and destroy the French who were living there. On December 11, 1729, Yazoo and Koroa insurgents (possibly with Natchez assistance) killed their Jesuit missionary, Jean-François Souel, and the next day wiped out the seventeen-man garrison at nearby Fort St. Pierre.[36]

CONSPIRACY THEORY

The idea that the Natchez revolt may have been part of a larger conspiracy instigated by the English first appears in a letter from Governor Perier to the minister of the French navy, written just seven days after the massacre:

> The Natchez, pretending to be going hunting, fell upon the settlement of this post on the 28th of the past month between nine and ten o'clock in the morning, and massacred not only all the men who were at the fort in our village, but in addition attacked the concessions from which no one was able to escape. They kept the women, the children and the negroes. They captured the galley that I had sent there with goods and which was to bring the tobacco that I had gathered there. The attack made in broad daylight, the conduct of the action and the

capture of the galley, together with the preservation of the negroes is not at all characteristic of the Indians; there is not even an example of it, and this does not permit me to doubt that there were some Englishmen in disguise with them. Three negroes who escaped and who told me the details of the action assured me that the commandant had been warned the day before and that he had neglected the information that was given him.

. . . Our neighbors [the English] see that our tobacco and our farming are successful. They have solicited the Choctaws by means of the Chickasaws to take their goods and to break off all relations with us. They have solicited the Natchez by the same means and unfortunately have succeeded in this direction.[37]

According to Perier, the existence of an inter-tribal conspiracy was supported by reports from Africans and women held hostage after the massacre, who said that the Natchez boasted to them that other French settlements in Louisiana were also under attack.[38] Certainly, Perier benefited from the conspiracy theory, which shifted attention away from his having supported the troublemaker Chépart and made the rebellion appear to have been instigated by the English. Likewise, Perier later reported that, during the confrontation between the Natchez and the Choctaw in early 1730 (to be described shortly), the Natchez reproached the Choctaw for not following through with their attacks on New Orleans and Mobile.[39] Dumont seems to back up Perier's claims by writing that the Choctaw were reportedly incensed that the Natchez struck their blow earlier than the agreed-upon date.[40] Both Le Petit and Charlevoix indicate that the Natchez had a definite timetable for their attack on the French and that they did indeed attack earlier than originally planned. Both writers state that it was the arrival of the galley full of merchandise that led the Natchez to move ahead of schedule. Charlevoix adds that Kolly's presence at the Natchez provided the Indians with an excuse to pretend to be preparing for a hunting trip in order to provide meat for a celebration.[41]

If there was indeed an inter-tribal conspiracy, its true nature may never be sorted out. The narratives of Le Petit, Charlevoix, and Du Pratz all agree that the Natchez launched their rebellion with the belief that other tribes would join them in attacking the French. Du Pratz, like Perier, names the Choctaw as co-conspirators, and says that the Tunica and Houma rejected the invitation by the Natchez to become part of the insurgency.[42] Swanton has pointed out that, if an inter-tribal conspiracy did exist, it is odd that the Yazoo and Koroa were not brought in, given their past pro-English leanings and their close proximity to the French military outpost at the Yazoo. Yet, it is clear from the narratives that these two tribes only joined the insurgency after they witnessed the success of the Natchez surprise attack.[43]

Dumont and Du Pratz also wrote that the Natchez attack was pre-meditated and set to occur at a specific time, and they introduce into the story an element that has become a part of the folklore that surrounds the Natchez: the counting sticks. The story of how the Natchez used the sticks to time their attack on the French apparently came from Du Pratz's interview with the old female chief, Tattooed Arm, while she was imprisoned in New Orleans in 1731.[44] She told Du Pratz that the Natchez planned to coordinate their attack on the French with other tribes by delivering to each tribe a bundle of sticks, with each bundle containing the same number of sticks. The chiefs of the conspiring tribes were instructed to remove one stick each day from the bundle and when the last stick was withdrawn, the tribes would all attack the French simultaneously. In his narrative, Du Pratz recounts Tattooed Arm's tale of how she discovered her tribe's plot to attack the French and learned of the employment of the counting sticks to determine when to strike the blow.[45] Curiously favoring the French over her own people, Tattooed Arm said that she had warned several Frenchmen, who were all rebuffed by Chépart. She then surreptitiously removed some of the sticks from the bundle in the Natchez temple. According to Du Pratz, her reason for removing the sticks was to cause the Natchez to strike early and thus allow the French at other outposts the time to be on guard against the rest of the tribes in the confederacy.[46] Confusingly, Du Pratz goes on to say that the Natchez chiefs then *delayed* their attack to await the arrival of the galley and oar boat.

Dumont also incorporates the bundle of sticks into his narrative. In his version of the story, a young boy happened to see the Great Sun removing a stick from the bundle in the tribal temple, and the boy later imitated the chief by removing some sticks in secret, causing the Natchez to attack early.[47] Le Petit, who wrote his narrative before Du Pratz's interview with Tattooed Arm, does not mention the sticks. Likewise, Charlevoix, whose narrative is probably based on Le Petit's writing, does not contain the counting stick story. However, all accounts agree that the French were forewarned of the attack and that Chépart and others failed to take the necessary precautions. Despite the shortage of troops at the Natchez, a show of vigilance and resolve on the part of Chépart and the concessionaires might have deterred the Indians from attacking.

Perhaps the last word on the conspiracy question comes from the Natchez chief called Saint-Cosme, the namesake of the priest who had attempted to missionize the Natchez some thirty years earlier. Saint-Cosme, a member of the Sun family, told Bienville in 1733 that there had been no inter-tribal conspiracy. The chief said that his people had been forced to revolt in response to "harsh treatment," an apparent reference to Chépart's indignities and the 1723 war.[48]

FRENCH RETALIATION

The first French survivors from the Natchez revolt straggled into New Orleans on December 2 to spill out their stories to a stunned colonial population.[49] Governor Perier, a relative newcomer to Louisiana, tried to grasp what was happening as a wave of panic began to spread through the colony.[50] Overnight, every Indian around New Orleans became suspect, and the frightened colonists jumped at each other's shadows. The outlook went from bad to worse when the news from the Yazoo post reached the capital.[51] Perier sent word of the disaster to the Company of the Indies via a ship departing for France and set the African slaves in New Orleans to work digging a defensive entrenchment around the city.[52]

Far from being enlightening, the intelligence that Perier was able to gather from Native American sources only served to confound the governor. A lone Choctaw traveling downriver told Perier about a report coming from the Chickasaw that an Indian revolt against the French was in the making; however, the Choctaw assured the governor of his own people's innocence. Soon after, representatives of the *petites nations*, the small tribes living along the Mississippi River, visited Perier to inform him that indeed the Choctaws were a part of the conspiracy. Then, from Mobile came the news that two Frenchmen had been killed there and that a Choctaw attack on the fort and settlement was imminent. If that wasn't enough, a Choctaw chief who had been on a hunting trip near New Orleans told Perier that he should be wary of the small tribes, for they were in on the conspiracy with the Natchez.[53] Driven by panic instead of logic, Perier armed a party of African slaves and made them attack one of the small tribes, a defenseless people living below New Orleans known as the Chaouachas, composed of only about thirty households.[54]

While he probably wished that he could send his African slaves to serve the Natchez as they had the Chouachas, Perier realized that only a force of superior numbers could put down the rebellion. With less than sixty men in his New Orleans garrison, the governor had little choice but to enlist the help of the Choctaw. Although Perier mistrusted them as much as he did the small tribes, the Choctaw could field an army of several hundred fighters. Charles Le Sueur, Bienville's relative and an old Louisiana hand, was assigned to go to the Choctaw and invite them to make war on the Natchez.[55] As it turned out, the Choctaw were easily persuaded to undertake this mission. Not long after the massacre, they had sent two successive envoys to the Natchez seeking a share of the French booty. To their disappointment, the Natchez only offered them trifles and withheld the real prize—the stockpile of guns, powder, and bullets. The Natchez also angered the Choctaw by killing some of the French hostages, whom the Choctaw regarded as potentially valuable slaves. According to Dumont, and going back to the conspiracy question, the Choctaw were also quite disgruntled about the Natchez attacking the French ahead of schedule. Therefore, when Le Sueur arrived among the Choctaw to sell them on the idea of war, he found them ready and willing.[56] Immediately, some five to seven hundred Choctaw armed themselves and set out for the Natchez, and another 150 men went to the Yazoo to intercept any French or African hostages who might be transferred to the Chickasaw.[57]

Around this same time, a small party of Choctaws, unaware of what had just transpired, arrived at the Natchez from the Mobile post with a letter for Chépart. One of the Natchez chiefs showed off the severed heads of the Frenchmen, which were arranged in two rows on the ground, and advised the Choctaws to trade with the English "who sold their goods at a small price whereas the French did not give proper compensation." The Natchez also gave their Choctaw visitors two slaves—"a little French boy of nine or ten years old [and] a negro"—along with some horses, articles of clothing, and other items. The Choctaws also saw three French women who were being held captive. On their way back to their villages, these Choctaws met Le Sueur's Choctaw army on its way to attack the Natchez.[58]

While the Choctaws were being mobilized, Perier ordered Henry de Louboey, in command of a detachment of French soldiers encamped at Point Coupee, to proceed to the Natchez and "take measures to recover the French women, their children and our negroes." Louboey was a newcomer to the region and perhaps not the best choice for the job at hand. He was told that Choctaw reinforcements were coming, but he had no idea when or where the rendezvous would occur.[59]

With another Natchez war under way, the Tunicas were probably expecting additional traffic at their river landing. On December 9, a party of Tiou Indians arrived from the Natchez to try to enlist the Tunica in their confederacy against the French. Despite the offer of a share of the confiscated loot, the Tunica declined the invitation. Although they had no appetite for war against the French, the Tunica failed to protect two Frenchmen, probably escapees from the massacre, whom the Tiou found and killed at their village. Only a day or two after the Tiou visit, the first detachment of Louboey's troops reached the Tunica.[60] By the beginning of January 1730, Louboey's force at the Tunica included 90 soldiers, 110 settlers, and some 300 Indians from the *petites nations*.[61]

Once again, the Tunica found themselves beset by a diverse gang of French soldiers, settler militia, and Indian mercenaries, all gathered at their home fires readying for hostilities up river. Instead of pressing the offensive, Louboey set his men to work digging trenches and throwing up redoubts.[62]

Back at the Natchez, the post-massacre celebrations had ended with the news that a French and Indian army was gathering at the Tunica settlement to stage a retaliatory strike. The Natchez chiefs probably also expected to have to defend their newfound European merchandise and hostages from the Choctaw, who would be returning in force and without their calumet. At this juncture, it would seem that the Natchez chiefs committed a strategic blunder. Instead of withdrawing into the rugged hill country bordering their settlements, where they might have held out indefinitely using guerilla tactics, the Natchez—at least part of the tribe—elected to make a defensive stand inside two forts. However, the Natchez were farmers who were tied to the land they had occupied for centuries. Indeed, their cornfields were not simply a part of their sustenance but were a part of their spiritual lives as well.[63] The use of forts allowed them some measure of defense while they were within easy reach of their settlements and fields.

The two Natchez forts were constructed beside St. Catherine Creek, about 500 yards south of the Grand Village (Figure 8).[64] The French named these two forts "Fort de la Farine" (Fort Flour) and "Fort de la Valeur" (Fort Valor). In all probability, people from the Flour settlement (and possibly the Tiou) occupied Fort de la Farine under the Flour chief's command.[65] The identity of the occupants of Fort de la Valeur is less certain; however, the White Apple chief probably was in command of this fort, with elements of the White Apple, Jenzenaque, and Grigra settlements. It is unlikely that the entire tribe was crowded into the forts. The fort's defenders may have been mostly men, along with women from the adjacent Flour settlement who would have been exposed to the coming attack.

The Fort Farine archaeological site, discovered by Joseph Frank, has been tentatively identified as the location of the Natchez fort. The site is on the east side of St. Catherine Creek, about 1,500 feet south of the Grand Village. In the 1960s, Frank found gun flints, lead balls, and Natchezan ceramics at the site, although the area was eroding away due to scouring by the creek. Likewise, flooding and erosion on the west side of the creek may have erased the archaeological remains of Fort de la Valeur.[66] The knowledge of building forts was certainly in the tribe's repertoire, having provided the labor to erect Fort Rosalie. In addition, Dumont wrote that a previous commandant at Fort Rosalie, Charles Du Tisné, also instructed the Natchez on how to build palisaded forts.[67]

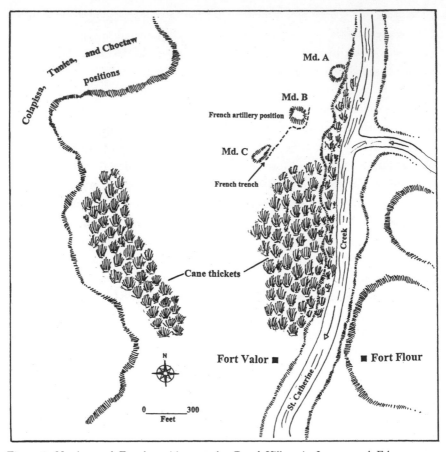

Figure 8. Natchez and French positions at the Grand Village in January and February 1730. (Composite map based upon Neitzel 1983, Figure 2 and an anonymous 1730 French military map entitled *Plan des Deux Forts des Natchez Assiegez* in the d'Anville Collection [code: IFN-7883572], Bibliothéque nationale de France.)

The historian Charles Gayarré gives the following description of the Natchez fortifications:

Trunks of trees, of a circumference of six feet, were driven five or six feet into the ground, leaving ten feet out with sharpened tops. The joints of these posts were strengthened inside by the application of other posts of the diameter of one foot. This wooden wall was protected outside by towers erected at a distance of forty steps from one another. Its inside was supported by an elevation or bank of earth three feet wide by three feet in height, which bank was lined, to keep the earth compact, with green branches and leaves serried together by strong stakes. They showed great intelligence in opening loopholes, and all along their wall, about five feet above the parapet of earth of which I have spoken, they had a sort of pentice made with branches and splinters of wood, as a protection against grenades. In the center of the fort, they planted a tree, the branches of which had been lopped off about nine inches from the trunk, so that they might serve to go to the top, where, when necessary, the Indians placed a sentinel to watch the movements of the enemy. Round this tree, or ladder, they constructed several cabins, or sheds, as an asylum for the women and children against falling arrows. Round the fort were several fortified houses, which were its outposts and dependencies: they were useful in times of peace, as relieving the fort of many of its encumbrances; but when a serious attack was made, they were generally abandoned after a short resistance. If you cut the wicker strings which bind the hoop of a barrel, and if you fling that hoop on the ground, the figure which it will form, when both extremities of the hoop lie apart and get loose from each other, will represent the fort and its entrance. This entrance always fronted some stream or spring from which water was procured, and was defended by a truncated tower. In cases of extreme danger, this passage was blocked up with every kind of briars and thorny shrubs.[68]

In preparation for the coming siege, the Natchez moved the cannons and cannonballs from Fort Rosalie to their new forts. The Indians had been around the French long enough to know how to load and fire the cannons, and some of the African insurgents may have also had experience with artillery. As will be seen, the Natchez artillery would be at least as effective as that of the French in the coming confrontation.

While awaiting the Choctaw reinforcements, Loubocy sent five soldiers under the command of Sieur Mesplex to the Natchez to meet with the chiefs and negotiate for the release of the hostages. The patrol was also instructed to size up the strength of the enemy. Not long after Mesplex and his men stepped ashore in Natchez country, a party of Natchez ambushed them and killed three of their number before the Frenchmen surrendered. Enlisting the help of one of the French women being held hostage, the Natchez chiefs drafted a written message for Louboey with the Indians' ransom terms:

[The Natchez] sent back one of these prisoners the next day with a letter demanding as hostages Sieur Broutin, who had been in command [at Fort Rosalie], and the Chief of the Tunicas. Besides this, they demanded as ransom for the women, children, and slaves the following: 200 muskets, 200 casks of powder, 200 casks of balls, 2000 musket-flints, 200 knives, 200 axes, 200 mattocks, 20 casks of brandy, 20 barrels of wine, 20 casks of vermillion, 200 shirts, 20 bolts of limbourg, 20 bolts of linen, 20 coats with laced seams, 20 hats bordered with plumes, and a hundred ordinary coats.[69]

Du Pratz indicates that the Natchez still sought revenge for Old Hair's execution, and perhaps they looked to gain satisfaction by killing Broutin.[70] Likewise, the Tunica chief's execution would avenge the death of the Little Sun, whom he had killed in 1723. The ransom note also appears to betray a critical bit of information about the Natchez insurgency. The note might be interpreted to mean that the Natchez force numbered two hundred warriors. Estimates of population numbers published by Swanton indicate that the Natchez tribe had from five hundred to seven hundred warriors in 1729 and 1730. Even if the lower estimate is used, then a significant portion of the population seems to have opted out of the rebellion or at least decided not to leave their homes to enter the forts.[71] The Natchez ransom demand gave Louboey three days in which to make a response. When no word came to the Natchez after the allotted time, the soldier with Mesplex was executed, and Mesplex himself was tortured to death.[72]

If the Natchez chiefs entertained any serious hope of ransoming their hostages, those hopes were shattered on the morning of January 27, 1730, when the Choctaws made their attack. According to Perier's official report, the Choctaws killed a hundred Natchez and took fifteen to twenty prisoners.[73] Among those killed in the battle was the White Apple chief. With this chief dead and the young Great Sun unable to form a coalition, the Flour chief apparently seized control of the tribe.[74] As the remainder of the insurgents withdrew into their forts, they inadvertently left some of their hostages unguarded. A few French women and children and about a hundred African men, women, and children soon found themselves in Choctaw custody. According to Du Pratz, the Choctaws stripped the hostages of what little clothing and possessions they had and herded them to a campsite on the grounds of the old St. Catherine concession.[75] From this point on, it is apparent that the Choctaws, by virtue of sheer numbers, had taken control of the situation and lowered the siege on the Natchez forts.

When Louboey received word that the Choctaws were at the Natchez, he finally came out from behind his fortifications at the Tunica settlement and moved his force upriver. Arriving at the Natchez on February 8, Louboey cautiously landed most of his men on the west bank of the river until he was assured by the Choctaws that the Natchez were being held in their forts. Louboey's force came ashore in a heavy rainstorm and marched to the Choctaw encampment at the St. Catherine concession.[76] Warriors from the Tunica and Colapissa tribes accompanied the French troops and militia.[77] On the February 9, an attempt by a combined party of French and Choctaws to capture the Great Sun during a parlay failed when one of the Choctaws opened fire on the Natchez group.[78]

More skirmishing and fruitless parlays continued on February 12 and 13 while Louboey's men brought in their cannons and established a battery and command post at the Grand Village.[79] On February 15, a few of the French women managed to escape from the forts during an attempt by the French to hold a parlay. According to Du Pratz, the Natchez reacted by killing some of the hostage children and displaying their bodies on their palisade wall.[80] For the next six days, the Natchez and French fired their cannons at each other with little effect. Taking advantage of the concealment offered by a heavy canebrake along St. Catherine Creek, the Natchez staged several sorties but were driven back. With the French army keeping the Natchez occupied, the Choctaws apparently helped themselves to whatever loot was left behind in the Natchez settlements. A French officer's journal indicates that alcohol was plentiful: "Returning to camp, had the pleasure of finding the head chief of the Choctaws in full possession of my tent and very drunk."[81] By February 20, the French had six cannons in action and were beginning to dig a sap trench from their position at the Grand Village mounds south toward the Natchez forts.[82] The cannons of the early eighteenth century were made of brass and fired a round cast-iron or lead shot weighing from two pounds up to about eighteen pounds. Louboey's cannons were probably in the two- to four-pounder range because it would have been difficult to transport larger field pieces. A four-pounder cannon weighed a thousand pounds. The cannons commandeered by the Natchez Indians from Fort Rosalie were probably similar in size to those of the French.[83] Trenching was a part of the classic siege strategy used by European armies of the day, and it allowed for a very methodical and controlled offense. The trenches were begun just out of effective musket range (about 50 yards) and were progressively extended toward the fort in a zig-zag pattern. Portable mantelets (armored or wooden shields) and gabions (wicker baskets to be filled with dirt for shoring up parapets) were standard equipment for besieging a fort.[84]

In the 1972 excavations at the Grand Village of the Natchez Indians, Robert S. Neitzel found approximately 550 feet of the French trench extending from the east side of Mound B (the Great Sun's Mound) to near the northern end of Mound C (the Temple Mound). This stretch of the trench, which was well within the French battery and infantry positions, presumably would have helped protect the soldiers from gunfire by the Natchez Indians in the canebrake along St. Catherine Creek.[85]

In the midst of a driving rain on the night of February 22, the Natchez staged an all-out attack that almost succeeded in routing the French. With their muskets wrapped in wool to protect them from the downpour, about two hundred Natchez fighters emerged from the canebrake near the Grand Village and stormed the French battery and defensive positions. According to Charlevoix, Louboey was quartered on Mound C and had probably commandeered the temple as his head-quarters.[86] Part of the French battery, or cannon emplacement, was on Mound B (the Great Sun's Mound). Neitzel speculated that the disturbance to the north face of Mound B, as seen in the archaeological investigation of the earthwork, was the result of modifications by the French to construct a parapet for the placement of cannons.[87] The fighting lasted almost four hours before the French were able to drive the attackers back into the canebrake. The fury of the Natchez fighters is understandable given the religious significance of the Grand Village.[88]

The Choctaws had been encamped at the Natchez for almost a month and were growing weary of Louboey's overly cautious soldiering. The morning after the Natchez attack described above, they informed Louboey that they were ready to return home.[89] Importantly, the Choctaws still maintained custody of the French and African hostages liberated from the Natchez during the January 27 attack. These unfortunate people were confined at the Choctaws' main camp at the St. Catherine concession, where they were forced to endure the cold, rainy January weather in whatever crude accommodations their captors provided.

In a final attempt to break the Natchez resistance, the French moved three cannons to within 80 yards of Fort de la Valeur and began firing. The Natchez cannoneers returned the fire, wounding four French soldiers. With Loubouy's men already beset with sickness and fatigue, and with dwindling provisions and ammunition, the effectiveness of the Natchez artillery broke the spirit of the French.[90] To end the stalemate, the Choctaw chief, Alibamon Mingo, negoti-ated the terms with the Natchez to terminate the siege.[91] According to Du Pratz, it was Bienville's former scout Ette-actal who represented the Natchez in these negotiations.[92]

Louboey agreed to move his men and artillery three miles away to the bank of the Mississippi River. In return, the Natchez agreed to release their hostages. What happened next proves that, despite the presence of a French army on the field, the Choctaws were in fact holding the reins of power. On the morning of February 24, while the French soldiers dismantled their cannons, the Choctaws and not the French took possession of the hostages released by the Natchez.[93]

During the night of February 25–26, while the French were encamped around the ruins of Fort Rosalie and the Choctaws were presumably at their

St. Catherine camp, the Natchez Indians quietly left their forts and absconded to safety. Du Pratz expressed the incredulity of many regarding the unbelievable overnight disappearance of over two hundred people:

> Thinking about this escape, I cannot see how it was possible. I know the Naturals and I know that their usual belongings and implements are all that they can carry. One must not forget that they had the weapons, clothing and goods of the French; it is impossible that they could have transported all of this in a single trip. They must have returned several times and made several trips. I conclude from this that they could not have gone far with their children and all of the elders of the Nation. Where, then, did they go? Frankly, I will say that I know nothing; I simply know from what I have been told that they became invisible.[94]

The Natchez Indians' overnight escape, apparently without detection by either the French or the Choctaws, is verified by the French officer's narrative: "They had crossed the river or sought the cover of swamps and cane-breaks, and were beyond pursuit.[95] Like Du Pratz, Swanton found it difficult to imagine how the insurgents managed to slip away unnoticed and speculated that perhaps the Choctaws allowed the Natchez to get away in exchange for the hostages.[96] With the Natchez gone, Louboey found himself in the humiliating position of having to bargain with individual Choctaw chiefs and warriors to recover the French and African hostages. As Du Pratz put it, "these allies demanded a ransom greater than they would have ever asked of sworn enemies." With French provisions and ammunition running low, Louboey had little merchandise with which to pay the Choctaws.[97]

Fortunately for the French, the Tunica chief assisted with the negotiations. At the end of the day, most of the hostages were turned over to the French for a partial payment of the ransom demand, and the Choctaws were promised that they would receive the balance of the merchandise the next day. During the night, the French quietly sent most of the women and children downriver in canoes. The next morning, the Choctaws were understandably angry to learn that they would have to trust the French to pay them the rest of the ransom later. Despite being shorted on their ransom, the Choctaws, helped by the African slaves they had retained, returned to their home villages with all the spoils of war that they could carry.[98]

The aforementioned Captain de Lusser was at the Choctaw villages when the warriors returned home from the Natchez campaign and tried without success to talk the Choctaws into turning over to him the remaining African and French hostages from the Natchez. He also found a few hostages, both French and African, which the Choctaws had taken from the Yazoo. For their part, the Choctaws gladly promised to return the hostages to the French at some future date, but not without being paid for them. In fact, some Choctaws apparently went directly to New Orleans from the Natchez to demand payment for hostages.[99]

Back at the Natchez, Louboey returned to New Orleans leaving one of his officers, Baron de Cresnay, with one hundred and twenty men to construct an earthen fort near the ruins of Fort Rosalie.[100] When word began to circulate through Louisiana (and later in France) that the French army had let the Natchez Indians escape, Perier wasted no time in laying the blame on the rank and file soldiers; Louboey and his officers received glowing commendations.[101] Perier also praised the performance of the fifteen Africans who fought alongside the French troops, saying that they "did deeds of surprising valor."[102] Of course, the Choctaws were vilified, despite the fact that they had kept the Natchez bottled up in their forts for two weeks before Louboey arrived.[103]

As winter gave way to spring in 1730, the general consensus in Louisiana was that the Chickasaw and English were somehow behind the Natchez uprising and that Chépart deserved much of the blame for his abusive behavior and his failure to heed the warnings of his officers. All of this aside, Perier voiced what was perhaps the root of the trouble at the Natchez: "One of the great mistakes that we have yet made has been to settle with the Indians themselves. When we are several leagues distant they come [to our settlements] only for the sake of their affairs and are not every day mingling indiscriminately and drinking with the settlers as did those of the Natchez. This made it easy for them to destroy our people without difficulty and without running any risk."[104]

By March 1730, Perier had learned from the Tunica that the Natchez were west of the Mississippi River. Although their exact location remained a mystery, the French now knew that they were somewhere up one of the tributaries to the Red River, possibly near the area formerly occupied by the Taensa.[105] Around this time, a small number of Yazoos and Koroas joined the Natchez after the Acansa destroyed their villages.[106] In spite of their weakened condition, Natchez war parties ventured out of the tribe's hiding place to strike at the French. In July 1730, one hundred Natchez warriors surprised a work detail of African slaves guarded by French soldiers about five miles from Fort Rosalie, killing everyone except two whites and five blacks.[107] Not long after this attack, six Natchez Indians passing themselves off as Choctaws entered Fort Rosalie speaking the Mobilian trade language. Once inside, they killed the lone sentinel but were overpowered by the other soldiers on duty. Five of the intruders were killed in the fighting, and the sixth, according to Du Pratz, was "burned on the square frame."[108]

Whenever the Natchez ventured close to the Mississippi River, they risked capture by the Tunica and other tribes allied to the French.[109] In the summer of 1730, around fifty Natchez captives were sold to the French, who re-sold them to the sugarcane concessionaires on the island of Santo Domingo. Some of the Natchez captives were also publicly tortured to death on the frame at New Orleans.[110] Du Pratz described a scene that he probably witnessed first-hand:

> A group of Tunicas, having captured alive a Natchez woman, took her to New Orleans. They presented her to the Commandant General, who resigned her to their hands. They put her in the square frame, where they killed her inch by inch, for the purpose of showing the French how they treated their enemies, for I can assure you that they were really enemies to the enemies of the French. This execution happened between the town and the levee at the edge of the river. Despite all of the suffering this woman endured, despite the cruel torments the Tonicas made her suffer, she didn't shed a tear. She contented herself with pronouncing their imminent destruction.[111]

THE LAST STAND

In December 1730, a French expedition commanded by Governor Perier himself set out from New Orleans to destroy the Natchez Indians. The Natchez were reported to be awaiting the French with five hundred warriors in three forts somewhere up the Black River, a tributary of the Red River.[112] Having learned a hard lesson from the previous campaign, the French army carried with it considerable firepower and provisions to support, if necessary, a lengthy siege. Perier's threadbare colonial army was supplemented by 150 marines from the Fort at Brest and 200 soldiers recruited by the Company of the Indies. Providing additional support was a company of colonial militia and about 150 Indian mercenaries drawn from the Tunica, Colapissa, and other Mississippi tribes.[113] Although Perier had met with some of the Choctaw chiefs in Mobile a month earlier, the Choctaw still had not returned all of the Africans captured at the Natchez, and the governor decided to leave them out of the coming campaign.[114] Several large boats, probably similar in size to the company's galley that figured in the Natchez uprising, provided transportation for men and supplies.[115]

It was snowing and sleeting when the expedition reached the Tunica landing on December 28.[116] While waiting for the Tunicas to organize their warriors for departure, Perier learned that the Natchez had attacked a party of twenty Africans and Indians commanded by a French officer traveling by pirogue up the Mississippi River, killing or wounding at least ten. The ambushed party was on its way to rendezvous with Acansa warriors, who were waiting upstream to join the expedition. When the news of this brazen assault reached the army encamped at the Tunicas, some of the Indian mercenaries quit the expedition.[117]

At the mouth of the Red River, the force was joined by troop detachments from the Natchez and Natchitoches forts. On January 11, 1731, the French galleys entered the Red River with some of the troops on board and others following the flotilla in pirogues and on land. As a ruse, Perier sent a detachment of the militia to Fort Rosalie to make it appear to the Natchez as though the French army was approaching them from that point. In spite of having sent twenty Indian search parties into the lower Tensas Basin, Perier still did not know the location of his quarry. His best intelligence had come from a captured ten-year-old Natchez boy.[118] Evidently following the Natchez boy's directions, Perier's force entered the Black River on January 12 and began moving slowly northward. Along the way, the Indian mercenaries were unable to resist shooting at game, despite orders that the army should proceed as quietly as possible to avoid detection.[119]

Once the French army began its ascent up the Black River, its exact route becomes somewhat speculative. The historian John A. Green, after looking at the available documentation, reconstructed the expedition's route up the Black River and into the Tensas River at the present town of Jonesville. From there, the army moved up the Tensas River to Tensas Lake, just below the mouth of Bayou Macon, and from Tensas Lake, they traveled west following the Fool River to its head, about two miles northeast of the present town of Sicily Island, Louisiana (Figure 9).[120] The expedition's advance forces reached this point on January 19. That same day, Indian scouts encountered two parties of Natchez Indians and reported that they had killed a Natchez man and woman. Perier's men camped that night unaware of how close they were to their enemy. Not far away, the Natchez certainly knew of the French army's presence and probably spent the night moving their people and possessions into their fort.[121]

On January 20, Indians and French soldiers reconnoitering the area quickly found a well-worn path that led them to their objective, roughly an hour's walk from the previous night's camp. Wet season water levels in the Tensas Basin's bayous and streams were sufficiently high to allow the boats transporting the army's siege supplies and artillery to land about a mile and a half from the Natchez fort. Perier reported that the landing site was within earshot of their objective: "Our bateaus and pirogues were hardly landed until we heard the musketry of the fort and that of the skirmishers."[122] Contrary to the earlier reports, Perier and his men found the Natchez in one fort instead of three. In his official report on

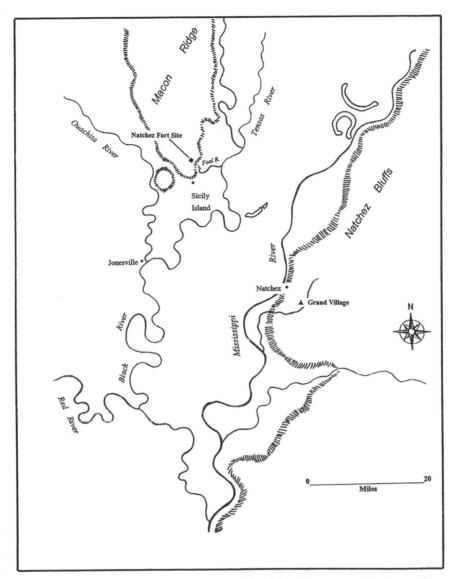

Figure 9. French approach route to the Natchez Indians' fort, January 1731. (Based upon Green "Perier's Expedition" 1936, 575.)

the campaign, Perier called Natchez fort "Fort Valeur," repeating the name given to one of the forts at the Natchez. Some of the Indians' abandoned houses near the fort were burned, and others served to screen the incoming French troops from Natchez musket fire. Perier set up his headquarters behind a mound, about 350 yards from the fort.[123]

The archaeological site known as the "Natchez Fort site" has been tentatively identified as the location of this encounter between the French and the Natchez, although the footprint of Fort Valeur remains to be found. An anonymous 1731 map entitled *Plan du Fort des Sauvages Natchez*, which shows the fort and its relationship to an adjacent lake and streams, bears a close resemblance to modern maps of the area (Figure 10). The site is situated on the eastern side of Macon Ridge, with the fort placed near the edge of the bluff about ten feet higher in elevation than the Tensas River bottomland to the east. In addition to eighteenth-century musket parts, grape shot, cannon balls, and various other military accoutrements found at the site, archaeologists have found Plaquemine and Coles Creek pottery pieces, including the Leland/Fatherland type. If the Natchez Fort site is indeed the location of Perier's Fort Valeur, then the mound that Perier described was gone by 1935, probably lost to plowing and erosion.[124] The presence of Natchezan ceramics and possibly a ceremonial mound provides an explanation for the Natchez Indians' choice of this spot as their place of refuge. The eastern edge of Macon Ridge was an attractive settlement location in prehistoric times, and this particular place would undoubtedly have been well-known in the Natchez villages, only twenty-five miles to the southeast.

On January 21, Perier raised a white flag and demanded that the Natchez release their African hostages.[125] The Natchez responded with musket fire, and the French began launching grenades into the fort. Fortunately for the Natchez, some of the wooden mortars used to launch the grenades soon began to fall apart. Following the time-honored European procedure for besieging a fort, the French officers set their men to work excavating trenches. For their part, the Natchez were not content to sit back and watch all this activity in front of them. At 5:30 in the afternoon, a squad of soldiers working a trench only about 120 feet from the fort were surprised by a party of Natchez attacking them from their rear. The French suffered two or three casualties, including an African laborer. Gunfire from neighboring French positions eventually drove the Natchez back into the fort. Since they attacked from the rear of the French position, this group of warriors may not have come directly from the fort, but were perhaps a group of hunters returning to find their tribesmen besieged.[126] Both the Natchez and the French had plenty of muskets and ammunition, but the continuous heavy rains would have made it difficult to maintain dry powder and gunflints. Despite the weather conditions, the combatants kept up a steady exchange of musket fire into the night.

After a difficult time moving their field pieces from the galleys up to the fort through the swampy bottomland, Perier's cannons inflicted little damage on the Natchez fort. Most of the action on January 22 involved French efforts to disable

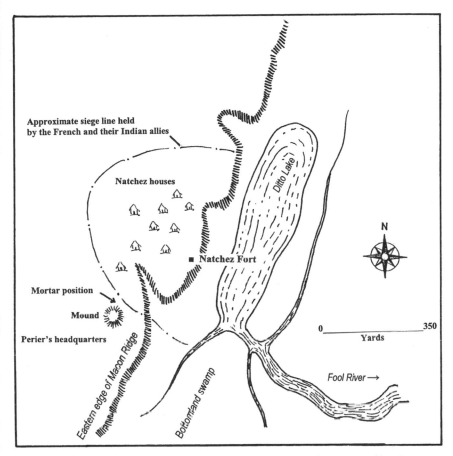

Figure 10. Approximate locations of Natchez and French positions in January 1731. (Based upon 1731 map entitled *Plan du Fort des Sauvages Natchez* in the Bibliothéque nationale de France, Paris.)

a Natchez musket position that was harassing the trenching operations. The Natchez fort incorporated a few of these palisaded redoubts outside the walls proper, from which the defenders could fire on the trench works. After two assaults by the French, the Natchez were forced to abandon the redoubt, which was then occupied by the attackers. Throughout the day on the January 23, the French continued to extend their trenches toward the fort and reached the captured redoubt.[127]

Apparently weary of the intermittent cannon and grenade attacks and concerned about the approaching trenches, the Natchez raised a white flag in the rain on the morning of January 24. An Indian messenger emerged from the fort and crossed the battle lines. Although the army employed an interpreter,

Perier reported that the Natchez man could speak a little French. The governor demanded the release of the Africans before any other discussions were held and stated that he wished to discuss the terms of peace with the chiefs themselves. The messenger assured Perier that the chiefs would not come out of the fort, but the Africans, numbering eighteen or nineteen men and one woman, were delivered into French custody a half hour later.[128]

As the day wore on and the weather grew worse, Perier stubbornly refused to negotiate peace with anyone but the Great Sun. Eventually, the messenger returned to Perier's headquarters accompanied by the young chief named Saint-Cosme. The chief apologized for what his people had done to the Natchez colony and told Perier that, since the Choctaws had killed the chief who had led the revolt (the White Apple chief), the French should cease their attack. Again, Perier insisted upon meeting face to face with the Great Sun.

Apparently convinced of having diplomatic immunity and despite Bienville's lesson in trickery in 1716, the young Great Sun finally left the fort and crossed over to the French lines. With him were Saint-Cosme and the Flour chief. With the rainstorm raging harder, the negotiating party was ushered into one of the Natchez houses and immediately placed under armed guard. Perier called on the Tunica chief and Le Sueur to interrogate the hostages regarding the number of warriors remaining inside the fort, but the Natchez chiefs were unresponsive. Charlevoix says that the Tattooed Serpent (the successor to the chief who had died in 1725), was also summoned to help with the questioning. Anticipating the obvious question, Charlevoix adds "my authorities do not state whether Tattooed Serpent was then in [the French] camp as a friend or as a prisoner."[129] In fact, Saint-Cosme's role as the negotiator for the Great Sun may indicate that he now held the title of Tattooed Serpent.

In the early hours of January 25, soldiers were awakened by gunfire around the house where the prize hostages were being held. Upon arriving at the makeshift jail, the marines found Le Sueur and his men holding Saint-Cosme and the Great Sun at gunpoint. Despite the presence of armed sentries, the Flour chief had vanished into the stormy night. In his report, Perier said that twelve men were guarding the prisoners that night, while Charlevoix's source (probably Le Sueur) said that six guards were on duty—three standing watch while three slept.[130]

With the early morning rain came more bad news: A messenger from the Natchez fort reported that the Flour chief had entered the fort before dawn and had induced his nephew and ten other warriors and their families to escape the siege. Exasperated and prepared to lie to the Natchez in order to bring the siege to a conclusion, Perier promised the Great Sun that all of the Natchez who came out of the fort unarmed would be spared and protected from persecution from the mercenary Indians. After first refusing to accept the offer, the Great Sun's wife came forward with some of their relatives. During the rest of the day, more defenders left their weapons and emerged from the fort in little groups. Upon reaching the French lines, the Natchez were placed under guard. According to Charlevoix, the "woman chief," Tattooed Arm, refused to leave the fort, but we know that she did because Du Pratz later spoke with her in New Orleans. Perier's report states that four hundred and fifty women and children and forty-five men surrendered, and sixteen men and four women remained inside the fort after sundown. Charlevoix said that thirty-five men and two hundred women (children aren't mentioned) gave themselves up, leaving seventy warriors inside the fort. Around 8:00 P.M., Perier received word that the Natchez had escaped from the fort, having taken advantage of the steady rainstorm and slipped past the sentry positions. Troops were immediately sent into the fort, where they found only a Natchez woman and her newborn child, along with a man who had apparently remained to assist her.[131]

The next morning, Perier's Indian mercenaries refused to pursue the Natchez, pointing out to Perier that it was the French who had allowed the defenders to escape; however, two Natchez men were apparently captured and killed. The soldiers spent the next two days burning the fort, along with the Natchez houses and canoes. On January 29, the army returned to the boats with the prisoners, whom Perier referred to as "slaves." Charlevoix wrote that the Natchez prisoners, numbering 387, were bound and loaded into the galleys for transport to New Orleans.[132] Ironically, many of these people had comprised the pro-French faction of the Natchez tribe.

The governor's official campaign report ends on a note of feigned optimism: "One cannot praise too highly those who served this expedition. Each strove to equal the other and desired to distinguish himself by his bravery and work, the officer always setting the example and giving a hand to everything necessary to terminate promptly and happily this expedition."[133]

THE RETROCESSION OF LOUISIANA TO THE KING OF FRANCE

On January 21, 1731, while the French besieged the Natchez fort in the Tensas Basin, the Company of the Indies officially relinquished its Louisiana concession to the King of France. By Royal Decree, the Louisiana province was "reunited to the domain of his Majesty together with all the fortresses, forts, buildings, artillery, arms, and troops that are there at the present time."[134] The directors of the company were thinking about getting out of the Louisiana business before the Natchez revolt, because the hoped-for profits had not been forthcoming. It was simply too difficult to manage the colony at long-distance and much more costly to protect its population from the native inhabitants than the directors had been led to believe. After 1729, the company's Louisiana project became untenable.[135]

As news of the Natchez disaster and the botched sieges reached the people in France, Perier received much of the blame, having placed Chépart in authority at the Natchez and then having allowed the enemy to escape destruction. Although the governor subsequently lost his Louisiana post, he still had some support in Paris. Upon his return to France in 1733, Perier was promoted to the rank of lieutenant general.[136]

By 1731, the French in Louisiana were looking past the war with the Natchez to an inevitable confrontation with the Chickasaws, who were seen as the motivating force behind the Natchez Revolt.[137] To prosecute these wars and bring the colony back into order, the king sent for Bienville, who had been living in Paris since 1725. One wonders how the Canadian-born voyageur, who had caused countless Indians to be enslaved, scalped, burnt on the frame, and beheaded, had adjusted to life in Parisian society. At any rate, the fifty-three-year-old Indian fighter gamely accepted the governorship of Louisiana and sailed from France in December 1732.[138]

EXILE TO SANTO DOMINGO

The Natchez Indians who laid down their muskets and crossed over to Perier's army at Fort Valeur were taken to New Orleans. Among those making the long voyage south were the young Great Sun, his mother, Tattooed Arm, and Saint-Cosme, the last title-holders of the elite Sun lineage. Perier's count of four hundred and ninety-five prisoners is probably somewhat high, but perhaps more accurate than Charlevoix's estimate of two hundred and thirty-five without counting children. At New Orleans, the Natchez people were jailed while they awaited deportation. It was then that Du Pratz sought out Tattooed Arm and recorded her story of the conspiracy, the counting sticks, and the massacre. Some of the Natchez children and women may have been sold as slaves in New Orleans, and many of the people apparently died in prison.

In May 1731, two hundred and ninety-one Natchez men and women were herded onto the ship *Venus* for the voyage to Santo Domingo. According to the ship captain's records only one hundred and sixty reached the port of Cape Français. There, the Natchez people were auctioned to the sugar-cane concessionaires to pay the cost of their passage.[139] One of those who survived the passage was Saint-Cosme. In January 1733, en route to Louisiana from France, Bienville's ship docked at Cape Français and the Natchez chief was somehow able to meet and speak with his tribe's old nemesis. Of the encounter, Bienville had this to say to Maurepas, the minister of marine:

> I have seen here, my lord, the chiefs of the Natchez who are slaves, among others the man named St. Cosme, who had been made to hope that they would be able to return with me. They assured me that it was only their nation that had entered into the revolt and that the harsh treatment that had been given them had forced them to it and that they had decided upon it without taking council of the other nations, and if I am willing to believe them about it, my arrival in the colony will restore to it the tranquillity that I had left there.[140]

GUERILLA WARFARE AND ATTRITION

Perier's report that only sixteen Natchez warriors escaped from Fort Valeur was no doubt intended to stem the criticism he knew would be forthcoming regarding his handling of the campaign. Charlevoix's estimate of seventy warriors and their families is probably closer to the truth. Under interrogation, the Great Sun told Le Sueur that many of his people were not in the fort when it became besieged. The chief admitted that two hundred warriors, including Yazoos and Koroas, were still at large with another two hundred boys who could, if push came to shove, handle a musket. Le Sueur was also given the following distribution of many of these warriors in various Natchez bands and their tentative locations: one chief and forty warriors with their families had gone to the Chickasaws; sixty or seventy warriors and their families were camped three days journey from Fort Valeur on the shore of a lake; twenty men, ten women, and six Africans were at the Ouachita tribe; a small band had been sighted by Perier's scouts south of Fort Valeur on January 18; twenty warriors were in the neighborhood of their old villages; the Flour chief was leading sixty or seventy warriors and their families; and a contingent of Yazoos and Koroas were in a fort three days journey from Fort Valeur.[141]

After January 1731, going by Le Sueur's information, the Natchez tribe appears to have split into three main groups. The smallest of these three, forty warriors and their families led by an anonymous chief, was spotted en route to the Chickasaws in March 1731 with fifteen Chickasaw warriors traveling with them. Choctaws who encountered this party deemed them too formidable to attack and let them pass unmolested. A smaller Yazoo party that later passed through Choctaw country following the same route was not treated with the same respect. The Choctaws killed all of the Yazoo warriors and took their wives for slaves.[142]

The other two large Natchez groups, one of which was led by the Flour chief, remained in the area and were soon causing considerable havoc to French interests. In April 1731, a large Natchez force attacked a group of seventy Frenchmen going upriver to the Acansa. According to Diron d'Artaguette, an officer under Perier's command, the news of the attack led the governor to conspire with the Tunica chief to draw the Natchez into a trap and destroy them once and for all. The plan called for the Tunica chief to inform the Natchez that they were to be granted amnesty and allowed to settle with the Tunicas, provided they give up their weapons. With the Natchez disarmed, they would be dealt with at a time to be chosen by the French. The Natchez apparently suspected foul play. In June, the Tunicas received a party of one hundred and fifty Natchez in their village, and the two tribes spent the night dancing and celebrating their union. At daybreak, the Natchez fell on the sleeping Tunicas and killed many of them, including their chief and several Frenchmen who were in the village. At the same time, another Natchez force temporarily besieged the little garrison at Fort Rosalie, preventing them from coming to the Tunicas' assistance.[143] In addition to thwarting Perier's scheme, the massacre was retribution for the many Natchez Indians who had been killed or enslaved by the Tunicas in French-sanctioned wars and raids.

Following the attack on the Tunica, the Flour chief led a large Natchez force against the Natchitoches tribe but was outnumbered and overpowered by a coalition of Indian, French, and Spanish fighters. The Flour chief was killed in the confrontation, and between seventy and eighty Natchez warriors were reportedly killed or captured.[144] Two months later, a report from one of Perier's officers, Pierre Gabriel Juzan, mentioned that the Flour chief's daughter was a slave at the Natchitoches fort, apparently captured in the fighting. She told Juzan that a group of Natchez Indians had gathered near their old villages. The group was comprised of thirty warriors with their families, under the leadership of "the little chief of Corn." Patricia Galloway has speculated that this chief might represent a Natchez village not mentioned in the 1720s narratives.[145] If so, then the heretofore-unnamed village may have been the settlement district to the north of Jenzenaque and White Apple, discussed earlier as the Fairchilds Creek/ Coles Creek area.

It may have been a part of this same group that was coaxed into Fort Rosalie and then placed in the guardhouse by the commandant, Baron de Cresnay. The Indians somehow managed to commandeer some muskets and kill seven or eight soldiers. Several more were wounded, including some African workers. The situation became so serious that De Cresnay had to use the fort's artillery at close range within the enclosure to prevent the Natchez from overpowering the garrison. Charlevoix reports that the chief of this group, possibly the little chief of the Corn, had gone to New Orleans at the time, ostensibly to seek peace, but he was imprisoned and killed.[146]

Although the Natchez guerilla parties seemed to be striking French outposts and river convoys at will, plenty of evidence indicates that a substantial number of Natchez refugees left the area and went to join their old comrades, the Chickasaw. In late 1731, Perier was informed that as many as two hundred and fifty to three hundred Natchez men with their families were already established at the Chickasaw villages; however, later information makes these numbers seem too high.[147] Around this time, the English were reported to have convinced about eighty Natchez families to relocate in Carolina, a move that foreshadowed later migrations.[148]

Despite the losses of the Flour chief and the little chief of the Corn, Natchez guerillas along the Mississippi River fought on under new leaders during 1732 and 1733. In one notable incident, a strong Natchez party attacked a 170-man French convoy on its way up to the Illinois country. Elsewhere, a group of Natchez, Chickasaws, and Yazoos raided a Chachiuma village and took eleven women. Increasingly, however, participation in raiding parties like this put the Natchez at risk of being killed or captured by tribes allied to the French, including the Choctaws, Acansas, and Illinois.[149]

While most of the Natchez refugee groups scattered throughout the Lower Mississippi Valley, one small group of Natchez Indians dared to return to their old homeland. In 1732, a small Mississippi tribe called the Ofogoula was induced to settle beside Fort Rosalie to hunt for the garrison and perform all of the support services once handled by the Natchez. After Bienville's return to Louisiana, he began to suspect that the Ofogoula were in contact with a Natchez band that was thought to be living in hiding somewhere near their old haunts. Pressured by Bienville to prove their loyalty to the French, an Ofogoula and Choctaw search party discovered a Natchez man tending a large field of planted vegetables less than two day's march from the fort. They beheaded the unfortunate gardener and told the commandant of the fort that, judging from the size of the field, the associated Natchez village might contain as many as fifty warriors. Upon receiving this news, the commandant assayed his meager garrison and lack of provisions and decided against attacking the Natchez.[150]

Some months later, a French and Tunica force found and burned this Natchez village with its cornfields. The Natchez people in this group fled to the Chickasaws, leaving behind an old woman who told the French that the village had consisted of twenty warriors and their families. She said that about forty warriors and their families still lived in hiding in the hills nearby. Based upon this intelligence and another report by a Natchez woman captured by the Avoyels, Bienville estimated that the two hundred Natchez men capable of bearing arms were still at large, including thirty who had gone with the English to Carolina. Besides the small group remaining near Fort Rosalie and those Natchez who had gone to the Chickasaw, a Natchez group was also suspected to be in the Tensas Basin, possibly in the area of the fort that Perier had attacked.[151]

The small Natchez band living near their old homeland apparently persisted into the spring of 1734, when the smoke from their cooking fires was sighted in the rugged bluff hills between Fort Rosalie and the Yazoo River.[152] Three years later, the Ofogoulas burned a Natchez settlement and cornfields near the tribe's old settlement area; however, the people again managed to flee to another hiding place.[153] Although most of the Natchez refugees had relocated to the Chickasaw villages by the mid-1730s, a group of Indians thought by Bienville to be Natchez were sighted on the Big Black River in the bluff hills some fifty miles above Fort Rosalie.[154]

Joseph Frank has pointed out that a small faction of the Natchez tribe may have remained in southwestern Mississippi until the 1770s, based upon a memoir by Colonel Anthony Hutchins, a retired British army officer who settled in the Natchez area in 1772. According to Hutchins, a man who identified himself as a Natchez Indian led the colonel to a place the Indian called "White Apple Village," some twelve miles south of Fort Rosalie on Second Creek. By the time that Hutchins arrived in the Natchez area, the 1763 Treaty of Paris had given the English control of the Natchez area, making it safe for the first time in over thirty years for Natchez Indians to reveal their identity in their old homeland.

As previously discussed, the White Apple settlement of the 1720s was located on St. Catherine Creek northeast of Fort Rosalie; however, examples from accounts of the Chickasaw indicate that, as the people who occupied a particular village were forced to move to a new location, they often gave their new village the same name as the old one.[155] A third "White Apple" place name is associated with a small community about twenty miles southeast of Fort Rosalie, in northwestern Franklin County. Although at this point we can only speculate, the possibility exists that a small band of Natchez Indians chose to risk capture and remain in the Natchez area. If so, then the group may have been a remnant of the renegade White Apple settlement district.[156]

As already mentioned, the majority of Natchez Indian refugees sought safety with the Chickasaws, arguably the most powerful military force in the region. During the 1730s, the Chickasaws had to fend off numerous raids by their neighbors the Choctaws, which were actively encouraged by Bienville. The governor's overriding motivation for promoting Choctaw-Chickasaw enmity was his fear that the two nations might unite under English leadership, with predictable consequences for French Louisiana. Now that the majority of Natchez refugees were residing in the Chickasaw villages, Bienville had yet another reason to promote the Choctaw raiding parties. By the mid-1730s, the Choctaws were growing weary of doing all of Bienville's fighting for him, and some of the Chickasaw chiefs were favoring the idea of surrendering the Natchez to the French to establish peace. As James Atkinson has observed, all of the parties involved seemed to wish for an end to the fighting except Bienville and the French. Bienville apparently rejected a 1733 peace proposal from the Chickasaws, although the circumstances surrounding the terms of the proposal are unclear.[157]

By 1735, in response to pressure from the Choctaw raids and from some of the Chickasaws themselves, many of the Natchez had moved further east and eventually settled among the tribes close to the English, notably the Cherokees and Creeks.[158] Perhaps as many as one hundred Natchez men and their families remained with the Chickasaws in 1735, forming a separate village.[159] The following year, the French and Choctaws launched the war with the Chickasaws that Bienville had advocated since his return to Louisiana.[160] For the first time in his long career, Bienville was handed a defeat, a victory over the French that the Chickasaws would repeat in 1740 with Bienville's second Chickasaw campaign.[161]

CONCLUSION

>→ ———————————————————————— ←←

AFTER THE CHICKASAW WARS, few Natchez Indians remained in the Lower Mississippi Valley. In addition to the remnant of the tribe discussed above, which may have held on until the end of the eighteenth century in their old home place, a few Natchez families apparently remained with the Chickasaws into the 1740s. In 1764, a remnant of the Natchez tribe was located in the western edge of Chickasaw country, on the east bank of the Mississippi River above the mouth of the Arkansas River.[1]

The Natchez group with the Cherokees eventually formed its own village, called Notchee Town, located on the Hiwassee River in North Carolina. There they developed a reputation as dance leaders.[2] According to the historian James Mooney: "[The Natchez] seem to have been regarded by the Cherokee as a race of wizards and conjurers, probably due in part to their peculiar religious rites and in part to the interest which belonged to them as the remnant of a broken tribe."[3] With the Creeks, the Natchez also formed a village named after them on Tallahatchie Creek (formerly Natchez Creek) in Talladega County, Alabama.[4] By the end of the eighteenth century, the Natchez were established in their Cherokee and Creek towns and had found an important niche as spiritual leaders.

The other two Natchezan groups, the Avoyel and Taensa, also succumbed to the pressures brought on by the influx of European and African settlers. The Avoyel remained along the Red River in Rapides and Avoyelles parishes in Louisiana, where they became known as horse and cattle traders between the Spanish to their west and the French and English to their east. After the Treaty of Paris, the Avoyel allied with the Spanish against English encroachment in the Lower Mississippi Valley. With their numbers declining in the early nineteenth century, they intermarried with the Chitimacha, Atakapa, Alabama, and Tunica-Biloxi. Throughout the twentieth century, Avoyel descendants living near Marksville,

Louisiana, managed to preserve their genealogical history and maintain a sense of tribal identity.[5] From 1715 to 1764, the Taensa lived near the French post on Mobile Bay. In 1725, their numbers had dwindled to seventy men and their families. Following the Treaty of Paris, the Taensa chose to avoid English dominion and moved west of the Mississippi River, settling near the Apalachee tribe in Rapides Parish, Louisiana. Between 1803 and 1812, they moved south to Grand Lake in Cameron Parish.[6] In recent years, the Taensa and Avoyel have merged to form the Avoyel-Taensa Tribe/Nation of Louisiana, Inc., which is actively seeking federal recognition.[7]

As for the Natchez Indians who joined the Cherokees and Creeks, their nineteenth- and twentieth-century history became fused with that of their host tribes. The pro-English sentiments among the Natchez in the east led them to fight alongside the Red Sticks in the Creek War of 1813–1814, a theater of the War of 1812.[8] Through a series of treaties between 1815 and 1828, the Cherokees and Creeks lost practically all of their lands, paving the way for their forced removal to reservation lands in Oklahoma between 1832 and 1838.[9] Many of the Natchez descendants ended up settling near Tallequah and Muskogee in eastern Oklahoma. In the 1870s, a Natchez descendant by the name of Creek Sam was instrumental as a religious leader in the formation of the conservative Keetoowah and Four Mothers societies. These societies, formed around the Natchez sacred fire that Sam's ancestors had brought from the east, sought to resist changes in tribal government promoted by more liberal factions. The conservative societies also struggled in vain to avoid the consequences of the Dawes Severalty Act of 1887 and the Curtis Act of 1889, which divided the tribal land held in common into individual allotments. These two reprehensible pieces of legislation cheated the Cherokees and Creeks in Oklahoma out of millions of acres of land. During the first decade of the twentieth century, the infamous Dawes Commission decided who was, and who was not, considered to be a member of the few tribes recognized by the federal government. As a result, the Natchez and hundreds of other small tribes were left without any of the benefits that eventually accrued to the recognized tribes.[10]

In 1907, John R. Swanton found a small group of Natchez Indians living near Braggs, Oklahoma. At that time, at least five people were able to speak the Natchez language, although most of the group spoke both Creek and Cherokee as well. Swanton made notes on the Natchez language and wrote down some of the stories told by the speakers. Among the Natchez speakers at Braggs were two members of the Sam family, Creek Sam, mentioned earlier as a ceremonial leader, and his son, Watt Sam. Ethnologist and archaeologist Hiram Gregory has emphasized the importance of religious activity and language maintenance in cultural survival.[11] The Sam family, it seems, carried the torch of Natchez culture that had been nurtured and passed along from generation to generation since the breakup of the tribe in the 1730s.

In 1931, an anthropologist, Dr. Victor Riste, made several wax cylinder recordings of Watt Sam speaking the Natchez language. At least one of these cylinders has survived in the Voice Library at Michigan State University. Watt Sam was interviewed again in 1934 by the anthropologist/linguist Mary Haas, who collected Natchez stories and word lists. These recordings and notes about the Natchez language are remarkable because they document the tenacious survival of a language for two hundred years after the tribe that spoke it ceased to function. By the 1950s, all known Natchez language speakers were gone.[12]

The Medicine Springs ceremonial ground, associated with the mixed Natchez, Cherokee, and Creek community known as Notchee Town, near Gore, Oklahoma, was active until the 1930s. Watt Sam's nephew Archie Sam, also recognized as a leader in the knowledge of ritual, revived the Medicine Springs ceremonial ground in 1969.[13] Before his death in 1986, Sam spent several years searching unsuccessfully for surviving speakers of the Natchez language. Although he could not speak the language himself, he said that he would be able to recognize it if he heard it. K. T. (Hutke) Fields, a descendant of the Sam family, currently lives in eastern Oklahoma and is a leader in a movement to gain recognition for the Natchez Indians. His grandmother, Eliza Jane (Sourjohn) Fields-Sumpka, was Archie Sam's sister. His father, the late Jobie Levi (Naui) Fields, was a professional dancer, choreographer, and actor in Los Angeles, California, appearing in television and films.[14]

Anthropologists Sharlotte Neely and Wendall H. Oswalt recently documented a group of Natchez descendants living near Charleston, South Carolina. These people, who call themselves the Edisto-Natchez-Kusso, are descended from Natchez Indians who lived with the Cherokees. In the 1830s, when many Cherokees were sent to reservations in Oklahoma, some members of this group of Cherokee-Natchez were permitted to remain in South Carolina as settlers.[15]

Approximately 1,600 miles southeast of Natchez, Mississippi, is the Caribbean island of Hispaniola, where perhaps as many as one hundred and sixty Natchez Indians, including the last Great Sun, arrived as slaves in the 1730s. Although no ethnological research has been done on this segment of the Natchez refugee population, the tenacious survival of language and genealogy demonstrated by the Sam family in Oklahoma and the Edisto-Natchez-Kusso in South Carolina certainly makes it seem likely that a Caribbean branch of the Natchez family tree still exists.

With the advent of the Internet, an eventual reunion of these disparate groups of Natchez descendants seems inevitable. Indeed, this process has already begun with Hutke Fields' leadership of the Natchez Nation at Notchee Town.[16] Fields' efforts have brought the Natchez heightened public recognition—if not the federal recognition they desire, taking the story that began with the meeting between De Soto's *conquistadores* and Quigualtam's warrior boatmen into the twenty-first century.

The history of the Natchez Indians is an account of a Native American society evolving in response to the relentless impact of European contact. In that first encounter in 1542–1543, the Quigualtam chiefdom was powerful enough to easily take the dominant role. One hundred and thirty-nine years later, when La Salle's party descended the Mississippi River, the late prehistoric chiefdoms had all been swept away by disease and environmental factors. In their place were smaller populations organized along simpler lines.

The political organization of the Natchez at the end of the seventeenth century offers a unique example of this simplification process. They were a multi-ethnic confederation of autonomous settlement districts that retained vestiges of chiefdom ceremonialism. They recognized the Great Sun's ritualistic role but invested him with no real power. The political power in the tribe rested with the settlement district chiefs, who enjoyed the freedom to act independently to reinforce their leadership positions and to come together in council for mutual support.

The confederation of autonomous settlements proved to be adaptive during the period 1682–1716, when agents of France and England were pulling the allegiance of the Natchez in two directions. Although they managed to avoid extended European settlement during these three decades (with the exception of Saint-Cosme), the Natchez people suffered from exposure to disease and were inexorably drawn into the European economic web through the slave-catching business and the deerskin trade.

The founding of Fort Rosalie and the establishment of the agricultural colony at the Natchez in 1716, with the influx of hundreds of European and African settlers, hastened the tribe's destruction. Between 1716 and 1729, the coveted European trade merchandise offered by the settler population brought many Natchez Indians into daily contact with the colonists by supplying food, labor, and companionship. Thus three very different cultural groups—Native American, European, and African, became dangerously intertwined at the Natchez colony, even as they remained strangers to each other. In the tragic aftermath of the Natchez Rebellion of 1729, the Natchez Indians vanished as a people; however, their descendants have not relinquished their tribal identity.

NOTES

Note: Complete publication information is available in the bibliography.

INTRODUCTION

1. Alternate spellings of Theloel include Challaouelles, Chelouels, Techloel, Théloël, Theloelles, and Thecoél. See John R. Swanton *Indian Tribes of the Lower Mississippi Valley* 25, 45; for details of Iberville's 1700 Mississippi expedition, see Swanton *Indian Tribes of the Lower Mississippi Valley* 45–46, 190–191, 219, 277, 286–287, 347; Richebourg McWilliams *Iberville's Gulf Journals* 1–3, 49, 67, 114, 124–127.

2. Le Page du Pratz *History of Louisiana or of the Western Parts of Virginia and Carolina* (Claitor's); Charles E. O'Neill *Charlevoix's Louisiana*; François-René de Chateaubriand *Atala and René*. These are only a few of the many published works, both fact and fiction, about the Natchez Indians.

3. Warren K. Moorehead "Explorations of the Etowah Site" 160–161.

4. James A. Ford "Analysis of Indian Village Site Collections" 50–65.

5. Robert S. Neitzel "Archeology of the Fatherland Site"; Robert S. Neitzel "The Grand Village of the Natchez Revisited."

6. Robert S. Neitzel "Archeology of the Fatherland Site" 50–51, 86; Philip Phillips "Archaeological Survey in the Lower Yazoo Basin" 949.

7. Ian W. Brown "Plaquemine Culture in the Natchez Bluffs" 147–149.

8. Ian W. Brown, personal communication 7/31/2006. For a detailed look back at the beginnings of modern archaeology in the Lower Mississippi Valley, see Stephen Williams "Introduction to 2003 Edition" xi–xxxii.

9. A forthcoming book on the archaeology of the Natchez Bluffs by Brain, Brown, and Steponaitis will shed further light on the prehistoric roots of the historic Natchez tribe. Jeffrey P. Brain, Ian W. Brown, and Vincas Steponaitis *Archaeology of the Natchez Bluffs*.

10. Swanton *Indian Tribes of the Lower Mississippi Valley* 45–186.

11. Ian W. Brown "Natchez Indians and the Remains of a Proud Past" 8–9. Also see Vincas Steponaitis "Location Theory and Complex Chiefdoms" 53; Ian W. Brown "Natchez Indian Archaeology" 2.

12. Marcel Giraud *A History of French Louisiana, Volume One*; Marcel Giraud *A History of French Louisiana, Vol. Five*; Marcel Giraud *A History of French Louisiana, Volume Two: Years of Transition*; Verner W. Crane *The Southern Frontier*; Jack D. Elliott Jr. *The Fort of Natchez*.

13. Cf. Patricia Galloway and Jason Baird Jackson "Natchez and Neighboring Groups" 598–615.

14. Marvin T. Smith "Aboriginal Population Movements 18–19; Karl G. Lorenz "A Re-Examination of Natchez Sociopolitical Complexity 97–112.

15. Russell Thornton "Demographic History" 51.

CHAPTER ONE. WARRIOR BOATMEN

1. Of the five known narratives of the De Soto expedition, only three describe the expedition's adventures in the realm of Quigualtam. These are the narratives of Luys Hernández de Biedma, The Gentleman from Elvas (anonymous), and Garcilaso de la Vega. A fourth narrative, by Rodrigo Rangel, does not cover the activities of the expedition in 1542 and 1543. The fifth narrative is a very brief abstract of a lost account of the expedition by a priest named Sebastián de Cañete, which does not provide any information about the events of interest here. John E. Worth "Relation of the Island of Florida" (Biedma), James Alexander Robertson "The Account by a Gentleman from Elvas," Charmion Shelby and David Bost "La Florida by Garcilaso de la Vega," John E. Worth "Account of the Northern Conquest and Discovery" (Rangel), Eugene Lyon "The Cañete Fragment." The Biedma narrative is a primary source and is considered to be the most reliable; however, Biedma's relation of the army's contact with Quigualtam is extremely brief, with only a few lines describing the Indians of Quigualtam. Elvas and Garcilaso are somewhat less reliable, being memoirs collected several years after the events described. Of these two sources, Elvas's account (published in 1557) is considered to be more reliable than Garcilaso's (published in 1605). Therefore, I will present Biedma's quotes about the Quigualtam episode, use Garcilaso sparingly, and rely mainly on the Gentleman from Elvas, who provides a good day-to-day account. For an in-depth evaluation of the De Soto narratives, see Patricia Galloway *The Hernando de Soto Expedition*. English translations of all of the De Soto narratives are available in Lawrence A. Clayton et al. *Volumes I and II, The De Soto Chronicles*. For simplicity's sake, I sometimes refer to the De Soto army as "Spaniards," although soldiers from other countries, including Portugal and Italy, took part in the expedition.

2. James Alexander Robertson "The Account by a Gentleman from Elvas" 112, 128, 129, 131, 133.

3. Clayton et al. *The De Soto Chronicles*. For an up-to-date summary of the expedition's exploits, see: Charles Hudson "The Hernando De Soto Expedition" 74–103.

4. Brian M. Fagan *The Little Ice Age*; David S. Brose "From the Southeastern Ceremonial Complex to the Southern Cult"; Hudson "The Hernando De Soto Expedition," 93.

5. Robertson "The Account by a Gentleman from Elvas," 132–133.

6. Charmion Shelby and David Bost "La Florida by Garcilaso de la Vega" 443–446.

7. Robertson "The Account by a Gentleman from Elvas," 134. According to Patricia Galloway, the Spaniards adopted the term "cacique" (meaning chief) from the Indians of the Caribbean Islands. Galloway *Choctaw Genesis* 114.

8. Robertson "The Account by a Gentleman from Elvas," 151–152.

9. Hudson "The Hernando De Soto Expedition" 94–98.

10. De Soto scholar and archaeologist Charles Hudson places Guachoya in Desha County and Aminoya in Phillips County, Arkansas. Ibid. 94, 98. Hudson's reconstruction the route of De Soto's army west of the Mississippi River differs considerably from the route proposed by Jeffrey P. Brain. Brain's reconstruction of the route places Guachoya and Aminoya in northeastern Louisiana, in Tensas and Madison parishes. Jeffrey P. Brain "Introduction: Update of De Soto Studies" xl–xlvi.

11. John E. Worth "Relation of the Island of Florida"; Robertson "The Account by a Gentleman from Elvas," 151–153.

12. An Indian woman from a village loyal to Chief Quigualtam told the Spaniards on July 3 that the chief was prepared to meet them. Robertson "The Account by a Gentleman from Elvas," 155; Shelby and Bost "La Florida," 503–507.

13. Worth "Relation of the Island of Florida" 245.

14. Robertson "The Account by a Gentleman from Elvas," 153–154.

15. Ibid. 154.

16. Ibid. 154–155.

17. Ibid. 155.

18. Ibid.

19. Ibid. 155–156; Worth "Relation of the Island of Florida" 245; Shelby and Bost "La Florida," 507.

20. Robertson "The Account by a Gentleman from Elvas," 156.

21. Ibid.

22. Shelby and Bost "La Florida," 503; Worth "Relation of the Island of Florida" 245.

23. Robertson "The Account by a Gentleman from Elvas," 157–158; Shelby and Bost "La Florida," 507, 509, 518.

24. Robertson "The Account by a Gentleman from Elvas," 158.

25. Worth "Relation of the Island of Florida" 245

26. Shelby and Bost "La Florida," 518

27. Hudson "The Hernando de Soto Expedition," 99.

28. Robertson "The Account by a Gentleman from Elvas," 158.

29. Hudson "The Hernando de Soto Expedition," 99.

30. Jeffrey P. Brain "Late Prehistoric Settlement Patterning" 338, 340–343, 349.

31. Ibid.; Stephen Williams and Jeffrey P. Brain "Excavations at the Lake George Site; Jeffrey P. Brain "Winterville."

32. Marvin D. Jeter "From Prehistory through Protohistory to Ethnohistory" 211–213. Recent archaeological investigations at Winterville by the University of Southern Mississippi also indicate that site may have been occupied during the De Soto timeline. H. Edwin Jackson "The 2005 Excavations at Winterville Mounds."

33. Charles Hudson *Knights of Spain, Warriors of the Sun* 389–390.

34. Robertson "The Account by a Gentleman from Elvas," 155.

35. Ian W. Brown "Excavations at the Anna Site" 4; personal communication 7/31/2006.

36. Brain "Late Prehistoric Settlement Patterning," 356–358; Brain "Introduction: Update of De Soto Studies," xl–xlvi.

37. David J. Hally *The Upper Tensas Basin* 347, 480, 533, 536, 580–586, 602.

38. Ian W. Brown, personal communication 7/31/2006; Vincas P. Steponaitis, Stephen Williams, R. P. Stephen Davis Jr., Ian W. Brown, Tristram R. Kidder, Melissa Salvanish (eds.) 2002 *LMS Archives Online* 12/27/2004 and 8/22/2006, 24-M-1 pages 1–4, 24-M-2 pages 1–33, 22-M-5 page 2.

39. Galloway *Choctaw Genesis* 315–320; Jeffrey P. Brain "Tunica Archaeology" 318. I speak of the Natchez language in the past tense because there are no known speakers alive at the time of this writing.

40. Charles D. Van Tuyl "A Short English-Natchez Dictionary"; Swanton *Indian Tribes of the Lower Mississippi Valley* 256–257.

41. John R. Swanton *Final Report of the United States De Soto Expedition Commission* 54. For a detailed discussion of Swanton's Natchezan place names in southeastern Arkansas, see Jeter "From Prehistory through Protohistory to Ethnohistory" 206–213.

42. Robertson "The Account by a Gentleman from Elvas," 112.

43. John M. Barry *Rising Tide* 38, 39.

44. Robertson "The Account by a Gentleman from Elvas," 153.

45. Randolph J. Widmer "The Structure of Southeastern Chiefdoms" 128.

46. Ibid. 144.

47. John E. Worth "Account of the Northern Conquest and Discovery" 300.

48. Ibid. 300; Robertson "The Account by a Gentleman from Elvas," 112; Hudson "The Hernando De Soto Expedition," 91.

49. John F. Scarry "The Late Prehistoric Southeast" 26.

50. Galloway *Choctaw Genesis* 78–85, 143–160.

51. Ibid. 160–161; Paul E. Hoffman "Lucas Vázquez de Ayllón's Discovery and Colony" 38–49.

52. Hudson "The Hernando De Soto Expedition," 74. Ian Brown questions the assumption that the De Soto army was capable of spreading diseases among the Indians after having been separated from Europe and the sources of the sicknesses for such a long time. Personal communication 7/31/2006.

53. Galloway *Choctaw Genesis* 133–134.

54. Ibid. 137.

55. Williams and Brain "Excavations at the Lake George Site," 414; Ann F. Ramonofsky "Death by Disease" 47–49.

56. Melvin L. Fowler "Cahokia and the American Bottom" 468; Galloway *Choctaw Genesis* 139.

57. Galloway *Choctaw Genesis* 71; Galloway "Colonial Period Transformations" 230–231; Fagan *The Little Ice Age*.

58. Brain "Late Prehistoric Settlement Patterning," 354–365.

59. Neitzel "Archeology of the Fatherland Site" and "The Grand Village of the Natchez Revisited."

60. Ibid. 360; Vincas P. Steponaitis "The Late Prehistory of the Natchez Region" 192.

61. Karl G. Lorenz "The Natchez of Southwest Mississippi" 146–150.

62. Brain "Late Prehistoric Settlement Patterning," 358.

63. Galloway *Choctaw Genesis* 308–309; Swanton *Indian Tribes of the Lower Mississippi Valley* 334–336.

64. Jeter "From Prehistory through Protohistory to Ethnohistory," 198.

65. Galloway *Choctaw Genesis* 66.

66. Swanton *Indian Tribes of the Lower Mississippi Valley*, Plate I.

67. Jeffrey P. Brain *Tunica Archaeology* 15, 21–44.

68. Jeter "From Prehistory through Protohistory to Ethnohistory," 208.

69. Swanton *Indian Tribes of the Lower Mississippi Valley* 258.

70. Ibid. 272–273.

71. Jeter "From Prehistory through Protohistory to Ethnohistory," 210–211.

72. Galloway *Choctaw Genesis* 347–349.

73. Swanton *Indian Tribes of the Lower Mississippi Valley*, Plate I

74. Patricia Galloway "Natchez Matrilineal Kinship" 5.

75. See Ann Linda Bell "Minet" 29–68.

CHAPTER TWO. EUROPEAN RECONNAISSANCE

1. For background on the origins of French and English colonialism in North America, see Giraud *A History of French Louisiana, Volume One*; Francis Parkman *La Salle and the Discovery of the Great West*; Crane *The Southern Frontier*. Background on the Catholic orders and missionaries in Louisiana is found in Roger Baudier *The Catholic Church in Louisiana*. Protestant missionaries to the tribes in and around English Carolina in the early eighteenth century made little headway and had no effect on the tribes in the Lower Mississippi Valley. Alan Gallay *The Indian Slave Trade* 223–240. "Carolana" was the name of the original English colonial province from which the Carolina colony was later derived. See William S. Powell "Carolana and the Incomparable Roanoke; additional background information on the distinction between Carolana and Carolina can be found at http://www.carolana.com/carolana_vs_carolina.html.

2. Galloway *Choctaw Genesis* 166–167, 169; William C. Foster *The La Salle Expedition on the Mississippi River* 38–41.

3. Parkman *La Salle and the Discovery of the Great West* 122–123. Parkman's book adequately covers the extraordinary life and accomplishments of René-Robert Cavelier de La Salle, so I will confine my remarks to La Salle's dealings with the Mississippi Indians.

4. Bell "Minet" 42. The French refer to the Mahicans as "Loups" or wolves. John R. Swanton places them in the Algonquian language family. They were originally located on the upper Hudson River. John R. Swanton *Indian Tribes of North America* 41–42. Other expedition sources indicate that members of three other tribes, Huron, Chippewa, and Abnaki, may have also been part of La Salle's Indian contingent. Foster *The La Salle Expedition on the Mississippi River* 27.

5. Parkman *La Salle* 467–468n; Jay Higginbotham *Old Mobile* 55, 195, 196n. Tonti's reports are found in four documents: a letter dated July 23, 1682; in the anonymous report entitled *Relation de la découverte de l'embouchure du Mississippi, faite par De La Salle, en 1682*; Tonti's 1684 memoir; and his 1691 memoir. English translations of excerpts from Tonti's reports are found in Swanton *Indian Tribes of the Lower Mississippi Valley* 187–189. Also see Galloway "Sources for the La Salle Expedition" 11–40. The two brief *procès-verbal* documents by the expedition's notary Jacques de La Métairie represent a compilation of information supplied by the group's principal members. William C. Foster "Appendix A. Official Report" and "Appendix B. Official Report" 127–136.

6. Nicolas de La Salle is the only member of the expedition known to have kept a daily journal of the trip. Although the original journal appears to be lost, one version of his journal was published in the late nineteenth century by Pierre Margry. English translations of excerpts from Margry's version are found in Swanton *Indian Tribes of the Lower Mississippi Valley*. The journal of Jean-Baptiste Minet's 1684 voyage to the Gulf of Mexico contains Nicolas' reminiscences of the 1682 expedition. Bell "Minet" 29–68. Galloway "Sources for the La Salle Expedition." In 1998, another version of Nicolas's journal was discovered in the Texas State Archives. Foster *The La Salle Expedition on the*

Mississippi River. Two other members of La Salle's party, Father Zenobius Membré and Gabriel Barbier, contributed additional information about the 1682 expedition. See Galloway "Sources for the La Salle Expedition" 11–40.

7. Foster *The La Salle Expedition on the Mississippi River* 123. The Mosopelea, a Siouan-speaking group, were first documented in southwestern Ohio. In the Lower Mississippi Valley, they were more commonly known as the Ofogoula (or Ofo) and were longtime allies of the French. Swanton *Indian Tribes of North America* 235, 273, 314.

8. Foster "Appendix C" 106–107.

9. Ibid. 140–142.

10. Swanton *Indian Tribes of the Lower Mississippi Valley* 186–189.

11. Ibid. 187.

12. Foster *The La Salle Expedition on the Mississippi River* 108.

13. Swanton *Indian Tribes of the Lower Mississippi Valley* 188.

14. Foster *The La Salle Expedition on the Mississippi River* 108.

15. Ibid.; Bell "Minet," 51; Swanton *Indian Tribes of the Lower Mississippi Valley* 187–188.

16. Swanton *Indian Tribes of the Lower Mississippi Valley* 327–328; Foster *The La Salle Expedition on the Mississippi River* 109.

17. The Quinipissa, also known as the Mugulasha or Mongulasha, was a Muskogean language group located on the lower Mississippi River between Baton Rouge and New Orleans. By 1699, the Quinipissa were decimated by disease and had merged with another Muskogean tribe, the Mugulasha, for mutual protection. Within a year, this amalgamated group was broken up by conflicts with neighboring tribes. Swanton *Indian Tribes of the Lower Mississippi Valley* 9, 279–281.

18. Foster *The La Salle Expedition on the Mississippi River* 112, 118; Swanton *Indian Tribes of the Lower Mississippi Valley* 279–280.

19. Foster *The La Salle Expedition on the Mississippi River* 120.

20. Bell "Minet," 59.

21. Ibid.; Swanton *Indian Tribes of the Lower Mississippi Valley* 327–328.

22. Foster *The La Salle Expedition on the Mississippi River* 121.

23. This National Historic Landmark archaeological site will be discussed in more detail in a succeeding section.

24. Swanton *Indian Tribes of the Lower Mississippi Valley* 48.

25. Ibid. 45. The present mouth of St. Catherine Creek, located only about two miles south of the City of Natchez, is the result of the artificial diversion of the stream in the late 1800s. Originally, the creek was much longer, flowing along the base of the bluffs and entering the Mississippi River just north of Hutchins Landing. The lower drainage course is now called "Old St. Catherine Creek." See Neitzel "Archeology of the Fatherland Site," 11–12.

26. Ibid. Plates 14–16.

27. Jeffrey P. Brain "La Salle at the Natchez" 56–58.

28. Steponaitis "The Late Prehistory of the Natchez Region," 192. Of course, negative evidence— the failure of archaeologists to find European trade items at a site—doesn't prove that Emerald and Foster were completely abandoned before French contact. However, the absence of contact period artifacts makes these two sites unlikely candidates for places occupied by the Natchez during and after La Salle's time.

29. Foster *The La Salle Expedition on the Mississippi River* xiii–xiv, 10, 29, 39.

30. Gallay *The Indian Slave Trade* 102–105.

31. Bell "Minet," 52n, 60.

32. Ian W. Brown "The Calumet Ceremony" 311.

33. Gallay *The Indian Slave Trade* 105–110.

34. Hally *Upper Tensas Basin* 689, 690, 692–693; Steponaitis et al. 12-27-2004, 24-L-9, p. 1, 2, 24-L-14, p. 2.

35. Joseph V. Frank personal communication 12/22/2004.

36. Steponaitis et al. 2002 *LMS Archives Online* 25-K-4, p. 1, 25-K-14, p. 1, 25-K-15, p. 1.

37. See Robert S. Weddle et al. *Three Primary Documents.*

38. Swanton *Indian Tribes of the Lower Mississippi Valley* 188.

39. Ibid.

40. Gallay *The Indian Slave Trade* 49. Crane *The Southern Frontier* 18–19.

41. Gallay *The Indian Slave Trade* 56, 103–104.

42. Thomas Nairne *Nairne's Muskhogean Journals* 50; Gallay *The Indian Slave Trade* 56.

43. Gallay *The Indian Slave Trade* 130.

44. James R. Atkinson *Splendid Land Splendid People* 4–5, 27.

45. Robert A. Brightman and Pamela S. Wallace "Chickasaw" 486, 487.

46. Galloway *Choctaw Genesis* 200, 313–314.

47. Crane *The Southern Frontier* 46.

48. Gallay *The Indian Slave Trade* 297. James R. Atkinson believes that the numbers of slaves attributed to the Chickasaw are exaggerated and points out that the Chickasaw themselves were the target of Choctaw slave raids. Atkinson *Splendid Land Splendid People* 18, 29.

49. Carl A. Brasseaux "The Moral Climate of French Colonial Louisiana 526, 527.

50. Gallay *The Indian Slave Trade* 308–311; Giraud *Vol. I* 177–179.

51. Dunbar Rowland and Albert G. Sanders *Mississippi Provincial Archives Vol. II* 23, 28, 32, 37, 45–46. In 1708, Bienville wrote that one African slave was worth two Indian slaves in Santo Domingo. Rowland and Sanders *Vol. II* 37; Rowland and Sanders *Mississippi Vol. III* 47, 53.

52. Swanton *Indian Tribes of the Lower Mississippi Valley* 39.

53. Rowland and Sanders *Vol. III*, 23; for information on the Atakapa, see Swanton *The Indian Tribes of North America* 197–199; Swanton *Indian Tribes of the Lower Mississippi Valley* 360–363.

54. Nairne *Muskhogean Journals* 3, 14–16, 74; Gallay *The Indian Slave Trade* 291, 297, 318.

55. Rowland and Sanders *Vol. III* 144, 151, 171–173.

56. Crane *The Southern Frontier* 65.

57. See Nairne *Muskhogean Journals.*

58. Gallay *The Indian Slave Trade* 315–318, 322, 327, 328.

59. Parkman *La Salle* 121, 134–135; Bell "Minet," 240 n18, n20; Jerald T. Milanich "Franciscan Missions" 276–303.

60. See Weddle et al. *La Salle, the Mississippi, and the Gulf.*

61. Baudier *The Catholic Church in Louisiana* 17.

62. See Weddle et al. *La Salle, the Mississippi, and the Gulf.*

63. Parkman *La Salle* 37–47, 88, 102–105.

64. Giraud *A History of French Louisiana, Vol I* 26–30.

65. John Gilmary Shea (ed. and trans.) "Letters." Both Shea and John R. Swanton assumed that the La Source who accompanied the Seminarian priests that year was the Seminarian Thaumer de

La Source, who served in the Illinois country in the 1720s; however, Jeffrey P. Brain points out that it was the lay adult J.-B. La Source who traveled with Davion, Saint-Cosme, and De Montigny during the winter of 1698–1699. Brain *Tunica Archaeology* 17.

66. Swanton *Indian Tribes of the Lower Mississippi Valley* 308–311.

67. Ibid. 189.

68. Giraud *A History of French Louisiana, Vol I* 57.

69. Shea "Letters" 72, 81.

70. Ibid. 82.

71. John Gilmary Shea "Letters" 82.

72. McWilliams *Iberville's Gulf Journals* 128; McWilliams *Pénicaut* 33–34.

73. Swanton *Indian Tribes of the Lower Mississippi Valley* 189; Rowland and Sanders *Vol. III* 38.

74. Giraud *A History of French Louisiana, Vol I* 54.

75. Baudier *The Catholic Church in Louisiana* 21–22.

76. Swanton *Indian Tribes of the Lower Mississippi River Valley* 22.

77. Ibid. 75, 93.

78. Ibid. 139n.

79. Ibid. 190.

80. McWilliams *Iberville's Gulf Journals* 129, 131–132. The Jesuit missionary Jacques Gravier indicates that the Taensa gave De Montigny a young female slave, who was one of the people that the vicar had saved from sacrifice during the chief's funeral. According to Gravier, the gift of the slave girl was part of a clever ruse to divert the missionary from the tribe's intent to carry out the other funerary sacrifices without De Montigny's knowledge. Swanton *Indian Tribes of the Lower Mississippi Valley* 140. Iberville's operations in the Lower Mississippi Valley will be detailed in a later section.

81. McWilliams *Iberville's Gulf Journals* 114.

82. Ibid. 146. According to John G. Shea, Du Montigny refused further assignments in America and was sent to China. He died in Paris in 1725 at the age of 64. Shea "Letters" 52n.

83. For a summary of Iberville's impressive military career, see Tennant S. McWilliams "Pierre LeMoyne and the Competition for Empire" 1–16. Some have characterized Iberville and his brothers as being nothing short of pirates, whose own self-interest happened to coincide with the empirical interest of France. Gwendolyn Midlo Hall *Africans in Colonial Louisiana* 12–13.

84. McWilliams *Iberville's Gulf Journals* 2–4.

85. Father Hennepin had explored the upper Mississippi. Upon his return to France, he somehow gained access to La Salle's 1682 letters and used the information to publish a book in 1683, in which the priest claimed to have accompanied La Salle to the mouth of the Mississippi. Parkman *La Salle* 281–282; Crane *Southern Frontier* 56–57.

86. Crane *Southern Frontier* 54–57; Giraud *A History of French Louisiana, Vol I* 22; Charles Elliott "Bienville's English Turn Incident" 11–12.

87. McWilliams *Iberville's Gulf Journals* 20. Iberville's fleet consisted of the *Badine* and the *Marin*, two armed frigates, the *François*, a warship assigned as escort, and two smaller transport vessels. Ibid. 20n, 23n, 23n, 25n.

88. McWilliams *Iberville's Gulf Journals* 33.

89. Ibid. 34–39.

90. Ibid. 43–44.

91. Ibid. 46–48.

92. Ibid. 72–73. Richebourg McWilliams, who provides the English translation quoted here, points out that Iberville has listed nine villages instead of eight.

93. McWilliams *Iberville's Gulf Journals* 109.

94. Swanton *Indian Tribes of the Lower Mississippi Valley* 22.

95. Swanton *Indian Tribes of the Lower Mississippi Valley* 45–48. The Tiou settlement district at the Natchez will be discussed in more detail in a later section.

96. Swanton *Indian Tribes of the Lower Mississippi Valley* 46. See James M. Crawford *The Mobilian Trade Language.*

97. Swanton *Indian Tribes of the Lower Mississippi Valley*, 46; Ignace-François Broutin *Carte des environs du fort Rosalie aux Natchez* 1723; Vincas P. Steponaitis personal communication 1/3/2007.

98. McWilliams *Iberville's Gulf Journals* 70–77.

99. Ibid. 114.

100. Ibid. 117.

101. Ibid. 120.

102. Ibid. 119–122.

103. Ibid. 122; Swanton *Indian Tribes of the Lower Mississippi Valley* 272–274.

104. McWilliams *Pénicaut* 147; Swanton *Indian Tribes of the Lower Mississippi Valley* 9, 17, 272–274; Galloway and Jackson "Natchez and Neighboring Groups," 598.

105. McWilliams *Iberville's Gulf Journals* 123.

106. Swanton *Indian Tribes of the Lower Mississippi Valley* 191. Because the chief's mound and the temple mound are only separated by a distance of about 325 feet, I've used Swanton's translation for this passage instead of McWilliams'. The latter gives the dimensions of the space between the chief's mound and the temple mound in "yards," which is too large an area. Swanton's use of the term "paces" may be a little more accurate, since Iberville's stride was probably something less than a yard. Neitzel "Archaeology of the Fatherland Site," 13.

107. McWilliams *Iberville's Gulf Journals* 125.

108. Ibid. 125–126.

109. Ibid. 132.

110. Ibid. 143–145. The English party at the Acansa was led by Jean Couture, a Frenchman who had been in Tonti's employ, but had deserted and joined the English in Carolina. Elliott "Bienville's English Turn Incident" 15.

111. McWilliams *Iberville's Gulf Journals* 137; Giraud *Vol. I* 84–85; Galloway *Choctaw Genesis* 322–323. Higginbotham lists the names of some of Iberville's cabin boys who were stationed with Mississippi Indian tribes in 1700–1702: St. Michel, Pierre Huet, Gabriel Marcal, Jean Joly, Jacques Charon, and Pierre Le Vasseur. Jay Higginbotham *Fort Maurepas* 85. Of these, only St. Michel can be linked to a specific tribe; he was sent to live with the Chickasaw in April 1702. McWilliams *Iberville's Gulf Journals* 176.

112. Swanton *Indian Tribes of the Lower Mississippi Valley* 187.

113. Foster The La Salle Expedition on the Mississippi River 108.

114. McWilliams *Iberville's Gulf Journals* 72–73.

115. The specific locations of these villages or settlement districts have not been positively identified. The general locations shown in Figure 4 are based upon inferences drawn from French colonial narratives, maps, and archaeological data. See Andrew C. Albrecht "The Location of the Historic

Natchez Villages" 67–88; Brown "Natchez Indian Archaeology; Broutin *Carte des environs du fort Rosalie aux Natchez* 1723.

116. Swanton *Indian Tribes of the Lower Mississippi Valley* Plate 7a.

117. Steponaitis et al. *LMS Archives Online*: 26-K-22 (22-AD-590) p. 1; Brown *Natchez Indian Archaeology* Figure 3.

118. Jean Baptiste d'Anville *Essai d'une Carte de la Louisiane*.

119. Broutin *Carte des environs du fort Rosalie aux Natchez* 1723.

120. Swanton *Indian Tribes of the Lower Mississippi Valley* 45–48; Marvin D. Jeter "Grigra" 179; Marvin D. Jeter and Ives Goddard "Tiou" 188.

121. Swanton *Indian Tribes of the Lower Mississippi Valley* 9, 33; Galloway *Choctaw Genesis* 308–309.

122. Jeter and Goddard "Tiou," 188.

123. Broutin *Carte des environs du fort Rosalie aux Natchez* 1723.

124. See Brain *Tunica Archaeology*.

125. Swanton *Indian Tribes of the Lower Mississippi Valley* 336.

126. Brown *Natchez Indian Archaeology* 99–176; Broutin *Carte des environs du fort Rosalie aux Natchez* 1723.

127. Swanton *Indian Tribes of the Lower Mississippi Valley* 189, 327; Galloway *Choctaw Genesis* 174. Jeter and Goddard "Tiou," 188.

128. Swanton *Indian Tribes of the Lower Mississippi Valley* 330.

129. Jeter and Goddard "Koroa," 180.

130. Swanton *Indian Tribes of the Lower Mississippi Valley* 330–332.

131. Swanton *Indian Tribes of the Lower Mississippi Valley* 46–48.

132. Brown *Natchez Indian Archaeology* 75–97.

133. Broutin *Carte des environs du fort Rosalie aux Natchez* 1723; Swanton *Indian Tribes of the Lower Mississippi Valley* 213.

134. Swanton *Indian Tribes of the Lower Mississippi Valley* 214.

135. Brown *Natchez Indian Archaeology* 190.

136. Smith "Aboriginal Population Movements," 18–19.

137. Marvin D. Jeter "Protohistoric and Historic Native Americans" 241; Swanton *Indian Tribes of the Lower Mississippi Valley* 9, 327–332, 334–336, 336.

138. Douglas R. White et al. "Natchez Class and Rank" 382.

139. According to White et al., the rebellious chief of the Jenzenaque settlement district, whom we will meet in Chapter Three, was probably a member of the Sun lineage. White et al. "Natchez Class and Rank," 382.

140. Du Pratz (Claitor's), 79; Swanton *Indian Tribes of the Lower Mississippi Valley* 198–199.

141. Brown "Natchez Indian Archaeology," 5, 6.

142. Swanton *Indian Tribes of the Lower Mississippi Valley* 47.

143. Based upon archaeological findings, the Fairchilds Creek/Coles Creek settlement district was pro-English. Brown *Natchez Indian Archaeology* 12.

144. Galloway *Choctaw Genesis* 314.

145. Neitzel "Archeology of the Fatherland Site," 15–16, 63–64.

146. Ibid. 16–26. James F. Barnett Jr. "Natchez House Reconstruction."

147. Neitzel "Archeology of the Fatherland Site," 22, 40–41; Du Pratz (Claitor's), 334, 339; O'Neill *Charlevoix's Louisiana* 242, 247.

148. Neitzel "Archeology of the Fatherland Site," 27–39.

149. Neitzel "The Grand Village of the Natchez Revisited," 26–65.

150. James F. Barnett Jr. "A New Building Location at the Fatherland Site" 2–11.

151. Giraud *Vol I.* 55; Swanton *Indian Tribes of North America* 241. The missionary's name is sometimes given as "St. Côme." Jean-François Buisson de Saint-Cosme's younger brother, Michel Buisson de Saint-Cosme, also became a Seminarian priest and made a brief foray into Louisiana. He is sometimes referred to as Saint-Cosme "the younger." Giraud *Vol. I* 55–56; Céline Dupré *Dictionary of Canadian Biography Online.*

152. Giraud *Vol I.* 9, 55, 57–58.

153. As of this writing, Saint-Cosme's letters from his Natchez mission are only accessible to English-speaking researchers through all-too-brief excerpts quoted and referenced in publications such as Swanton *Indian Tribes of the Lower Mississippi Valley* 49, 93, 172–173, 269–270; and Giraud *Vol I* notes on pages 53,54,56, 57, 58, 59. Six letters from the priest's Natchez period are referenced by Swanton and Giraud: August 1701, December 1701, April 1702, October 1702, March 1705, and January 1706. Ibid.

154. Swanton *Indian Tribes of the Lower Mississippi Valley* 178–181.

155. Giraud *Vol I* 55–56, 76–77.

156. Céline Dupré *Dictionary of Canadian Biography Online;* Rowland and Sanders *Vol. III* 120.

157. John Gilmary Shea (ed. and trans.) "Journal of the Voyage of Father Gravier."

158. Ibid. 136.

159. Ibid. 140. Gravier also made reference to a Natchez chief's funeral held one month before the funeral described by the cabin boy. From the context of his journal, however, Gravier is obviously referring to the Taensa chief's funeral: "Mr. de Montigni, who has left this country to go to Siam, being informed of what they [the Taensa] were accustomed to do, made them promise not to put any one to death." Ibid.

160. Swanton *Indian Tribes of the Lower Mississippi Valley* 22.

161. See Ibid. 258.

162. Giraud *Vol. I* 232.

163. Swanton *Indian Tribes of the Lower Mississippi Valley* 329.

164. Ibid. 310, 330. The narrative of André Pénicaut records the names of the two Frenchmen who were traveling with Foucalt as Dambouret and de St. Laurent. McWilliams *Pénicaut Narrative,* 98–99; Giraud *Vol. I* 276.

165. Giraud *Vol. I* 55, 86. According to Giraud, Davion's servant remained with the Tunica during the priest's sojourn in Mobile. Ibid 238.

166. Ibid. 86, 207.

167. Swanton *Indian Tribes of the Lower Mississippi Valley* 310–311.

168. Ibid. 39.

169. Ibid. 310–311.

170. Bienville claims to have sent the Acansa against the Koroa. Rowland and Sanders *Vol. III* 22–23. The missionary De la Vente wrote that the Illinois joined the Acansa in the attack on the Koroa, while the memoir of the soldier De Richebourg indicates that the Koroa chiefs took it upon themselves to punish the murderers. Swanton *Indian Tribes of the Lower Mississippi Valley* 331.

171. McWilliams *Pénicaut Narrative* xxx, xxxi.

172. See Swanton *Indian Tribes of the Lower Mississippi Valley* 4; Giraud *Vol. I.* 49; and McWilliams *Pénicaut Narrative* xxiii–xxxviii. Pénicaut's name is sometimes written as Pénicault, Pénicaud, Pénigaut, or Pénigault.

173. Ibid. 80. In this instance, Pénicaut's date of 1704 is correct since he associates his Natchez sojourn with the arrival of the French supply ship *Le Pélican*, which, according to Swanton, arrived in Mobile in July 1704. Ibid. 96–97; Swanton *Indian Tribes of the Lower Mississippi Valley* 192; Giraud *Vol. I* 141.

174. McWilliams *Pénicaut Narrative* 27–49, 82–83. Pierre-Charles Le Sueur had arrived in Louisiana with Pénicaut on Iberville's second voyage. Le Sueur's expedition ascended the Mississippi River all the way to its headwaters in what is now Minnesota, where the men spent the winter of 1700–1701 mining copper.

175. Ibid. 81.

176. Ibid. 87.

177. Ibid. 87–88.

178. Ibid. 90.

179. Ibid. 89–90.

180. Galloway and Jackson "Natchez and Neighboring Groups," 603. Any discussion of Natchez society is incomplete without some mention of the so-called "Natchez Paradox." During the 1960s and 1970s, a few scholars raised the issue that, by following the custom of nobles marrying commoners, the number of commoners would, over time, decrease to the point that the practice would no longer be viable without the infusion of more commoners. This eventuality was cited as a possible motive for the Natchez Indians' adoption of refugee groups such as the Koroa, Tiou, and Grigra, who might have replenished the shrinking commoner ranks. However, a reevaluation of Natchez society by Douglas R. White, George P. Murdock, and Richard Scaglion, of the University of Pittsburg, convincingly argued that the Natchez social system was, in fact, quite balanced and capable of maintaining an equilibrium between the numbers of nobles and commoners. In this writer's opinion, the Natchez Paradox has been happily moot for many years; however, for readers who wish to delve into its intricacies, I can recommend the following articles: White et al. "Natchez Class and Rank Reconsidered," 369–388; Jeffrey P. Brain "The Natchez Paradox" 215–222; Galloway and Jackson "Natchez and Neighboring Groups," 602–603; George I. Quimby "Natchez Social Structure" 134–137.

181. Galloway and Kidwell "Choctaw in the East" 504; Walker "Creek Confederacy Before Removal" 383; Brightman and Wallace "Chickasaw" 485.

182. Ibid. 485.

183. Du Pratz in Swanton *Indian Tribes of the Lower Mississippi Valley* 117; Hudson *The Southeastern Indians* 237, 410.

184. Galloway and Kidwell "Choctaw in the East," 504; Swanton *Indian Tribes of the Lower Mississippi Valley* 185, 356.

185. McWilliams *Pénicaut Narrative* 84–85, 88–89.

186. Ibid. 92–96.

187. Cf. Du Pratz and Dumont in Swanton *Indian Tribes of the Lower Mississippi Valley* 143–157.

188. See Hudson *The Southeastern Indians* 328.

189. McWilliams *Pénicaut Narrative* 97, 97n.

190. Ibid. 83–84.

191. Giraud *Vol. I* 192.

192. Rowland and Sanders *Vol. II* 166.

193. McWilliams *Pénicaut Narrative* 96–97.

194. Giraud *Vol. I* 177–179; see Brasseaux "The Moral Climate of French Colonial Louisiana," 526, 527.

195. Swanton *Indian Tribes of the Lower Mississippi Valley* 337–338.

196. Du Pratz in Ibid. 340.

197. Ibid. 245–247; White et al. "Natchez Class and Rank Reconsidered," 382.; Dupré *Dictionary of Canadian Biography Online*; McWilliams *Pénicaut Narrative* 70n. McWilliams *Iberville's Gulf Journals* 176n; Brasseaux "The Moral Climate of French Colonial Louisiana," 536n; Rowland and Sanders *Vol. III* 58n; Giraud *Vol. I* 335. The Saint-Cosme rumor may have been fueled in part by Du Pratz's claim that the female chief Tattooed Arm told him in 1731 that one of her sons was fathered by a Frenchman (whom she apparently didn't name). Du Pratz (Claitor's) 80.

198. O'Neill *Charlevoix's Louisiana* xviii, 258.

199. Giraud *Vol. I* 110, 173.

200. Rowland and Sanders *Vol. III* 112; McWilliams *Pénicaut Narrative* 14n, 18–19.

201. Giraud *Vol. I* 75, 80; Rowland and Sanders *Vol. III* 152, 158–159.

202. Rowland and Sanders *Vol. II* 20–29, 60–66.

203. Crane *The Southern Frontier* 90–91.

204. Rowland and Sanders *Vol. II* 39, 40, 126, 128, 129, 130; Rowland and Sanders *Vol. III* 113, 159, 160.

205. Galloway and Kidwell "Choctaw in the East," 512.

206. Crane *The Southern Frontier* 86.

207. Swanton *Indian Tribes of the Lower Mississippi Valley* 259–270, 307–313.

208. Brain *Tunica Archaeology* 297–298; Fred B. Kniffin, Hiram F. Gregory, and George A. Stokes *The Historic Indians of Louisiana* 76–77; Swanton *Indian Tribes of the Lower Mississippi Valley* 289. In 1715, the Taensa moved from the Mississippi River to the French post at Mobile. Rowland and Sander *Vol. III* 183.

209. Although they remained ensconced in the king's court in France, Jérôme and his father Louis were in continuous contact with the movers and shakers of the Louisiana colony, and were influential behind-the-scenes players in the colony's politics and strategies. Giraud *Vol. I*.

210. Rowland and Sanders *Vol. II* 177; Rowland and Sanders *Vol. III* 59, 66; Giraud *Vol. I* 249–251.

211. Rowland and Sanders *Vol. II* 162; McWilliams *Pénicaut Narrative* 158; Swanton *Indian Tribes of the Lower Mississippi Valley* 192; Giraud *Vol. I* 305.

212. McWilliams *Pénicaut Narrative* 170, 173. The exact location of Crozat's trading post may never be known.

213. McWilliams *Iberville's Gulf Journals* 62.

214. Claudio Saunt "History Until 1776" 133–134.

215. Rowland and Sanders *Vol. II* 81–82; Crane *Southern Frontier* 109. To protect New France's flourishing beaver skin trade, the French Crown prohibited the sale of beaver pelts in Louisiana, leaving the Mississippi tribes to focus on deer, bear, otter, and fox. Rowland and Sanders *Vol. III* 49, 59–60; Giraud *Vol. I* 146, 146n, 170–171.

216. Based upon a example involving bearskins detailed by Jean-Baptist du Bois du Clos, commissary general of Louisiana, profit on deerskin sales to Spanish and French buyers ran between 17 and 34 percent, netting the Mobile residents between four and eight sous per skin. Rowland and Sanders *Vol. II* 85–87.

217. Rowland and Sanders *Vol. II* 149, 150, 153.

218. Saunt "History Until 1776," 133.

219. Ibid. 133–134.

220. Rowland and Sanders *Vol. II* 84–87.

221. Saunt "History Until 1776," 133.

222. Giraud *Vol. II* 74.

223. Rowland and Sanders *Vol. II* 177–178, 180–181.

224. See McWilliams *Pénicaut Narrative* 98–157.

225. Ibid. 159. Pénicaut says that this event occurred in 1713; however, it is clear from other sources that he found the Englishmen with the Natchez in 1715. Rowland and Sanders *Vol. III* 186–187. The Chaouachas (alternately spelled "Chawasha") were allied to the French and living on the Mississippi River below New Orleans in 1715. Swanton *Indian Tribes of North America* 201.

226. Crane *Southern Frontier* 102.

227. McWilliams *Pénicaut Narrative* 160.

228. Ibid. 160–162.

229. Rowland and Sanders *Vol. III* 182, 187.

230. Gallay *Indian Slave Trade* 328. Bienville's nephew Sieur de St. Hélène was killed in the Yamasee War backlash by Indians who thought that he was English. Rowland and Sanders *Vol. III* 168–169.

231. McWilliams *Pénicaut Narrative* 163.

232. Crane *Southern Frontier* 170.

233. Rowland and Sanders *Vol. III* 194. It is interesting that Bienville refers to both "chiefs and headmen," possibly recognizing a distinction between hereditary chiefs and big-men.

234. Rowland and Sanders *Vol. III* 198, 208–209.

235. Ibid. 209.

CHAPTER THREE. EUROPEAN OCCUPATION

1. Ibid. 198.

2. McWilliams *Pénicaut Narrative* 167.

3. Ibid. 169.

4. Ibid. 168. By this time, Pénicaut had served in Louisiana for fifteen years and was proficient in the Mobilian trade language. He also seems to have acquired some grasp of the Natchez language from his time spent with the tribe. Ibid. 81, 105.

5. Ibid. xxxi.

6. Ibid. 169. Le Petite Gouffre, or Petit Gulf, is the site of the nineteenth-century river town of Rodney, Mississippi, some twenty-five miles above Natchez. J. F. H. Claiborne *Mississippi as a Province, Territory, and State* 109.

7. White et al. "Natchez Class and Rank," 382.

8. Andrew C. Albrecht "Indian-French Relations at Natchez" (*American Anthropologist* Vol. 48, No. 3, July–September, 1946) 334.

9. McWilliams *Pénicaut Narrative* 170–173.

10. Ibid. 174.

11. Giraud *Vol. II* 151–152.

12. Rowland and Sanders *Vol. III* 184–185. King Louis XIV died September 1, 1715.

13. Letters written by Bienville indicate that he received the news of the deaths of the four voyageurs between January 2 and 20, 1716. Rowland and Sanders *Vol. III* 191–200.

14. Pénicaut inflates the number of Natchez warriors to twelve hundred. McWilliams *Pénicaut Narrative* 177. Bienville's estimate is probably also too high, although the exact number of Natchez fighting-age men in 1716 is unknown.

15. De Richebourg in Swanton *Indian Tribes of the Lower Mississippi Valley* 197; Rowland and Sanders *Vol. II* 205, 214–216; Rowland and Sanders *Vol. III* 213.

16. The English translation of the De Richebourg Memoir in Swanton *Indian Tribes of the Lower Mississippi Valley* is taken from the *Historical Collections of Louisiana* 241–252, published between 1846 and 1875. Rowland and Sanders *Vol. III* 203. Giraud *Vol. I* 276; De Richebourg in Swanton *Indian Tribes of the Lower Mississippi Valley* 196–197.

17. Brain *Tunica Archaeology* 31, 298.

18. McWilliams *Pénicaut Narrative* 176.

19. Both Pénicaut and De Richebourg seem to indicate that Bienville's island encampment was fairly close to the Tunica village. Pénicaut says "we went to camp on an island in the middle of [the Tunicas'] bay." De Richebourg writes: "Bienville . . . had all the Tonikas assembled, and . . . told them . . . he was going to encamp on an island a third of a league from their village." However, the Tunica village was some fifty to sixty river miles downstream from the Natchez, seemingly too great a distance for the back-and-forth negotiations by canoe between the Natchez and the French that took place over the next few weeks. The position of Bienville's island on a 1731 map by Broutin correlates closely with that of Natchez Island and the latter location fits well with the rest of the narrative about the first Natchez war. McWilliams *Pénicaut Narrative* 176; De Richebourg in Swanton *Indian Tribes of the Lower Mississippi Valley* 198; Broutin *Carte Particuliere du Cours du Fleuve Missisipy ou St. Louis a la Louisiane depuis la Nouvelle Orleans*.

20. Joanne Ryan "Cultural resources Investigation of West Bank Mississippi River 16, Figure 4–23b.

21. De Richebourg in Swanton *Indian Tribes of the Lower Mississippi Valley* 198. Rowland and Sanders *Vol. III* 194. Pénicaut claims to have served as a Natchez interpreter during this campaign. McWilliams *Pénicaut Narrative* 181.

22. Pénicaut does not mention this first visit by the Natchez to the island.

23. De Richebourg in Swanton *Indian Tribes of the Lower Mississippi Valley* 198–199.

24. Ibid. 337–342.

25. Ibid. 199.

26. Ibid.

27. This list of Natchez chiefs is based upon the Natchez genealogical reconstruction in White et al. "Natchez Class and Rank," 382. Pénicaut says that the Grand Chief did not accompany the other chiefs to Bienville's island. McWilliams *Pénicaut Narrative* 178. Almost nothing is known about how names were bestowed on individuals in the Natchez tribe. Great Sun and Tattooed Serpent were apparently titles of office and not personal names. The Bearded, Old Hair, Yakstalchil, and Alahoflechia may have been personal names.

28. Gallay *Indian Slave Trade* 193.

29. De Richebourg in Swanton *Indian Tribes of the Lower Mississippi Valley* 200.

30. Pénicaut says that the Little Sun tried to pass off the head of a "feeble-minded person" as that of the chief of the White Earth settlement. McWilliams *Pénicaut Narrative* 178. Duclos says that the innocent man's head was that of a man who was dead or dying of disease. Rowland and Sanders *Vol. III* 210.

31. De Richebourg in Swanton *Indian Tribes of the Lower Mississippi Valley* 200–201.

32. Ibid. 201. Pénicaut's narrative does not mention the flood.

33. Oyelape has also been called "The Arrow." See Swanton *Indian Tribes of the Lower Mississippi Valley* 201n; White et al. "Natchez Class and Rank," 382. Despite De Richebourg's earlier statement that Bienville recognized all of the Natchez chiefs at the time that he took them hostage, the commander apparently was not aware that The Bearded was in his jail until the three suns informed him.

34. De Richebourg in Swanton *Indian Tribes of the Lower Mississippi Valley* 201–202.

35. Pailloux arrived in Louisiana in 1707 and is credited with constructing the French fort at Mobile. Rowland and Sanders *Vol. II* 44.

36. De Richebourg in Swanton *Indian Tribes of the Lower Mississippi Valley* 203.

37. This passage may have been written by Bienville; a previous entry says that De Richebourg was ill and left the island to return to Mobile on June 11. Ibid. 203–204.

38. Ibid. 202. Pénicaut indicates that The Arrow was the Grand Chief's nephew, while White et al. show him as a possible first cousin. McWilliams *Pénicaut Narrative* 178–179; White et al. "Natchez Class and Rank," 382.

39. De Richebourg in Swanton *Indian Tribes of the Lower Mississippi Valley* 202–204.

40. Ellwood S. Harrar and J. George Harrar *Guide to Southern Trees* 371–373.

41. De Richebourg in Swanton *Indian Tribes of the Lower Mississippi Valley* 204.

42. Ibid. 204; Dumont in Ibid. 205; Giraud *Vol. II* 155.

43. Rowland and Sanders *Vol. III* 161–162.

44. Swanton *Indian Tribes of the Lower Mississippi Valley* 337–342; Rowland and Sanders *Vol. II* 75, 126–127; Rowland and Sanders *Vol. III* 19–22, 113, 114, 128, 136, 139, 161.

45. Rowland and Sanders *Vol. II* 24; Rowland and Sanders *Vol. III* 33–34

46. Rowland and Sanders *Vol. III* 137.

47. Galloway "Natchez Matrilineal Kinship," 5–6.

48. Du Pratz in Swanton *Indian Tribes of the Lower Mississippi Valley* 106.

49. Linda Schele and David Freidel *A Forest of Kings* 194.

50. Rowland and Sanders *Vol. III* 207.

51. Elliott *The Fort of Natchez* 10, 10n, Figures 1 and 2.

52. Pénicaut places one of the La Loires at Natchez in 1718, while Swanton indicates that the year may have been 1719. McWilliams *Pénicaut Narrative* 215; Swanton *Indian Tribes of the Lower Mississippi Valley* 205n.

53. Rowland and Sanders *Vol. III* 538.

54. Gregory Waselkov "Exchange and Interaction since 1500" 692–693.

55. Ibid. 692–693.

56. Daniel H. Usner *Indians, Settlers, and Slaves* 30–31.

57. Archaeologists suspect that this settlement district was pro-English. Brown "Natchez Indian Archaeology" 12.

58. McWilliams *Pénicaut Narrative* 183; Giraud *Vol. II* 8, 52.

59. Susan Gibbs Lehmann "The Problems of Founding a Viable Colony" 360–366.

60. Waselkov "Exchange and Interaction since 1500," 693.

61. Economic theorists continue to debate the merits of John Law's *Système*. See François R. Velde "Government Equity and Money."

62. McWilliams *Pénicaut Narrative* 203; Giraud *Vol. II* 52.

63. Rowland and Sanders *Vol. II* 237, 240.

64. Ibid. 219; Giraud *Vol. II* 31–33.

65. Giraud *Vol. II* 79–82.

66. McWilliams *Pénicaut Narrative* 206.

67. Rowland and Sanders *Vol. II* 249–250.

68. Giraud *Vol. II* 163–168. Bienville's being prohibited from making presents to the Indians may have stemmed from accusations—later proved to be false—that he was pilfering merchandise from the king's warehouse at Mobile. Rowland and Sanders *Vol. III* 76–106.

69. Giraud *Vol. II* 66–67.

70. Velde "Government Equity and Money"; Mathé Allain "French Emigration Policies" 97; Carl A. Brasseau "The Image of Louisiana" 156–157.

71. James D. Hardy Jr. "The Transportation of Convicts to Colonial Louisiana" 116–117; Carl A. Brasseau "The Administration of Slave Regulations in French Louisiana" 209.

72. Le Page du Pratz's book *Histoire de la Louisiane* (three volumes, Paris: De Bure, Delaguette, Lambert 1758) has become the best-known primary source of information about the Natchez Indians. In 1774, an English language version of the book was printed to acquaint Britons with the country acquired from France in the Treaty of Paris. The English edition has been reprinted twice in the United States: *The History of Louisiana or of the Western Parts of Virginia and Carolina.* (Claitor's Publishing Division, Baton Rouge 1972) and Joseph G. Tregle Jr. (ed.) *The History of Louisiana or of the Western Parts of Virginia and Carolina* (Facsimile reproduction of the 1774 edition; published for the Louisiana American Bicentennial Commission by the Louisiana State University Press, Baton Rouge 1976). These two reprints are a combination of literal translation and passages that merely paraphrase Du Pratz's original French publication. Literal translations of portions of Du Pratz's French-language narrative are provided by John R. Swanton, Gordon Sayre, and Patricia Galloway. Swanton's excerpts are from his 1911 *Indian Tribes of the Lower Mississippi Valley.* Sayre's translation is available at his web site dedicated to Le Page du Pratz: http://www.uoregon.edu/~gsayre/LPDP.html. Galloway's translations stem from her work with the original manuscript in the Mississippi Department of Archives and History's collection. Whenever possible, I rely on the literal translations.

73. According to Stanley C. Arthur, former director of the Louisiana State Museum, Du Pratz departed from La Rochelle, France, on May 25, 1718, and arrived at Louisiana on August 25 of that year. Stanley C. Arthur in "Foreword," Du Pratz (Claitor's). In addition to the slaves he acquired in Louisiana, Du Pratz apparently arrived in the colony with one or more indentured servants. Brasseaux "The Administration of Slave Regulations" 210; Du Pratz (Claitor's) 19.

74. McWilliams *Pénicaut Narrative* 219.

75. Du Pratz in Swanton *Indian Tribes of the Lower Mississippi Valley* 340–342.

76. Patricia Galloway "Natchez Matrilineal Kinship," 5–7.

77. Swanton *Indian Tribes of the Lower Mississippi Valley* 185, 356.

78. Du Pratz (Claitor's) 18.

79. Ibid. 20. For a description of the commissaire-ordonnateur's duties, see Donald J. Lemieux "Some Legal and Practical Aspects of the Office of Commissaire-Ordonnateur" 395–407.

80. Du Pratz (Claitor's) 22.

81. Du Pratz (Claitor's) 26.

82. McWilliams *Pénicaut Narrative* 204.

83. Du Pratz (Claitor's) 25.

84. Galloway and Jackson "Natchez and Neighboring Groups," 609.

85. Du Pratz (Claitor's) 25.

86. Dumont in Swanton *Indian Tribes of the Lower Mississippi Valley* 210.

87. McWilliams *Pénicaut Narrative* 241–242.

88. Ibid. 213–214. Also see Rowland and Sanders *Vol. II* 421. In 1721, while living on his farm at the Natchez, André Pénicaut lost his eyesight due to what he called "an inflammation of the eyes." Colonial doctors being unable to affect a cure, Pénicaut returned to France in October 1721, leaving behind his wife, Marguerite Catherine Prévôt, and two children, René André (baptized 1708) and Jacque (baptized 1710). According to his journal, he intended to return to Louisiana once his eyesight had been restored; however, Paris surgeons were unable to bring back Pénicaut's vision. It is doubtful that he ever returned to Louisiana and the fate of his family is unknown. McWilliams *Pénicaut Narrative* xxxii–xxxiii, 252–254.

89. Ibid. 237.

90. Velde "Government Equity and Money" 26.

91. Du Pratz (Claitor's) 25.

92. Rowland and Sanders *Vol. II* 533.

93. Giraud *Vol. II* 156.

94. McWilliams *Pénicaut Narrative* 239.

95. Ibid. 239.

96. Dawson Phelps (translator and editor) "Narrative of the Hostilities" 3–4; McWilliams *Pénicaut Narrative* 238. St. Catherine Creek is named for the St. Catherine Land Company.

97. Jean-Baptiste Bénard de La Harpe *Historical Journal* 170.

98. Du Pratz (Claitor's) 29.

99. See Giraud *Vol. V*.

100. Henry P. Dart and Heloise H. Cruzat (trans.) "The Concession at Natchez" 389–391; Giraud *Vol. V* 169–170.

101. Rowland and Sanders *Vol. II* 398–399.

102. O'Neill *Charlevoix's Louisiana* xvi–xviii.

103. Ibid. 241n.

104. Ibid. 260–261.

105. Father Maximin's order is given as Augustinian in several references (Rowland and Sanders *Vol. II* 526, 536; Giraud *Vol. V* 393–394); however, Vogel identifies Maximin as a Carmelite. Claude L. Vogel "The Capuchins in French Louisiana" 45n. Vogel's statement agrees with the following quote from the online Catholic Encyclopedia: "To [missions in the Near Orient, Constantinople and Turkey, Armenia and Syria] was added in 1720 'a new mission in America in the district called Mississippi or Lusitania [Louisiana], which was offered by Captain Poyer in the name of the French company, but under certain conditions.' If indeed this mission was accepted, it does not seem to have been long prosperous." Catholic Encyclopedia.

106. Giraud *Vol. V* 58–84.

107. Baudier *The Catholic Church in Louisiana* 22.

108. Giraud *Vol. V* 393–394.

109. Rowland and Sanders *Vol. II* 28, 37, 45.

110. La Harpe *Historical Journal* 87, 113, 154, 167, 168, 171, 173, 394.

111. Ibid. 168–169.

112. Ibid. 87, 113, 154, 167, 168, 171, 173, 394.

113. Allan Kulikoff *Tobacco Slaves* 317.

114. Rowland and Sanders *Vol. II* 358, 367, 372–373. For the history of the Company of the Indies' transition from regency control back to private ownership, see Giraud *Vol. V* xi–xii, 3–14.

115. Du Pratz (Claitor's) 26–27.

116. Rowland and Sanders *Vol. II* 420.

117. W. K. McNeil "Introduction" 20–23.

118. Du Pratz (Claitor's) 96.

119. Giraud *Volume V* 392.

120. La Harpe *Historical Journal* 216–217; Du Pratz in Swanton *Indian Tribes of the Lower Mississippi Valley* 207–208; Phelps "Narrative of Hostilities," 9. The numbering of the Natchez wars is not always consistent; for example, Du Pratz refers to the 1722 war as the "first war with the Natchez." Du Pratz in Swanton *Indian Tribes of the Lower Mississippi Valley* 209.

121. Dumont in Swanton *Indian Tribes of the Lower Mississippi Valley* 209–210.

122. Rowland and Sanders *Vol. III* 379, 382; Atkinson *Spendid Land Splendid People* 31–34.

123. La Harpe *Historical Journal* 156.

124. Dumont in Swanton *Indian Tribes of the Lower Mississippi Valley* 210.

125. Phelps "Narrative of Hostilities," 5–6.

126. Ibid. 5–10. Broutin *Carte des environs du fort Rosalie aux Natchez* 1723. The smoothbore muskets used by the Natchez Indians and the French were effective at ranges up to fifty yards and might have been capable of hitting a target at ranges up to one hundred yards; however, the Hill of Madame, as shown on Broutin's 1723 map, was around six hundred yards from the closest targets on the St. Catherine concession. At that distance, the Indians' fire may have been intimidating but certainly not lethal. Grover Stanton Jr. and Clark Burkett, personal communications 11/24/2005.

127. La Harpe and Du Pratz in Swanton *Indian Tribes of the Lower Mississippi Valley* 207, 209.

128. Dawson Phelps "Narrative of Hostilities," 5–7.

129. Swanton *Indian Tribes of the Lower Mississippi Valley* 207.

130. Ibid.

131. The narrative of the hostilities by four officers of the St. Catherine concession says that La Rochelle was beheaded. Phelps "Narrative of Hostilities," 6. Du Pratz wrote that "[the Indians] killed him and carried off his scalp." Du Pratz in Swanton *Indian Tribes of the Lower Mississippi Valley* 210.

132. Phelps "Narrative of Hostilities," 6–7.

133. Swanton *Indian Tribes of the Lower Mississippi Valley* 139, 208.

134. Phelps "Narrative of Hostilities," 6–7.

135. Ibid. 7.

136. Ibid.

137. Du Pratz (Claitor's) 96; Du Pratz in Swanton *Indian Tribes of the Lower Mississippi Valley* 208.

138. Ibid. 208–208.

139. Phelps "Narrative of Hostilities," 9.

140. White et al. "Natchez Class and Rank," 382.

141. Rowland and Sanders *Vol. III* 327–329. Worm-screws were used to pull wadding from gun barrels.

142. Phelps "Narrative of Hostilities," 6. La Harpe puts the Indian casualties at seven. La Harpe in Swanton *Indian Tribes of the Lower Mississippi Valley* 207.

143. Phelps "Narrative of Hostilities," 5–10.

144. Dumont in Swanton *Indian Tribes of the Lower Mississippi Valley* 210.

145. Ibid. 210–211.

146. Ibid. 73.

147. Lauren C. Post "The Domestic Animals and Plants of French Louisiana" 559.

148. See Foster *The La Salle Expedition on the Mississippi River* 10–11. Chicken remains (only two pieces of bone) were identified in the Grand Village archaeology. John T. Penman "Appendix II. Faunal Remains" 154.

149. Du Pratz and Dumont in Swanton *Indian Tribes of the Lower Mississippi Valley* 211, 215.

150. Rowland and Sanders *Vol. III* 386.

151. Phelps "Narrative of Hostilities," 3.

152. "Coup" is a French term for a custom among some Native American groups of exhibiting bravery by touching or striking an enemy. *The American Heritage Dictionary*. An incident in which a horse belonging to the White Earth or Belle Isle concession was struck with a war club and its tail cut off is attributed to a coup strike by a member of the Tiou settlement. Dumont in Swanton *Indian Tribes of the Lower Mississippi Valley* 216.

153. Rowland and Sanders, *Vol. II* 374. Dumont indicates that Bienville had five boatloads of company soldiers, plus the Canadians. Dumont in Swanton *Indian Tribes of the Lower Mississippi Valley* 211. Complaints about the Natchez Indians had been received in New Orleans as early as May 1723 and Bienville was criticized for not responding sooner to these complaints. Rowland and Sanders *Vol. II* 320.

154. Dumont in Swanton *Indian Tribes of the Lower Mississippi Valley* 211.

155. Galloway and Kidwell "Choctaw in the East," 501, 513; Galloway *Choctaw Genesis* 197.

156. Dumont in Swanton *Indian Tribes of the Lower Mississippi Valley* 211–212.

157. Dumont in Swanton *Indian Tribes of the Lower Mississippi Valley* 212. The route followed by Bienville's army in the third Natchez war is analyzed in Ian W. Brown "The Location of the Historic Natchez Villages."

158. Du Pratz in Swanton *Indian Tribes of the Lower Mississippi Valley* 215.

159. Ibid. 212.

160. Ibid. 215. Fans of Le Page du Pratz (and I am one myself) may take exception to my assumption that he was trying to catch these Natchez Indians to enslave them; however, it is hard to draw any other conclusion. Dumont makes it clear that Bienville's orders were to "give no quarter to males," and females deemed unsuitable for labor or concubinage were summarily scalped and killed. Du Pratz doesn't say whether he was chasing females or males, but I imagine that they were females—otherwise they would have been shot. Ibid. 212, 213.

161. Ian W. Brown "Natchez Indian Archaeology," 75–79.

162. Ibid. 189–190.

163. Dumont in Swanton *Indian Tribes of the Lower Mississippi Valley* 213.

164. Ibid. 213–214.

165. Ibid. 200, 202; White et al. "Natchez Class and Rank," 382.

166. White et al. indicate that the Little Sun killed in 1723 (they put the event in 1724) was a different person from Bienville's Little Sun. White et al. "Natchez Class and Rank," 382.

167. Brown "Natchez Indian Archaeology," 81, 195; Joseph V. Frank III "The Rice Site" 32–41.

168. The activities of Payon's detachment, which had returned to the White Apple area, are not mentioned in the narratives.

169. Rowland and Sanders *Vol. III* 386.

170. Ibid. 386–387; Rowland and Sanders *Vol. II* 421–422.

171. Dumont in Swanton *Indian Tribes of the Lower Mississippi Valley* 214–215; Rowland and Sanders *Vol. III* 387. Free blacks were living in the West Indies by 1700 and a small number were in New Orleans by the 1720s. They were either manumitted by former owners or born to free women. In a union between a free man and an enslaved woman, the children were slaves. On the other hand, the children of an enslaved man and a free woman were free. Although there is no record of free black men serving in the French military before 1735, Bienville's fear that the free black man living with the Natchez might teach the Indians military tactics indicates that the man may have been a soldier. Donald E. Everett "Free Persons of Color in Colonial Louisiana" 226–230. Because of the growing number of Africans in Louisiana, France's King Louis XV, at the request of the Company of the Indies, revised the *Code Noir* or Black Code that had been adopted for the West Indies in 1685 and extended it to Louisiana in March 1724. The Code defined the relationship between whites and blacks in the colony. Allain "Slave Policies in French Louisiana" 174. Article VI of the Code recognizes the status of manumitted or free-born blacks. *Afro-American Almanac.*

172. Dumont in Swanton *Indian Tribes of the Lower Mississippi Valley* 214–215.

173. Rowland and Sanders *Vol. II* 422.

174. Du Pratz in Swanton *Indian Tribes of the Lower Mississippi Valley* 106.

175. Although Oyelape (sometimes called "the Arrow") isn't named in the French colonial narratives after his 1720 pardon, Du Pratz, who perhaps knew the Natchez as well as any European, characterized the chief of the White Apple settlement as "a man of great abilities." Du Pratz (Sayre), 242. In their genealogical reconstruction of the Natchez sun lineage, White et al. identify the Arrow as Old Hair's successor. White et al. "Natchez Class and Rank," 382. In characterizing Old Hair's successor, Swanton says that "the chief of White Apple seems to have been a man of experience and one enjoying the confidence of the nation to a high degree. Swanton *Indian Tribes of the Lower Mississippi Valley* 221.

176. Dumont in Swanton *Indian Tribes of the Lower Mississippi Valley* 215.

177. Ibid. 216. Dumont doesn't give the date of this incident, but it probably occurred in 1724 or 1725.

178. Broutin (sometimes Brontin), an engineer, succeeded Sieur de Liette as commander of the fort. De Liette had succeeded Barnaval, the commander during the third Natchez war. Broutin was in command of Fort Rosalie until the end of 1726. Ibid. 216; Giraud *Vol. V* 170.

179. Benjamin Dumont de Montigny. The war club illustrated by Dumont is reminiscent of the spontoons or pikes carried by military officers in the eighteenth century. A spontoon similar to the one drawn by Dumont (but not identical) was found at a Chickasaw archaeological site in the Tupelo, Mississippi, area. Brad Lieb, personal communication 6/15/2005. For comparison, Du Pratz illustrated a war club that he called a "war club of the ancient pattern, made entirely of wood," consisting of a curved shaft with a carved ball to give weight to the weapon's business end. Du Pratz in Swanton *Indian Tribes of the Lower Mississippi Valley* 111.

180. Dumont in Swanton *Indian Tribes of the Lower Mississippi Valley* 149–150.

181. Shea "Letter of La Source," 82; "Journal of the Voyage of Father Gravier," 140.

182. Du Pratz in Swanton *Indian Tribes of the Lower Mississippi Valley* 111, 112.

183. Translation by Patricia Galloway from the original French publication.

184. Dumont in Swanton *Indian Tribes of the Lower Mississippi Valley* 149–157.

185. Ibid.; Du Pratz (Sayre) Chapters 3–4; Rowland and Sanders *Vol. I* 128.

186. Rowland and Sanders *Vol. III* 387.

187. Ibid. 385. Following the reorganization of the Company of the Indies in the early 1720s, Bienville was recalled to France and eventually replaced as Governor of Louisiana by Etienne de Périer. Giraud *Vol. V* 32–33, 53–54.

188. Natchezan pottery, primarily Fatherland and Leland decorative types found by relic collectors on Chickasaw archaeological sites in the Tupelo area, argue for sustained contact between the Natchez and Chickasaw. John O'Hear, personal communication 11/24/2004; Robert Prospere, personal communication 6/7/2005.

189. Du Pratz (Claitor's) 73–74.

190. Rowland and Sanders *Vol. II* 404–405.

191. Ibid. 609–610, 647–648, 663.

192. Ibid. 647–648; Roland and Sanders Vol. III 530.

193. Ibid. 419–421; Rowland and Sanders Vol. III 520–522.

194. Ibid. 396–397.

195. Ibid. 658, 602, 639, 663.

196. Ibid. 390, 398–399.

197. Ibid. 526; Giraud *Vol. V* 390, 391.

198. Ibid. 402, 492–493.

199. Ibid. 503–504, 547, 620.

200. Ibid. 525; Giraud Vol. V 393.

201. Ibid. 525.

202. The commanders at Fort Rosalie with their approximate years of service were: Bienville (1716–1717), Pailloux (1717–1718), Blondel (1718), Barnaval (1718–1723), Desliettes (1724–1725), Broutin (1724–1725), Du Tisné (1726–1729), Merveilleux (1726–1729), and Chépart (1729). Swanton *Indian Tribes of the Lower Mississippi Valley* 205–217; Giraud *Vol. V* 394–396.

203. Dart and Cruzat "The Concession at Natchez," 390–391; Rowland and Sanders *Vol. III* 496.

204. Swanton *Indian Tribes of the Lower Mississippi Valley* 220–221.

205. Two other post-1729 Natchez chiefs were Saint-Cosme, named for the tribe's former priest, and the new Tattooed Serpent. Ibid. 220–221; Charlevoix in Swanton *Indian Tribes of the Lower Mississippi Valley* 245–246.

CHAPTER FOUR. THE REBELLION

1. Rowland and Sanders *Vol. II* 567–569.

2. Dart and Cruzat "The Concession at Natchez," 391.

3. O'Neill *Charlevoix* 81.

4. Swanton *Indian Tribes of the Lower Mississippi Valley* 226.

5. Sometimes given as "Chopart" or "Detchéparre."

6. Swanton *Indian Tribes of the Lower Mississippi Valley* 221.

7. Dumont in Ibid. 221–222.

8. Du Pratz (Claitor's) 70–71; Swanton *Indian Tribes of the Lower Mississippi Valley* 221–222.

9. Du Pratz (Sayre) 231–237.

10. Rowland, Sanders, and Galloway *Vol. IV* 13–14, 17–18, 20–21, 25.

11. Ibid. 67, 144.

12. Rowland and Sanders *Vol. I* 54.

13. Swanton *Indian Tribes of the Lower Mississippi Valley* Plate 7a. New York State Museum "Batteau Fact Sheet."

14. O'Neill *Charlevoix* 83; Giraud *Vol. V* 117.

15. O'Neill *Charlevoix* 83.

16. Du Pratz (Sayre), 266.

17. Rowland and Sanders *Vol. I* 58, 62; O'Neill *Charlevoix* 81; Du Pratz (Sayre) 252–253.

18. Rowland and Sanders *Vol. I* 128.

19. Tattooed Arm was the sister of the Tattooed Serpent and Great Sun who died in 1725 and 1728 respectively. White et al. "Natchez Class and Rank," 382.

20. Du Pratz (Sayre) 254–255.

21. According to Du Pratz, who probably got his information from Tattooed Arm, the White Apple chief held a series of council meetings in which he convinced the other leaders of the Natchez tribe, including the Great Sun, to attack the French. Du Pratz (Sayre) 234–243.

22. Rowland and Sanders *Vol. I* 62.

23. The four principal references for the 1729 massacre are Du Pratz, Dumont, Le Petit, and Charlevoix. Du Pratz and Dumont were in New Orleans at the time of the massacre and their accounts were apparently compiled from the statements of survivors. Du Pratz also interviewed Tattooed Arm, the ranking female chief, following her capture by the French in 1731. Du Pratz (Claitor's) 87; Dumont and Du Pratz in Swanton *Indian Tribes of the Lower Mississippi Valley* 224–230; Du Pratz (Sayre) 252–261. The Jesuit missionary Mathurin Le Petit was with the Choctaws at the time of the Natchez Massacre. His account, written in New Orleans on July 12, 1730, was also compiled from survivors' reports. Richard H. Hart Mauthurin Le Petit "The Natchez Massacre"; Charlevoix was in France in 1729. His *Histoire et Description Général de la Nouvelle France* was published in 1744, prior to both Dumont's (1753) and Du Pratz's (1758) histories, and appears to be based largely on the Le Petit narrative. O'Neill *Charlevoix* xiii, xix, xixn, xx, 81–85.

24. Du Pratz (Sayre) 255–258; O'Neill *Charlevoix* 82–84; Swanton *Indian Tribes of the Lower Mississippi Valley* 225–226.

25. Swanton *Indian Tribes of the Lower Mississippi Valley* 227–229.

26. Rowland and Sanders *Vol. I* 122–126. Philibert's final total of 144 men included six who were killed in the subsequent campaign against the Natchez.

27. Rowland and Sanders, *Vol. I* 62; O'Neill *Charlevoix* 82.

28. O'Neill *Charlevoix* 84, 85n.

29. From a letter from Governor Perier, written in March 1730. Rowland and Sanders *Vol. I* 63.

30. Rowland and Sanders *Vol. I* 54; O'Neill *Charlevoix* 82–83.

31. Du Pratz (Sayre) 261.

32. Dart and Cruzat "The Concession at Natchez," 381; O'Neill *Charlevoix* 85; Du Pratz (Sayre) 261.

33. Swanton *Indian Tribes of the Lower Mississippi Valley* 229.

34. O'Neill *Charlevoix* 84.

35. Le Petit (Hart) 20.

36. O'Neill *Charlevoix* 85–86; Swanton *Indian Tribes of the Lower Mississippi Valley* 333.

37. Rowland and Sanders *Vol. I* 54, 55.

38. Ibid. 63; Hart Mauthurin Le Petit "The Natchez Massacre" 19.

39. Rowland and Sanders *Vol. I* 69, 73.

40. Dumont in Swanton *Indian Tribes of the Lower Mississippi Valley* 234.

41. Hart Mauthurin Le Petit "The Natchez Massacre" 17; O'Neill *Charlevoix* 81.

42. Hart Mauthurin Le Petit "The Natchez Massacre" 19; O'Neill *Charlevoix* 81; Du Pratz (Sayre) 250.

43. Swanton *Indian Tribes of the Lower Mississippi Valley* 223.

44. Du Pratz (Claitor's) 87.

45. Du Pratz indicates that the Natchez chiefs purposefully withheld the details of the plot from the women of the tribe. Du Pratz (Sayre) 242.

46. Du Pratz (Sayre) 252 255.

47. Swanton *Indian Tribes of the Lower Mississippi Valley* 224.

48. Rowland and Sanders *Vol. III* 580–581.

49. Rowland and Sanders *Vol. I* 61.

50. Giraud *Vol. V* 54; Rowland, Sanders, and Galloway *Vol. IV* 39.

51. One of those who brought the word about the Yazoo massacre was Father Stephen d'Outreleau, a Jesuit missionary to the Illinois who had come to visit Father Souel. The priest and some of his party were attacked by Yazoos and managed to escape in a canoe. Hart Mauthurin Le Petit "The Natchez Massacre" 21–22; O'Neill *Charlevoix* 86–87.

52. Rowland and Sanders *Vol. I* 65.

53. O'Neill *Charlevoix* 89–90. The small tribes on the lower Mississippi included the Bayogoula, Colapissa, and Houma. Rowland, Sanders, and Galloway *Vol. IV* 33; see Ives Goddard et al. "Small Tribes of the Western Southwest" 174–190.

54. Rowland and Sanders *Vol. I* 71; Ives Goddard "Washa, Chawasha, and Yakni-Chito" in *Handbook of North American Indians, Southeast* 188–190.

55. O'Neill *Charlevoix* 93–94; Giraud *Vol. V* 350.

56. Dumont in Swanton *Indian Tribes of the Lower Mississippi Valley* 234.

57. O'Neill *Charlevoix* 91.

58. Rowland and Sanders *Vol. I* 66n, 98.

59. Ibid. 65–66; Du Pratz (Sayre) 268–269. Louboey is sometimes spelled "Loubois."

60. Dumont in Swanton *Indian Tribes of the Lower Mississippi Valley* 236.

61. Giraud *Vol. V* 409.

62. Du Pratz (Sayre) 268.

63. See Swanton *Indian Tribes of the Lower Mississippi Valley* 111–123.

64. Rowland and Sanders *Vol. I* 68; Le Petit (Hart), 28; Swanton *Indian Tribes of the Lower Mississippi Valley* 237.

65. Ferdinand Claiborne (trans.), J. F. H. Claiborne 46–47, 47n.

66. Steponaitis et al. LMS Archives Online, 26-K-23, 7/15/2005, p. 1.

67. Swanton *Indian Tribes of the Lower Mississippi Valley* 217.

68. John A Green "Governor Perier's Expedition Against the Natchez Indians" 560.

69. Hart Mauthurin Le Petit "The Natchez Massacre" 27; Du Pratz (Sayre) 276–279.

70. Du Pratz (Sayre) 282.

71. Total population numbers are lacking; however, Swanton's demographic projections for Lower Mississippi Valley tribes (including the Natchez) at the beginning of the eighteenth century consistently estimate that warriors comprised about 29 percent of a tribe's total number. Using this as a guide, a population with 500 warriors could be estimated to have about 1,224 women and children and a total population of about 1,724. Swanton *Indian Tribes of the Lower Mississippi Valley* 40, 43.

72. Du Pratz (Sayre) 279–280.

73. Rowland and Sanders *Vol. I* 68.

74. O'Neill *Charlevoix* 110–111, 113; White et al. "Natchez Class and Rank," 382.

75. Du Pratz (Sayre) 284–285.

76. A detailed journal of Louboey's 1730 Natchez expedition by an anonymous French officer is published in Ferdinand Claiborne (trans.) J. F. H. Claiborne 46–47.

77. A French map of the siege of the Natchez forts shows Tunica and Colapissa camps near the French positions. Neitzel "The Grand Village of the Natchez Revisited," Plate 2a.

78. The Choctaw who fired on the Natchez was reported to have recognized a man who had killed one of his kinsmen. Ferdinand Claiborne (trans.) J. F. H. Claiborne 46.

79. Ibid. 46; O'Neill *Charlevoix* 104.

80. Du Pratz (Sayre) 289–290; Swanton *Indian Tribes of the Lower Mississippi Valley* 239.

81. Ferdinand Claiborne (trans.) J. F. H. Claiborne 46.

82. Ibid. 46–47.

83. Walter O'Meara *Guns at the Forks* 70–71; Samuel Wilson Jr. "Colonial Fortifications" 423.

84. Joseph L Peyser "The Chickasaw Wars" 13, 14, 15, 17, 20, 21; Donald B. Chidsey *The French and Indian War* 161; Rick Brainard "The Divisions of 18th Century Armies."

85. Neitzel "The Grand Village of the Natchez Revisited," 51–56; John D. Combes "Appendix V. Resistivity Survey at the Fatherland Site" 168–175.

86. O'Neill *Charlevoix* 98.

87. A French military map of the 1730 siege shows a battery placement on top of a mound. Neitzel "The Grand Village of the Natchez Revisited," 55, Plate IIa; Neitzel "Archeology of the Fatherland Site: The Grand Village of the Natchez," 18.

88. Ferdinand Claiborne (trans.) J. F. H. Claiborne 47.

89. Ibid.

90. Ibid.

91. Rowland and Sanders *Vol. I* 79.

92. Du Pratz (Sayre) 290–291.

93. Ibid. 80; O'Neill *Charlevoix* 100. According to the anonymous French officer's narrative, three of the Africans, recognized as participants in the Natchez attack of February 22, were turned over to the French. One of the Africans was subsequently killed while attempting to escape. Ferdinand Claiborne (trans.) J. F. H. Claiborne 47.

94. Du Pratz (Sayre) 291–293. Note that Du Pratz refers to the Indians as "Naturals" in an era when most European writers referred to them as "Savages."

95. The French officer's narrative gives the date of the Natchez escape as the night of February 25–26, which is probably correct. Ferdinand Claiborne (trans.) J. F. H. Claiborne 47. According to Charlevoix, the Natchez made their escape on the night of February 28–29. O'Neill *Charlevoix* 100.

96. Swanton *Indian Tribes of the Lower Mississippi Valley* 241.

97. Ferdinand Claiborne (trans.) J. F. H. Claiborne 47. A French boy among the hostages at the Natchez was carried away into slavery by the Choctaws because Louboey had been reluctant to offer more than one blanket in trade for him. Rowland and Sanders *Vol. I* 107–108.

98. Du Pratz (Sayre) 193–295.

99. While the main Choctaw force had been at the Natchez, a smaller force combined with Chakchiuma warriors had attacked the Yazoo and liberated three French women and three children. Rowland and Sanders *Vol. I* 97, 100, 103, 107, 110–112.

100. Du Pratz (Sayre) 295. The second Fort Rosalie (sometimes called the "Provisional Fort") was placed on a bluff a short distance to the southwest of the original fort and closer to the Mississippi River. Elliott *The Fort of Natchez* 16.

101. Rowland, Sanders, and Galloway *Vol. IV* 36–37; Rowland and Sanders *Vol. I* 70, 74, 75, 119–120.

102. Rowland and Sanders *Vol. I* 70.

103. Swanton *Indian Tribes of the Lower Mississippi Valley* 242.

104. Rowland and Sanders *Vol. I* 119.

105. Ibid. 70, 70n.

106. Ibid. 121.

107. Rowland, Sanders, and Galloway *Vol. IV* 37; Du Pratz (Sayre) 300–301.

108. Du Pratz (Sayre) 299–300.

109. Rowland, Sanders, and Galloway *Vol. IV* 40–41.

110. Ibid. 37.

111. Du Pratz (Sayre) 300–301.

112. Green "Perier's Expedition," 551.

113. Ibid. 551; O'Neill *Charlevoix* 107, 109.

114. Green "Perier's Expedition," 552. Perier's brother led the marines.

115. Ibid. 552.

116. Ibid. 553.

117. Ibid. 553. Charlevoix says that the ambushed party numbered twenty-four men and that sixteen were killed or wounded. O'Neill *Charlevoix* 108.

118. Green "Perier's Expedition," 553.

119. O'Neill *Charlevoix* 109.

120. Green "Perier's Expedition," 575.

121. Ibid. 553–554.

122. Ibid. 554.

123. Ibid. 553–554. Perier's report gives the mound's distance from the fort as 120 *toises*, or fathoms, a unit of measurement equal to six feet.

124. Ibid. 565–568, 574; Steponaitis et al. LMS Online, 7 –13–2005, 25-J-3, pp. 1–2.

125. These were African workers captured in the Natchez raid on the work crew near Fort Rosalie. Green "Perier's Expedition," 555.

126. Ibid. 555; O'Neill *Charlevoix* 109. African hostages later freed by the Natchez told the French that some of the tribesmen were away hunting when the French forces arrived. Green "Perier's Expedition," 556.

127. Green "Perier's Expedition," 555.

128. Ibid. 556; O'Neill *Charlevoix* 110. Although the messenger for the Natchez is not identified, his ability to speak French might indicate that this was Ette-actal, who would have learned to speak some French while in Bienville's service.

129. O'Neill *Charlevoix* 110–112; Green "Perier's Expedition," 556.

130. O'Neill *Charlevoix* 112; Green "Perier's Expedition," 556.

131. O'Neill *Charlevoix* 113–114; Green "Perier's Expedition," 556.

132. O'Neill *Charlevoix* 114; Green "Perier's Expedition," 556–557.

133. Green "Perier's Expedition," 557.

134. Rowland, Sanders, and Galloway *Vol. IV* 57–58.

135. Giraud *Vol. V* 430–431.

136. Rowland and Sanders *Vol. I* 20.

137. Rowland, Sanders, and Galloway *Vol. IV* 81.

138. Rowland and Sanders *Vol. III* 12, 540–556.

139. Giraud *Vol. V* 428. In addition to the voyage of the *Venus*, Giraud indicates that a small number of Natchez Indians was shipped out of New Orleans on the *Gironde* in January 1731, also bound for Santo Domingo. The prisoners on the *Gironde* revolted while at sea and were apparently all killed by the ship's crew. The *Gironde* prisoners could not have been part of the group who surrendered at Fort Valeur in the Tensas Basin, since the Fort Valeur group did not reach New Orleans until February 5, 1731. O'Neill *Charlevoix* 114.

140. Rowland and Sanders *Vol. III* 581.

141. O'Neill *Charlevoix* 115.

142. Rowland, Sanders, and Galloway *Vol. IV* 70.

143. Ibid. 76–80. According to Perier's official report to the Ministry of Marine, the Flour chief led the attack on the Tunica. Perier relates the story of the Natchez attack on the Tunica as though he and the Tunica chief genuinely hoped that the Natchez would settle peacefully at the Tunica, although, given past events, such a conciliatory attitude on the part of the governor seems highly unlikely. Rowland, Sanders, and Galloway *Vol. IV* 102–103. Charlevoix's account of this incident is taken from Perier's version of what happened. O'Neill *Charlevoix* 116–117.

144. Charlevoix, 117–118; Du Pratz (Sayre) 271–274.

145. Rowland, Sanders, and Galloway *Vol. IV* 112, 113n.

146. Ibid. 80; O'Neill *Charlevoix* 117.

147. Rowland, Sanders, and Galloway *Vol. IV* 80.

148. Rowland and Sanders *Vol. I* 314.

149. Ibid. 167, 196; Rowland, Sanders, and Galloway *Vol. IV* 122.

150. Rowland and Sanders *Vol. I* 196–197; Rowland and Sanders *Vol. III* 622.

151. Rowland and Sanders *Vol. I* 208 and *Vol. III* 622–624.

152. Ibid. *Vol. I* 227–228.

153. Ibid. *Vol. III* 708–709.

154. Ibid. 755–756.

155. John Dyson "In Search of Yaneka."

156. Joseph V. Frank III "In Defense of Hutchins's Natchez Indian" 7–12; Claiborne *Mississippi as a Province, Territory, and State* 123, 127n; Joseph V. Frank III, personal communication 6/7/2005.

157. Rowland and Sanders *Vol. I* 273 and *Vol. III* 632–635; Atkinson *The Chickasaw Indians to Removal* 38–40.

158. Swanton *Indian Tribes of the Lower Mississippi Valley* 251, 253, 254.

159. Rowland and Sanders *Vol. I* 256; Swanton *Indian Tribes of the Lower Mississippi Valley* 251.

160. Rowland and Sanders *Vol. I* 198–200.

161. Peyser "The Chickasaw Wars," 1–25.

CONCLUSION

1. Swanton *Indian Tribes of the Lower Mississippi Valley* 252.

2. Ibid. 255–256.

3. Ibid. 255; Rowland and Sanders *Vol. IV* 168.

4. Swanton *Indian Tribes of the Lower Mississippi Valley* 253.

5. Ibid. 274; Jeffrey P. Brain et al. "Tunica, Biloxi, and Ofo" 588; Galloway and Jackson "Natchez and Neighboring Groups," 600; Avoyel-Taensa Chief Romes Antoine personal communication 3/11/2004.

6. Rowland and Sanders *Vol. III* 183, 536; Swanton *Indian Tribes of the Lower Mississippi Valley* 271–272.

7. Chief Romes Antoine, personal communication 3/11/2004.

8. Walker "Creek Confederacy Before Removal," 389–390; Gregory E. Dowd "The American Revolution to the Mid-nineteenth Century" 145–146; Galloway and Jackson "The Natchez and Their Neighbors," 611.

9. Galloway and Jackson "The Natchez and Their Neighbors," 611; Walker "Creek Confederacy Before Removal," 390; Duane H. King "Cherokee in the West: History Since 1776," 375.

10. Galloway and Jackson "The Natchez and Their Neighbors," 612–613; Duane H. King "Cherokee in the West: History Since 1776," 362, 366–367.

11. Hiram F. Gregory Jr. "Survival and Maintenance Among Louisiana Tribes" 655.

12. Swanton *Indian Tribes of the Lower Mississippi Valley* 256.

13. Galloway and Jackson "The Natchez and Their Neighbors," 611–613; James F. Barnett Jr. *The Natchez Indians* 38.

14. Ibid.

15. Wendall H. Oswalt and Sharlotte Neely "The Natchez: Sophisticated Farmers of the Deep South" 498–499.

16. See http://groups.msn.com/NatchezNation.

BIBLIOGRAPHY

Afro-American Almanac. http://www.toptags.com/aama/docs/lublkcodes.htm June 4, 2005.

Albrecht, Andrew C. "The Location of the Historic Natchez Villages." *The Journal of Mississippi History* Vol. VI, No. 2, April 1944.

———. "Indian-French Relations at Natchez." *American Anthropologist* Vol. 48, No. 3, July–September 1946.

Allain, Mathé. "French Emigration Policies: Louisiana, 1699–1715." In Glenn R. Conrad (ed.) *The Louisiana Purchase Bicentennial Series in Louisiana History: Volume 1, The French Experience in Louisiana,* 106–114. Center for Louisiana Studies, University of Southwestern Louisiana, Lafayette 1995.

———. "Slave Policies in French Louisiana." In Glenn R. Conrad (ed.) *The Louisiana Purchase Bicentennial Series in Louisiana History: Volume 1, The French Experience in Louisiana,* 174–182. Center for Louisiana Studies, University of Southwestern Louisiana, Lafayette 1995.

The American Heritage Dictionary of the English Language, 4th ed. Houghton Mifflin Co. Boston, MA 2000.

Anonymous. *Plan du Fort des Savages Natchez 1731.* In the Bibliothéque nationale de France, Paris.

Arthur, Stanley C. "Foreword." In Antoine Simone Le Page Du Pratz *The History of Louisiana or of the Western Parts of Virginia and Carolina.* Originally published 1774, reprint by Claitor's Publishing Division, Baton Rouge 1972.

Atkinson, James R. *Splendid Land Splendid People: The Chickasaw Indians to Removal.* The University of Alabama Press, Tuscaloosa 2004.

Barnett, James F., Jr. "A New Building Location at the Fatherland Site (Grand Village of the Natchez)." *Mississippi Archaeology* Vol. 19, No. 1, June 1984.

———. "Natchez House Reconstruction, Grand Village of the Natchez Indians." On file, Grand Village of the Natchez Indians, 1988, revised 1996 and 2002.

———. *The Natchez Indians.* Mississippi Department of Archives and History Popular Report 1998, revised 2002.

Barry, John M. *Rising Tide: The Great Mississippi Flood of 1927 and How It Changed America.* Simon and Schuster 1997.

Baudier, Roger. *The Catholic Church in Louisiana.* A. W. Hyatt, New Orleans 1939.

Bell, Ann Linda (trans.) and Patricia Galloway (annotations). "Minet: Voyage Made from Canada Inland Going Southward during the Year 1682, By Order of Monsieur Colbert, Minister of State."

In Robert S. Weddle, Mary C. Morkovsky, Patricia Galloway (eds.) *Three Primary Documents, La Salle, the Mississippi, and the Gulf*, 29–68. Texas A&M University Press, College Station 1987.

Brain, Jeffrey P. "The Natchez Paradox." *Ethnology* Vol. 10, No. 2, 1971.

———. "Late Prehistoric Settlement Patterning in the Yazoo Basin and Natchez Bluff Regions of the Lower Mississippi Valley." In Bruce D. Smith (ed.) *Mississippian Settlement Patterns*, 331–368. Academic Press, New York 1978.

———. "La Salle at the Natchez: An Archaeological and Historical Perspective." In Patricia Galloway (ed.) *La Salle and His Legacy: Frenchmen and Indians in the Lower Mississippi Valley*, 49–59. University Press of Mississippi, Jackson 1982.

———. "Introduction: Update of the De Soto Studies Since the United States De Soto Expedition Commission Report." In John R. Swanton *Final Report of the United States De Soto Expedition Commission*, xi–xlvi. Smithsonian Institution Press, Washington D.C. 1985.

———. *Tunica Archaeology*. Peabody Museum of Archaeology and Ethnology, Harvard University, Cambridge 1988.

———. "Winterville: Late Prehistoric Culture Contact in the Lower Mississippi Valley." Archaeological Report No. 23, Mississippi Department of Archives and History, Jackson 1989.

Brain, Jeffrey P., Ian W. Brown, and Vincas P. Steponaitis. *Archaeology of the Natchez Bluffs*. Forthcoming. Steponaitis personal communication 3/24/2006.

Brain, Jeffrey P., George Roth, and Willem J. de Reuse. "Tunica, Biloxi, and Ofo." In William C. Sturtevant (gen. ed.) and Raymond D. Fogelson (vol. ed.) *Handbook of North American Indians, Vol. 14, Southeast*, 586–597. Smithsonian Institution, Washington, D.C. 2004.

Brainard, Rick. "The Divisions of 18th Century Armies and Their Weapons." http://www.history1700s.com/articles/article1115.shtml.

Brasseaux, Carl A. "The Image of Louisiana and the Failure of Voluntary French Emigration, 1683–1731." In Glenn R. Conrad (ed.) *The Louisiana Purchase Bicentennial Series in Louisiana History, Volume 1, The French Experience in Louisiana*, 153–162. Center for Louisiana Studies, University of Southwestern Louisiana, Lafayette 1995.

———. "The Moral Climate of French Colonial Louisiana, 1699–1763." In Glenn R. Conrad (ed.) *The Louisiana Purchase Bicentennial Series in Louisiana History, Vol. I, The French Experience in Louisiana*, 525–537. Center for Louisiana Studies, University of Southwestern Louisiana, Lafayette 1995.

———. "The Administration of Slave Regulations in French Louisiana, 1724–1766." In Glenn R. Conrad (ed.) *The Louisiana Purchase Bicentennial Series in Louisiana History, Vol. I, The French Experience in Louisiana*, 209. Center for Louisiana Studies, University of Southwestern Louisiana, Lafayette 1995.

Brightman, Robert A. and Pamela S. Wallace "Chickasaw." In William C. Sturtevant (gen. ed.) and Raymond D. Fogelson (vol. ed.) *Handbook of North American Indians, Southeast, Volume 14*, 478–495. Smithsonian Institution, Washington, D.C. 2004.

Brose, David S. "From the Southeastern Ceremonial Complex to the Southern Cult: You Can't Tell the Players without a Program.'" In Patricia Galloway (ed.) *The Southeastern Ceremonial Complex: Artifacts and Analysis, The Cottonlandia Conference*, 27–37. University of Nebraska Press, Lincoln 1989.

Broutin, Ignace-François. *Carte des environs du fort Rosalie aux Natchez 1723*. Bibliothéque nationale de France. http://visualiseur.bnf.fr/Visualiseur?Destination=Gallica&O=IFN-6700314.

———.*Carte Particuliere du Cours du Fleuve Missisipy ou St. Louis a la Louisiane depuis la Nouvelle Orleans jusqu'aux Natchez, leveé par setime en 1721, 1726, 1731, et dressée au mois d'Aoust 1731, par Broutin*. Bibliothéque nationale de France, Paris.

Brown, Ian W. "The Location of the Historic Natchez Villages." Paper on file at the Grand Village of the Natchez Indians 1973.

———. "Natchez Indian Archaeology: Culture Change and Stability in the Lower Mississippi Valley." Archaeological Report No. 15, Mississippi Department of Archives and History, Jackson 1985.

———. "Natchez Indians and the Remains of a Proud Past." In Noel Polk (ed.) *Natchez Before 1830*, 8. University Press of Mississippi, Jackson 1989.

———. "The Calumet Ceremony in the Southeast and Its Archaeological Manifestations." *American Antiquity* Vol. 54, No. 2, 1989.

———. "Plaquemine Culture in the Natchez Bluffs Region of Mississippi." In Mark Rees and Patrick Livingood (eds.) *Plaquemine Archaeology*, 147–149. The University of Alabama Press, Tuscaloosa 2006.

Brown, Ian W. (ed.). "Excavations at the Anna Site (22Ad500), Adams County, Mississippi: A Preliminary Report, with Contributions by Virgil R. Beasley, Tony Boudreaux, Richard S. Fuller, and John C. Hall." Gulf Coast Survey, The University of Alabama 1997.

Catholic Encyclopedia. http://www.newadvent.org/cathen/03354a.htm.

Chateaubriand, François-René de, and Raymer Heppenstall (trans.). *Atala and René*. Oxford University Press, London 1963.

Chidsey, Donald B. *The French and Indian War*. Crown Publishing, New York 1969.

Claiborne, J. F. H. *Mississippi as a Province, Territory, and State with Biographical Notices of Eminent Citizens*. The Reprint Company, Spartanburg, SC 1978.

Clayton, Lawrence A., Vernon J. Knight Jr., and Edward C. Moore (eds.). *Volumes I and II, The De Soto Chronicles: The Expedition of Hernando De Soto to North America in 1539–1543*. The University of Alabama Press, Tuscaloosa 1993.

Combes, John D. "Appendix V. Resistivity Survey at the Fatherland Site." Archaeological Report No. 12, Mississippi Department of Archives and History, Jackson 1983.

Crane, Verner W. *The Southern Frontier: 1670–1732*. Published 1929, reprinted by University of Alabama Press, Tuscaloosa 2004.

Crawford, James M. *The Mobilian Trade Language*. University of Tennessee Press, Knoxville 1978.

D'Anville, Jean Baptiste. *Essai d'une Carte de la Louisiane*. Bibliotheque Nationale. http://images. bnf.fr/jsp/index.jsp?destination=afficherListeCliches.jsp&origine=rechercherListeCliches. jsp&contexte=resultatRechercheSimple.

Dart, Henry P., and Heloise H. Cruzat (trans.). "The Concession at Natchez" *The Louisiana Historical Quarterly*, Vol. 8, No. 3, July 1925.

Dowd, Gregory E. "The American Revolution to the Mid-nineteenth Century." In William C. Sturtevant (gen. ed.) and Raymond D. Fogelson (vol. ed.) *Handbook of North American Indians: Vol. 14, Southeast*, 139–151. Smithsonian Institution, Washington 2004.

De Montigny, Benjamin Dumont. http://www.louisiana.culture.fr/en/som.html; http://www.louisiana.culture.fr/en/jds/jds_nat_tab_zoo.html#.

Du Pratz, Antoine Simon Le Page. *Histoire de la Louisiane*. Paris: De Bure, Delaguette, Lambert 1758, collection of the Mississippi Department of Archives and History.

————. *The History of Louisiana or of the Western Parts of Virginia and Carolina.* Originally published 1774, reprint by Claitor's Publishing Division, Baton Rouge 1972.

Du Pratz, Antoine Simone Le Page, and Joseph G. Tregle Jr. (ed.). *The History of Louisiana or of the Western Parts of Virginia and Carolina.* Facsimile reproduction of the 1774 edition, published for the Louisiana American Bicentennial Commission by the Louisiana State University Press, Baton Rouge 1976.

Du Pratz, Antoine Simone Le Page, and Gordon Sayre (trans.). *Histoire de la Louisiane.* Originally published in three volumes. Paris: De Bure, Delaguette, Lambert 1758. Available online at http://www.uoregon.edu/~gsayre/LPDP.html.

Dupré, Céline. *Dictionary of Canadian Biography Online.* http://www.biographi.ca/EN/ShowBioPrintable.asp?BioId=34801.

Dyson, John. "In Search of Yaneka." Paper presented at the 2005 meeting of the Mississippi Archaeological Association, Vidalia, Louisiana, March 5, 2005.

Elliott, Charles. "Bienville's English Turn Incident: Anecdotes Influencing History." *Gulf South Historical Review, The Journal of the Gulf South Historical Association*, Vol. 14, No. 2, Spring 1999.

Elliott, Jack D., Jr. *The Fort of Natchez and the Colonial Origins of Mississippi.* Eastern National 1998.

Everett, Donald E. "Free Persons of Color in Colonial Louisiana." In Glenn R. Conrad (ed.) *The Louisiana Purchase Bicentennial Series in Louisiana History: Volume 1, The French Experience in Louisiana*, 226–248. Center for Louisiana Studies, University of Southwestern Louisiana, Lafayette 1995.

Fagan, Brian M. *The Little Ice Age: How Climate Made History, 1300–1850.* Basic Books, New York 2000.

Ford, James A. "Analysis of Indian Village Site Collections from Louisiana and Mississippi." Anthropological Study, Department of Conservation, Louisiana Geological Survey No. 2, 1936.

Foster, William C. (ed.). *The La Salle Expedition on the Mississippi River: A Lost Manuscript of Nicolas de La Salle, 1682.* Texas State Historical Association, Austin 2003.

————. "Appendix A. Official Report of the Taking Possession of the Acansa Country, 13th and 14th March, 1682." In William C. Foster (ed.) *The La Salle Expedition on the Mississippi River: A Lost Manuscript of Nicolas de La Salle, 1682*, 127–130. Texas State Historical Association, Austin 2003.

————. "Appendix B. Official Report of the Taking Possession at the Mouth of the Sea or the Gulf of Mexico." In William C. Foster (ed.) *The La Salle Expedition on the Mississippi River: A Lost Manuscript of Nicolas de La Salle, 1682*, 131–136. Texas State Historical Association, Austin 2003.

————. "Appendix C. La Salle's 1682 Mississippi River Expedition Itinerary." In William C. Foster (ed.) *The La Salle Expedition on the Mississippi River: A Lost Manuscript of Nicolas de La Salle, 1682*, 137–147. Texas State Historical Association, Austin 2003.

Fowler, Melvin L. "Cahokia and the American Bottom: Settlement Archaeology." In Bruce D. Smith (ed.) *Mississippian Settlement Patterns*, 466–478. Academic Press, New York.

Frank, Joseph V., III. "In Defense of Hutchins's Natchez Indian." *Mississippi Archaeology*, Vol. 10, No. 4, April 1975.

————. "The Rice Site: A Natchez Indian Cemetery." *Mississippi Archaeology*, Vol. 15, No. 2, December 1980.

————. "The French House Site 22AD668: The White Earth Concession (1720–1729)." *Louisiana Archaeology*, Bulletin of the Louisiana Archaeological Society, No. 8, Lafayette 1981.

Gallay, Alan. *The Indian Slave Trade: The Rise of the English Empire in the American South, 1670 –1717.* Yale University Press, New Haven 2002.

Galloway, Patricia. "Sources for the La Salle Expedition of 1682." In Patricia Galloway (ed.) *La Salle and His Legacy: Frenchmen and Indians in the Lower Mississippi Valley*, 11–40. University Press of Mississippi, Jackson 1982.

———. *Choctaw Genesis.* University of Nebraska Press, Lincoln 1995.

———. "Natchez Matrilineal Kinship: Du Pratz and the Woman's Touch." Paper presented at the Natchez Literary Celebration, Natchez, Mississippi 1995.

———. "Colonial Period Transformations in the Mississippi Valley: Dis-integration, Alliance, Confederation, Playoff." In Robbie Ethridge and Charles Hudson (eds.) *The Transformation of the Southeastern Indians, 1540–1760*, 225–248. University Press of Mississippi, Jackson 2002.

Galloway, Patricia (ed.). *The Hernando de Soto Expedition: History, Historiography, and "Discovery" in the Southeast.* University of Nebraska Press, Lincoln 1997.

Galloway, Patricia, and Jason Baird Jackson. "Natchez and Neighboring Groups." In William C. Sturtevant (gen. ed.) and Raymond D. Fogelson (vol. ed.) *Handbook of North American Indians, Southeast, Volume 14*, 598–615. Smithsonian Institution, Washington, D.C. 2004.

Galloway, Patricia, and Clara Sue Kidwell. "Choctaw in the East." In William C. Sturtevant (gen. ed.) and Raymond D. Fogelson (vol. ed.) *Handbook of North American Indians, Southeast, Volume 14*, 499–519. Smithsonian Institution, Washington, D.C. 2004.

Giraud, Marcel, and Joseph C. Lambert (trans.). *A History of French Louisiana, Volume One: The Reign of Louis XIV, 1698–1715.* Louisiana State University Press, Baton Rouge 1974.

Giraud, Marcel, and Brian Pearce (trans.). *A History of French Louisiana, Volume Five: The Company of the Indies, 1723–1731.* Louisiana State University Press, Baton Rouge 1991.

———. *A History of French Louisiana, Volume Two: Years of Transition.* Louisiana State University Press, Baton Rouge 1993.

Goddard, Ives. "Washa, Chawasha, and Yakni-Chito." In *Handbook of North American Indians, Southeast, Volume 14*, 188–190. Smithsonian Institution, Washington, D.C. 2004.

Goddard, Ives, Patricia Galloway, Marvin D. Jeter, Gregory Waselkov, and John E. Worth "Small Tribes of the Western Southwest." In William C. Sturtevant (gen. ed.) and Raymond D. Fogelson (vol. ed.) *Handbook of North American Indians, Southeast, Volume 14*, 174–190. Smithsonian Institution, Washington, D.C. 2004.

Green, John A. "Governor Perier's Expedition Against the Natchez Indians: December 1730–January 1731." *The Louisiana Historical Quarterly*, Vol. 19, No. 3, July 1936.

Gregory, Hiram F., Jr. "Survival and Maintenance Among Louisiana Tribes." In William C. Sturtevant (gen. ed.) and Raymond D. Fogelson (vol. ed.) *Handbook of North American Indians, Southeast, Volume 14*, 653–658. Smithsonian Institution, Washington, D.C. 2004.

Hall, Gwendolyn Midlo. *Africans in Colonial Louisiana: The Development of Afro-Creole Culture in the Eighteenth-century.* Louisiana State University Press, Baton Rouge 1992.

Hally, David J. "The Plaquemine and Mississippian Occupations of the Upper Tensas Basin, Louisiana." Ph.D. dissertation, Harvard University, Cambridge, MA 1972.

Hardy, James D., Jr. "The Transportation of Convicts to Colonial Louisiana." In Glenn R. Conrad (ed.) *The Louisiana Purchase Bicentennial Series in Louisiana History: Volume 1, The French Experience in Louisiana*, 115–124. Center for Louisiana Studies, University of Southwestern Louisiana, Lafayette 1995.

Harrar, Ellwood S., and J. George Harrar. *Guide to Southern Trees*. Dover Publications, New York 1962.

Hart, Richard H. (trans.). Mauthurin Le Petit. *The Natchez Massacre*. Poor Rich Press, New Orleans 1950.

Higginbotham, Jay. *Fort Maurepas: The Birth of Louisiana*. Colonial Books, Mobile 1968.

———. *Old Mobile: Fort Louis de la Louisiane 1702–1711*. Museum Publication No. 4, Museum of the City of Mobile 1977.

Hoffman, Paul E. "Lucas Vázquez de Ayllón's Discovery and Colony." In Charles Hudson and Carmen C. Tesser *The Forgotten Centuries: Indians and Europeans in the American South, 1521–1704*, 36–49. The University of Georgia Press, Athens 1994.

Hudson, Charles. *The Southeastern Indians*. University of Tennessee Press 1976.

———. "The Hernando De Soto Expedition, 1539–1543." In Charles Hudson and Carmen C. Tesser *The Forgotten Centuries: Indians and Europeans in the American South, 1521–1704*, 74–103. The University of Georgia Press, Athens 1994.

———. *Knights of Spain, Warriors of the Sun: Hernando de Soto and the South's Ancient Chiefdoms, 389–390*. The University of Georgia Press, Athens 1997.

Jackson, H. Edwin. "The 2005 Excavations at Winterville Mounds (22Ws500), Washington County, Mississippi." Report submitted to the Mississippi Department of Archives and History, Jackson 2006.

Jeter, Marvin D. "Protohistoric and Historic Native Americans" in Marvin D. Jeter, Jerome C. Rose, G. Ishmael Williams Jr., and Anna M. Harmon. *Archeology and Bioarcheology of the Lower Mississippi Valley and the Trans-Mississippi South*. Arkansas Archeological Survey Research Series No. 37, Final Report submitted to the U.S. Army Corps of Engineers, Southwestern Division Study Unit 6 of the Southwestern Division Archeological Overview, Contract No. DACW63-84-C-0149, 1989.

———. "From Prehistory through Protohistory to Ethnohistory in the Northern Lower Mississippi Valley." In Robbie Ethridge and Charles Hudson (eds.) *The Transformation of the Southeastern Indians, 1540–1760*, 177–224. University Press of Mississippi, Jackson 2002.

———. "Grigra." In William C. Sturtevant (gen. ed.) and Raymond D. Fogelson (vol. ed.) *Handbook of North American Indians, Southeast, Volume 14*, 179. Smithsonian Institution, Washington, D.C. 2004.

Jeter, Marvin D., and Ives Goddard. "Tiou." In William C. Sturtevant (gen. ed.) and Raymond D. Fogelson (vol. ed.) *Handbook of North American Indians, Southeast, Volume 14*, 188. Smithsonian Institution, Washington, D.C. 2004.

Jeter, Marvin D., and G. Ishmael Williams Jr. "Late Prehistoric Cultures, A.D. 1000–1500." In William C. Sturtevant (gen. ed.) and Raymond D. Fogelson (vol. ed.) *Handbook of North American Indians, Southeast, Volume 14*, 174–177. Smithsonian Institution, Washington, D.C. 2004.

King, Duane H. "Cherokee in the West: History Since 1776." In William C. Sturtevant (gen. ed.) and Raymond D. Fogelson (vol. ed.) *Handbook of North American Indians, Southeast, Volume 14*, 354–372. Smithsonian Institution, Washington, D.C. 2004.

Kniffin, Fred B., Hiram F. Gregory, and George A. Stokes. *The Historic Indian Tribes of Louisiana*. Louisiana State University, Baton Rouge 1987.

Kulikoff, Allan. *Tobacco Slaves: The Development of Southern Cultures in the Chesapeake, 1680–1800*. University of North Carolina Press, Chapel Hill 1986.

De La Harpe, Jean-Baptiste Bénard, Virginia Koenig, and Joan Cain (trans.), Glenn R. Conrad (ed.) *Historical Journal of the Settlement of the French in Louisiana*. University of Southwestern Louisiana, Lafayette 1971.

Lemieux, Donald J. "Some Legal and Practical Aspects of the Office of Commissaire-Ordonnateur of French Louisiana." In Glenn R. Conrad (ed.) *The Louisiana Purchase Bicentennial Series in Louisiana History: Volume 1, The French Experience in Louisiana*, 395–407. Center for Louisiana Studies, University of Southwestern Louisiana, Lafayette 1995.

Lehmann, Susan Gibbs. "The Problems of Founding a Viable Colony: The Military in Early French Louisiana." In Glenn R. Conrad (ed.) *The Louisiana Purchase Bicentennial Series in Louisiana History, Vol. I: The French Experience in Louisiana*, 360–367. Center for Louisiana Studies, University of Southwestern Louisiana, Lafayette 1995.

Lorenz, Karl G. "A Re-Examination of Natchez Sociopolitical Complexity: A View from the Grand Village and Beyond." *Southeastern Archaeology*, Vol. 16, No. 2, Winter 1997.

———. "The Natchez of Southwest Mississippi." In Bonnie G. McEwan *Indians of the Greater Southeast: Historical Archaeology and Ethnohistory*, 142–177. University Press of Florida, Gainesville 2000.

Lyon, Eugene (trans. and ed.). "The Cañete Fragment: Another Narrative of Hernando De Soto." In Lawrence A. Clayton, Vernon J. Knight Jr., Edward C. Moore (eds.) *Volume I, The De Soto Chronicles: The Expedition of Hernando De Soto to North America in 1539–1543*, 307–310. The University of Alabama Press, Tuscaloosa 1993.

McNeil, W. K. "Introduction." In George E. Lankford (ed.) *Native American Legends, Southeastern Legends: Tales from the Natchez, Caddo, Biloxi, Chickasaw, and Other Nations*, 13–28. August House Publishers, Little Rock 1987.

McWilliams, Richebourg G. (trans. and ed.). *Fleur de Lys and Calumet: Being the Pénicaut Narrative of French Adventure in Louisiana*. The University of Alabama Press, Tuscaloosa 1953.

———. *Pierre Le Moyne d'Iberville, Iberville's Gulf Journals*. The University of Alabama Press, Tuscaloosa 1981.

McWilliams, Tennant S. "Pierre LeMoyne and the Competition for Empire." In Richebourg G. McWilliams (trans. and ed.) *Pierre Le Moyne d'Iberville, Iberville's Gulf Journals*, 1–16. The University of Alabama Press, Tuscaloosa 1981.

Milanich, Jerald T. "Franciscan Missions and Native Peoples in Spanish Florida." In Charles Hudson and Carmen C. Tesser (eds.) *The Forgotten Centuries: Indians and Europeans in the American South, 1521–1704*, 276–303. University of Georgia Press, Athens 1994.

Moorehead, Warren K. "Explorations of the Etowah Site in Georgia." In *Etowah Papers I*, 159–165. Department of Archaeology, Phillips Academy, Andover, MA 1932.

Nairne, Thomas (Alexander Moore ed.). *Nairne's Muskhogean Journals: The 1708 Expedition to the Mississippi River*. University Press of Mississippi, Jackson 1988.

Neitzel, Robert S. "Archaeology of the Fatherland Site: The Grand Village of the Natchez. (*Vol. 51, Part 1, Anthropological Papers of the American Museum of Natural History*, New York 1965).

———. "The Grand Village of the Natchez Revisited: Excavations at the Fatherland Site, Adams County, Mississippi, 1972." Archaeological Report No. 12, Mississippi Department of Archives and History, Jackson 1983.

New York State Museum. "Batteau Fact Sheet." http://www.nysm.nysed.gov/batteau/.

O'Meara, Walter. *Guns at the Forks*. Prentice-Hall, Englewood Cliffs, NJ 1965.

O'Neill, Charles E. (ed.), John Gilmary Shea (trans.), Pierre F. X. Charlevoix. *Charlevoix's Louisiana: Selections from the History and the Journal, Pierre F. X. de Charlevoix.* Louisiana State University Press, Baton Rouge 1977.

Oswalt, Wendall H., and Sharlotte Neely. "The Natchez: Sophisticated Farmers of the Deep South." In *This Land Was Theirs*, 477–500. Mayfield Publishing, Mountain View, CA 1996.

Parkman, Francis. *La Salle and the Discovery of the Great West: France and England in North America.* Corner House Publishers, Williamstown, MA 1980, originally published 1897.

Penman, John T. "Appendix II. Faunal Remains." In Robert S. Neitzel "The Grand Village of the Natchez Revisited: Excavations at the Fatherland Site, Adams County, Mississippi, 1972." Archaeological Report No. 12, Mississippi Department of Archives and History, 1983.

Peyser, Joseph L. "The Chickasaw Wars of 1736 and 1740: French Military Drawings and Plans Document the Struggle for the Lower Mississippi." *The Journal of Mississippi History*, Vol. XLIV, No. 1, February 1982.

Phelps, Dawson (trans. and ed.). "Narrative of the Hostilities Committed by the Natchez Against the Concession of St. Catherine." *Journal of Mississippi History*, Vol. VII, No. 1, January 1945.

Phillips, Philip. "Archaeological Survey in the Lower Yazoo Basin, Mississippi, 1949–1955." Papers of the Peabody Museum of Archaeology and Ethnology, Harvard University, Vol. 60, Part One and Part Two, Cambridge 1970.

Phillips, Philip, James A. Ford, and James B. Griffin. *Archaeological Survey in the Lower Mississippi Alluvial Valley, 1940–1947.* Papers of the Peabody Museum of American Archaeology and Ethnology Vol. 25, Harvard University, Cambridge, MA 1951, reprinted by University of Alabama Press 2003.

Post, Lauren C. "The Domestic Animals and Plants of French Louisiana as Mentioned in the Literature with Reference to Sources, Varieties, and Uses." *Louisiana Historical Quarterly*, Vol. 16, No. 4, 1933.

Powell, William S. "Carolana and the Incomparable Roanoke: Explorations and Attempted Settlements, 1620–1663." North Carolina Office of Archives and History, The Colonial Records Project, http://www.ah.dcr.state.nc.us/sections/hp/colonial/Nchr/Subjects/powell5.htm, 5/27/2006. Additional background on the distinction between Carolana and Carolina is found at: http://www.carolana.com/carolana_vs_carolina.html.

Quimby, George I. "Natchez Social Structure as an Instrument of Assimilation." *American Anthropologist*, Vol. 48, 1946.

Ramonofsky, Ann F. "Death by Disease." *Archaeology*, March/April 1992, Vol. 45, No. 2.

Robertson, James Alexander (trans. and ed.). "The Account by a Gentleman from Elvas." In Lawrence A. Clayton, Vernon J. Knight Jr., Edward C. Moore (eds.) *Volume I, The De Soto Chronicles: The Expedition of Hernando De Soto to North America in 1539–1543*, 19–220. The University of Alabama Press, Tuscaloosa 1993.

Rowland, Dunbar, and Albert G. Sanders (eds. and trans.). *Mississippi Provincial Archives, 1729–1740, French Dominion, Vol. I.* Mississippi Department of Archives and History, Jackson 1927.

———. *Mississippi Provincial Archives, 1701–1729, French Dominion, Vol. II.* Mississippi Department of Archives and History, Jackson 1929.

———. *Mississippi Provincial Archives, 1704–1743, French Dominion, Vol. III* (Mississippi Department of Archives and History, Jackson 1932.

Rowland, Dunbar, Albert G. Sanders, and Patricia Galloway (eds. and trans.). *Mississippi Provincial Archives, 1729–1748, French Dominion, Vol. IV.* Louisiana State University Press, Baton Rouge 1984.

Ryan, Joanne. "Cultural Resources Investigation of West Bank Mississippi River Levees, Items 365, 361, and 357-R, Vidalia-Moreville, Concordia Parish, Louisiana." Final report prepared for U.S. Army Corps of Engineers, Vicksburg District, Contract No. W912EE-04-D-0001, December 2004.

Saunt, Claudio. "History Until 1776." In William C. Sturtevant (gen. ed.) and Raymond D. Fogelson (vol. ed.) *Handbook of North American Indians, Southeast, Volume 14*, 128–138. Smithsonian Institution, Washington, D.C. 2004.

Scarry, John F. "The Late Prehistoric Southeast." In Charles Hudson and Carmen C. Tesser *The Forgotten Centuries: Indians and Europeans in the American South, 1521–1704*, 17–35. The University of Georgia Press, Athens 1994.

Schele, Linda, and David Freidel. *A Forest of Kings: The Untold Story of the Ancient Maya.* William Morrow, New York 1990.

Shea, John Gilmary (ed. and trans.). "Journal of the Voyage of Father Gravier." In *Early Voyages Up and Down the Mississippi.* Albany, Joel Munsell 1861.

———. "Letters of J. F. Buisson Saint-Cosme, Mr. De Montigny, and La Source." In *Early Voyages Up and Down the Mississippi.* Albany, Joel Munsell 1861.

Shelby, Charmion (trans.), and David Bost (ed.). "La Florida by Garcilaso de la Vega, the Inca." In Lawrence A. Clayton, Vernon J. Knight Jr., Edward C. Moore (eds.) *Volume II, The De Soto Chronicles: The Expedition of Hernando De Soto to North America in 1539–1543*, 25–559. The University of Alabama Press, Tuscaloosa 1993.

Smith, Marvin T. "Aboriginal Population Movements in the Postcontact Southeast." In Robbie Ethridge and Charles Hudson (eds.) *The Transformation of the Southeastern Indians, 1540–1760*, 3–20. University Press of Mississippi, Jackson.

Steponaitis, Vincas P. "The Late Prehistory of the Natchez Region: Excavations at the Emerald and Foster Sites, Adams County, Mississippi." B.A. Thesis, Harvard University, Cambridge 1974.

———. "Location Theory and Complex Chiefdoms: A Mississippian Example." In Bruce D. Smith (ed.) *Mississippian Settlement Patterns*, 417–454. Academic Press, New York 1978.

Steponaitis, Vincas P., Stephen Williams, R. P. Davis Jr., Ian W. Brown, Tristram R. Kidder, Melissa Salvanish (eds.). LMS Archives Online. http://rla.unc.edu/archives/lms1/ site files. 2002.

Swanton, John R. *Indian Tribes of the Lower Mississippi Valley and Adjacent Coast of the Gulf of Mexico.* Smithsonian Institution Bureau of American Ethnology Bulletin 43, 1911, reprinted by Dover Publications 1998.

———. *Indian Tribes of North America.* Original 1952, Smithsonian Institution Bureau of American Ethnology, Bulletin 145, Smithsonian Institution Press, Washington D.C. 1984.

———. *Final Report of the United States De Soto Expedition Commission.* Smithsonian Institution Press, Washington, D.C. 1985.

Thornton, Russell. "Demographic History." In William C. Sturtevant (gen. ed.) and Raymond D. Fogelson (vol. ed.) *Handbook of North American Indians, Southeast, Volume 14*, 51. Smithsonian Institution, Washington, D.C. 2004.

Usner, Daniel H. *Indians, Settlers, and Slaves: The Lower Mississippi Valley Before 1783.* University of North Carolina Press, Chapel Hill 1992.

Van Tuyl, Charles D. "A Short English-Natchez Dictionary." Series in Anthropology, Number 4, Oklahoma Historical Society 1979.

Velde, François R. "Government Equity and Money: John Law's System in 1720 France." Paper accessible at: http://www.velde.org/econ/law.pdf, version 1.1, May 2004.

Vogel, Claude L. "The Capuchins in French Louisiana, 1722–1766." Ph.D. diss. The Catholic University of America, Studies in American Church History, Vol. VII, Washington, D.C. 1928.

Walker, Willard B. "Creek Confederacy Before Removal." In William C. Sturtevant (gen. ed.) and Raymond D. Fogelson (vol. ed.) *Handbook of North American Indians, Southeast, Volume 14*, 373–392. Smithsonian Institution, Washington, D.C. 2004.

Waselkov, Gregory A. "Exchange and Interaction Since 1500." In William C. Sturtevant (gen. ed.) and Raymond D. Fogelson (vol. ed.) *Handbook of North American Indians, Southeast, Volume 14*, 686–698. Smithsonian Institution, Washington, D.C. 2004.

Weddle, Robert S., Mary C. Morkovsky, Patricia Galloway (eds.). *Three Primary Documents, La Salle, the Mississippi, and the Gulf.* Texas A&M University Press, College Station 1987.

White, Douglas R., George P. Murdock, Richard Scaglion. "Natchez Class and Rank Reconsidered." *Ethnology*, Vol. 10 No. 2, 1971.

Widmer, Randolph J. "The Structure of Southeastern Chiefdoms." In Charles Hudson and Carmen Chaves Tesser (eds.) *The Forgotten Centuries: Indians and Europeans in the American South, 1521–1704*, 128. The University of Georgia Press, Athens 1994.

Williams, Stephen. "Introduction to 2003 Edition." In Philip Phillips, James A. Ford, and James B. Griffin *Archaeological Survey in the Lower Mississippi Alluvial Valley, 1940–1947*, xi–xxxii. Original 1951, reprinted by University of Alabama Press 2003.

Williams, Stephen, and Jeffrey P. Brain. "Excavations at the Lake George Site, Yazoo County, Mississippi, 1958–1960." *Papers of the Peabody Museum of Archaeology and Ethnology, Vol. 74*, Cambridge 1983.

Wilson, Samuel, Jr. "Colonial Fortifications and Military Architecture in the Mississippi Valley." In Glenn R. Conrad (ed.) *The Louisiana Purchase Bicentennial Series in Louisiana History: Volume 1, The French Experience in Louisiana*, 378–394. Center for Louisiana Studies, University of Southwestern Louisiana, Lafayette 1995.

Worth, John E. (trans. and ed.). "Relation of the Island of Florida by Luys Hernández de Biedma." In Lawrence A. Clayton, Vernon J. Knight Jr., Edward C. Moore (eds.) *Volume I, The De Soto Chronicles: The Expedition of Hernando De Soto to North America in 1539–1543*, 221–246. The University of Alabama Press, Tuscaloosa 1993.

———. "Account of the Northern Conquest and Discovery of Hernando De Soto by Rodrigo Rangel." In Lawrence A. Clayton, Vernon J. Knight Jr., Edward C. Moore (eds.) *Volume I, The De Soto Chronicles: The Expedition of Hernando De Soto to North America in 1539–1543*, 247–306. The University of Alabama Press, Tuscaloosa 1993.

INDEX